THE MARTYRS OF COLUMBINE

Also by Justin Watson

The Christian Coalition:
Dreams of Restoration, Demands for Recognition

THE MARTYRS
OF COLUMBINE

FAITH AND THE POLITICS OF TRAGEDY

JUSTIN WATSON

palgrave
macmillan

First published 2002 by
PALGRAVE MACMILLAN™
175 Fifth Avenue, New York, N.Y. 10010 and
Houndmills, Basingstoke, Hampshire, England RG21 6XS.
Companies and representatives throughout the world.

PALGRAVE MACMILLAN is the global academic imprint of the
Palgrave Macmillan division of St. Martin's Press, LLC and of
Palgrave Macmillan Ltd. Macmillan® is a registered trademark in
the United States, United Kingdom and other countries. Palgrave is
a registered trademark in the European Union and other countries.

ISBN 0-312-23957-2 hardback

Library of Congress Cataloging-in-Publication Data
Watson, Justin, 1957–
The martyrs of Columbine : faith and the politics of tragedy / Justin
Watson.
    p. cm.
Includes bibliographical references and index.
ISBN 0–312–23957–2
    1. Scott, Rachel (Rachel Joy) 2. Bernall, Cassie, 1981–1999.
3. Columbine High School (Littleton, Colo.)—Students—
Biography.   4. Christian martyrs—Colorado—Biography.
I. Title.

BR1608.5.W38 2002
272'.9'0973—dc21

                                            2002016919

A catalogue record for this book is available from the British
Library.

Design by Letra Libre, Inc.

First edition: November 2002
10 9 8 7 6 5 4 3 2 1

Printed in the United States of America.

In memory of

Cassie Bernall
Steven Curnow
Corey DePooter
Kelly Fleming
Matthew Kechter
Daniel Mauser
Daniel Rohrbough
William "Dave" Sanders
Rachel Scott
Isaiah Shoels
John Tomlin
Lauren Townsend
Kyle Velasquez

Contents

PREFACE

Just as I was completing this manuscript, the world changed. After the events of September 11, 2001, the Columbine High School shooting of 1999 suddenly seemed to belong to a lesser order of public significance. As traumatic as Columbine continues to be for the families and friends of the victims, I wondered if Columbine was relevant in an era in which we counted our casualties in the thousands rather than the dozens. I wondered if anyone remembered Columbine, if anyone still cared.

I discovered, or rather rediscovered, the vitality of the memory of Columbine, and of its most celebrated victims, Cassie Bernall and Rachel Scott, at a church in rural Pennsylvania in late October 2001.[1]

The church was holding a "Hell House" event, an evangelical Christian alternative to the traditional Halloween haunted house. The church described it as, "A demon guided walk-through tour that *WILL* change your life." Visitors to the Hell House are led by a guide, costumed as a demon, through a series of decorated rooms in which scenes of evil, sin, and death are enacted. The demon-guide provides gleefully malicious commentary as visitors are shown the funeral of a gay man who has died of AIDS, a bloody abortion, a depressed teenager committing suicide, and the aftermath of a fatal car crash caused by alcohol.

The next scene begins with students sitting in a school library. From the dialogue, we learn that some are Christians and some are not. Then two teenage boys, one named Eric, burst into the room with guns. The students panic and scream. Two of the Christian girls, named Cassie and Rachel, are asked if they believe in God. When they say "Yes!" they are each shot in the head. Then the two boys ritualistically kill each other. The demon-guide proclaims, "Once again I win!"

The following scene is Hell, in which visitors meet Satan, who proudly claims credit for killing Cassie and Rachel, and see the damned in eternal torment. One of the damned cries out in regret, "Oh, why didn't I listen to Cassie?!" The final scene of the tour is Heaven. Here visitors see a skit and hear a short sermon that make clear that the only way to avoid Hell is to accept salvation through Jesus Christ.

There are hundreds of such Hell Houses conducted around the country each year using the "Hell House Outreach Kits" developed and distributed by a Denver-area church, located just 17 miles from Columbine High School. The kit contains many scenes and each church chooses among them according to its own needs, resources, and preferences.[2] There is no way of knowing how many churches have used the scene based on Columbine and its martyrs, or how many thousands of visitors have seen it. But the mere fact that a church on the other side of the continent would enact that scene hints that Columbine—its martyrs and its meaning—have entered the folk tradition of American evangelicalism by becoming part of the way the promise of salvation is presented to America. As such, Columbine and its supposed martyrs merit the attention of those who want to understand not only evangelicalism and American religion, but the human need and capacity to make suffering meaningful, the religious task par excellence.

In the course of this project, I have had to explore a record of atrocity: autopsy reports, police statements of children watching other children being slaughtered, and video images of blood-soaked carpet. To deal with such material on a daily basis poses the danger of desensitization to horror. In addition, the various personal, religious, and political responses to Columbine that I have examined have at times moved me and at times appalled me. This is all to say, I did not expect the journey I have taken.

The core struggle for me throughout this project was to maintain a fully humane empathy for the suffering that radiates from this event while dispassionately seeking answers to my questions. These dual commitments led to certain moral dilemmas.

On April 25, 2000, Jefferson County, Colorado, authorities released to the public a videotape containing graphic images from the day of the massacre and its aftermath. The following morning, I watched on television as an anguished Beth Nimmo, the mother of Rachel Scott, denounced the release of the tape. "I'm outraged," she said. "It does so much harm to the victims and their families. I don't see any good coming out of this."[3] I put down my coffee and looked at the "To Do" list that I had written the night before. The first item was "Order the tape." I asked myself if I was crossing a moral boundary between a legitimate intellectual curiosity and a morbid fascination that could serve no good purpose. After some hesitation, I did purchase the tape and used it in my research. But I have not employed it in public presentations about Columbine.[4]

I have also found myself in the course of this study talking to persons who have drawn inspiration, hope, and strength from the martyr stories of Cassie and Rachel. And my duty has been to ask, "What if it didn't happen that way?" I have always tried to ask that question as gently as possible. But often I have sensed in the moment those persons consider that question a subtle change, a loss of innocence, or a new strain on their faith. People are sometimes changed by my questions but I haven't stayed around to deal with the effects. I have moved on to ask someone else the same questions. Does my obvious responsibility to expand knowledge outweigh my less obvious responsibility to these persons?

Some may dismiss these reflections as excessively introspective and quite unnecessary. Perhaps they are right. But for me, the blood and grief of Columbine demand something extra. I can only hope that in the course of this study I have managed to be both a decent human being and a responsible scholar. Ultimately it is you, the reader, who must judge my efforts.

But before I begin, many people deserve my heartfelt thanks. I started this book while teaching in Tallahassee at Florida State University and I finished it while plying my trade at Lafayette College in Easton, Pennsylvania. Many an academic project has not survived such a transition, and the fact that this one has is testimony to the support and encouragement I received from the members of each school's Department of Religion. I'm particularly grateful to the chairmen of these programs, FSU's John Kelsay and Lafayette's Robert L. Cohn. Despite the fact that I was only a visiting member of the Lafayette faculty, I was provided with a full-time research assistant, Amy Dziekonski, during the summer of 2001 under the auspices of the College's Excel Scholar program. Without her diligence and dedication, I doubt if I could have finished this project in a timely fashion.

Many organizations, publications, and individuals aided in this project by providing materials and information that otherwise would have been unavailable to me. These include Yvonne Osmun, Ty Tyler, Alan Lampe, Connie Michalik, Kevin Simpson, The Columbine Redemption, Darrell Scott, Torchgrab Youth Ministries, Bruce Porter, *Christianity Today,* Wendy Murray Zoba, Plough Publishers, Chris Zimmerman, the Records Division of the Jefferson County, Colorado, Sheriff's Office, and the librarians of Strozier Library at FSU and Skillman Library at Lafayette. I am also grateful to my editor at Palgrave, Gayatri Patnaik, whose enthusiasm and professionalism made this book possible.

I'd like to extend a special thanks to Jennifer Fleischman, a dear friend for many years who created the diagram of the Columbine library in chapter 5.

Finally, I must also thank all of my friends, near and far, for the support and kindness that sustained me throughout this endeavor.

INTRODUCTION

"It Pierced the Soul of America"

On April 20, 1999, Eric Harris and Dylan Klebold killed 12 of their fellow students and 1 teacher at Columbine High School in Littleton, Colorado. They also wounded more than 20 others before turning their guns on themselves, committing suicide.

Media coverage of this event was massive, as was public interest. An estimated 750 news organizations from around the world sent representatives to cover the aftermath of the massacre.[1] Memorial services and funerals of the victims were broadcast live on national television, attracting large audiences. According to a survey by the Pew Research Center, the Columbine shooting "attracted by far the most public interest of any news story of 1999." On April 22–23, 1999, some 68 percent of Americans reported following news about the shooting "very closely" with an additional 24 percent following it "fairly closely."[2] (By way of contrast, the Pew Research Center later reported only slightly higher initial levels of public interest in the terrorist attacks of September 11, 2001, with 74 percent reporting that they followed the news "very closely" and 22 percent "fairly closely."[3])

Such interest is hardly surprising. The Columbine story was full of horror, pain, blood, and spectacle—things that naturally compel our attention. On the first anniversary of the shooting, President Bill

Clinton spoke for many when he asserted, "What happened in Littleton pierced the soul of America. Though a year has passed, time has not dimmed our memory or softened our grief at the loss of so many, whose lives were cut off in the promise of youth."[4]

Anecdotal evidence of Columbine's impact on individuals abounds. For instance, type "Columbine" into any Internet search engine and there will be thousands of hits, including hundreds of sites created by individuals touched by the events of April 20, 1999, and its aftermath. These sites range from a single page to elaborate sites with photographs, links to hundreds of Columbine-related sites, or discussion forums. Some are memorials to all of the dead, and, as we will see in what follows, many are shrine-like tributes to single victims. There are even web sites that memorialize the killers. And one particularly large and well-maintained site, the Columbine Research Task Force, is a forum for those examining evidence of a third gunman and evidence of government involvement in the massacre.[5] Some sites have not been changed since they were created, others were abandoned after a few months, while a few continue to be revised and updated years later. The individuals who created such sites do not apparently work for any political or religious organizations and very few claim to have friends or relatives among the Columbine victims and survivors. All of these web sites bear witness to the fact that Columbine was not just a news story but an event in the lives of their creators, and that this event required a personal response.

Another measure of Columbine's impact, of course, is the new meaning the name of the school itself has acquired. When I tell people I am "researching Columbine," for instance, they understand without additional explanation that I am not studying wild flowers. Perhaps it was the high death toll, or the massive coverage, but Columbine has become the template for such events. School shootings, such as in West Paducah, Kentucky, in 1997 or in Jonesboro, Arkansas, in 1998, are spoken of as leading up to Columbine in 1999, and subsequent shootings, such as in Santee, California, in 2001, are seen as copycat events. After the Santee incident, for instance, *Time* magazine's cover read, "The Columbine Effect."[6] And when the next school shooting occurs, as unfortunately it will, Columbine will be part of the public discussion again.

Columbine is also used as an axial event, to divide time into a before and an after. References to the "post-Columbine era" often appear in discussions of responses by educators and police to potential school violence—or what some critics call "post-Columbine hysteria."[7] And some in the entertainment industry also spoke of Columbine as at least a temporary turning point in the depiction of violence. A film producer told the *Los Angeles Times* why he decided not to film a violent sequence in the script of his current project. "We talked about it, post-Columbine, and decided the scene was inappropriate to the movie and inappropriate for the time."[8] Like Pearl Harbor, Jonestown, Auschwitz, and September 11, "Columbine" has become a byword, a shorthand supposedly laden with meaning and lessons. But what is the meaning of Columbine? What are its lessons?

MULTIPLE INTERPRETATIONS

In another Pew Research Center survey, conducted December 8–12, 1999, only 15 percent of Americans ranked Columbine as the most *important* story of 1999.[9] Given the interest the public initially showed in the story, why didn't more Americans see Columbine as important? Perhaps because seeing an event as important requires more than an emotional response or curiosity. It requires some reasonably coherent explanation of causes of an event and an interpretation of its meaning for society. But in the case of Columbine, with insane rage at its very heart, coherent explanation and interpretation has been difficult.

Many explanations and interpretations, of course, have been offered. Activists concerned with all sorts of issues—guns, entertainment violence, education reform, school prayer—treated Columbine as a national "wake-up call," an opportunity to enact their solution through a decisive public or governmental response. But aside from efforts to improve school security and to conduct "threat assessments," very little changed. "Columbine wasn't a watershed for anything," observed Frank Newport, editor in chief of the Gallup Poll. "That's because the economy was so important."[10] Partisan political struggles were also part of the story, as were constitutional restrictions on government action. But more essentially, in a highly pluralistic society, it was too difficult to mobilize a critical mass of public opinion behind a single understanding of Columbine or behind a particular kind of public action that should be taken to prevent another such incident. American public opinion was also divided on whether prevention was even possible. According to a Gallup poll taken in early April 2000, 47 percent of adult Americans believed preventive action by government and society could be taken, while 49 percent held the view that such shootings would happen anyway.[11] When Gallup asked the same question in March 2001, the results were virtually unchanged.[12]

EVANGELICALISM AND THE CHRISTIAN RIGHT

In what follows, I will examine a variety of efforts to establish the meaning of the Columbine massacre and advance a set of solutions that have emerged primarily, but not exclusively, from the American evangelical community. American evangelicalism is a broad Protestant transdenominational community that traditionally has emphasized: (1) the authority of scripture, (2) the necessity of a personal experience of salvation through Jesus Christ, and (3) the importance of evangelism—sharing the good news of salvation with others. Despite a multitude of denominational identities, and clashing variations in theology and practice, among evangelicals a substantial heritage of cooperation and fellowship exists not only for evangelism, but also for social and political activism.[13]

Since the 1970s, many evangelicals have entered into an even broader alliance with a smaller number of non-evangelicals, especially traditionalist Roman Catholics, on behalf of conservative political candidates and causes. Operating primarily through the institutional vehicle of the Republican Party, religious conservatism, often called the Christian Right or Religious Right, has been particularly concerned with issues, such as abortion, that they regard as indicative of cultural and moral breakdown in American society. This breakdown is rooted, religious conservatives argue, in America's rejection of traditional forms of religion and a turn toward secularism as the basis for public policy and moral standards. The only hope for America is a return to traditional forms of religion as the basis of law and morality.

This jeremiad-like analysis of contemporary American culture has been used to explain the causes and meaning of the Columbine massacre. This essentially religious or spiritual analysis, of course, has been used before to interpret previous "senseless school shootings" and other tragic incidents of mass violence. What has made the religious interpretation of Columbine different is its persistent focus on one of the most powerful and enduring themes in the Christian tradition: martyrdom.

THE MARTYRS:
CASSIE BERNALL AND RACHEL SCOTT

In early media coverage of Columbine, the story of one of the victims, 17-year-old Cassie Bernall, became a staple of press reports and part of the stock of popular knowledge about the massacre. At the nationally televised April 25 memorial service for all of the victims, the two most prominent speakers, Vice President Al Gore and the Reverend Franklin Graham, the son and heir apparent of evangelist Billy Graham, mentioned Cassie's story in their remarks. "As the killer rushed into the library," said Graham, "and pointed his gun and asked her the life-or-death question, 'Do you believe in God?' she paused and then answered, 'Yes, I believe.' Those were the last words this brave 17-year-old Christian would ever say."[14]

Another victim, 17-year-old Rachel Scott, was also reported to have been asked by Harris if she believed in God. According to one version of the story, already wounded, she replied, "You know that I do." Harris then said, "Then go be with him now!" and shot her in the head, killing her instantly.[15] While less prominent in the early coverage of the Columbine shooting, the story of Rachel Scott had become as celebrated as that of Cassie Bernall by the first anniversary of the shooting.

Within days of their deaths, Cassie and Rachel were being hailed as modern-day martyrs and were seen by some, especially within the American evangelical community, as the sparks for a potential religious revival among teenagers. Based on the efforts of their grieving families,[16] both became the focus of what might be described as popular martyr cults. Cassie and Rachel also became useful symbols in a broader struggle over the meaning of the massacre and the state of American culture. Religious and social conservatives argued that this horrific event was not about gun control or high school cliques, but about religion, morality, and cultural decay. Cassie and Rachel, innocents martyred for their affirmation of God, stood in stark contrast to Harris and Klebold, the embodiments of a secular and evil "culture of death."

VICTIMS OR MARTYRS?

The symbolic potency of Cassie, however, was threatened when serious questions began to emerge in September 1999 as to whether she had been interrogated by her killer about her belief in God. It was alleged that the stories of this conversation were the result of confusion by some of the witnesses.[17] The story of Rachel's declaration of faith at gunpoint was also questioned. In December 1999, the only witness who could have heard her final words, another student who was severely wounded in the attack, said he could not remember the exchange.[18] The official report on the shooting by the Jefferson County Sheriff's Office, released on May 15, 2000, flatly contradicts the martyr stories about Cassie's death and makes no mention of any conversation between Rachel and her killers.[19] Both girls, therefore, may have been slaughtered without any opportunity to bear witness. Both may have been victims of a crime rather than martyrs to a cause.

What impact will these questions about the reputed martyrs of Columbine have? For some, Cassie and Rachel may entirely cease to be significant, and be forgotten. Others may discount these questions as the cynicism of the secular/liberal media and continue to tell the martyr stories. Still others may engage in various reinterpretations in order to preserve the spiritual and political meanings that have become attached to the awful events of April 20, 1999. And given the ever-shorter attention span of American popular culture, the martyrs of Columbine may not be discredited but simply fade away, their 15 minutes of fame over. While at present it seems that the martyr stories will live on indefinitely, the future significance of "the martyrs of Columbine" remains an open question.

With all this in mind, I will examine the developing story of Cassie Bernall and Rachel Scott and the meanings attached to both their lives and their deaths. My central concern is not to establish who said what at the moment of death (although I will examine the available evidence in detail) or to validate or invalidate claims of martyrdom. I will also not try to determine what caused Harris and Klebold's actions or how to prevent "another Columbine." I will discuss these questions but only insofar as they shed light on how Columbine is remembered and interpreted through the prism of Christian martyrdom. What I hope to understand is something about the larger meanings that have been found in, or assigned to, the lives and deaths of these two 17-year-old girls. My concern is not what happened at Columbine High School on April 20, 1999, but what that event has come to mean.

CHAPTER 1

MARTYRDOM

"The Blood of the Christians Is the Seed"

Emerging from the Columbine massacre, there were multiple stories about Eric Harris or Dylan Klebold asking for a confession of
faith from some of their victims. In June 1999, Kenneth Woodward of
Newsweek mentioned four such stories: Cassie Bernall and Rachel
Scott, who were killed, and Valeen Schnurr and Kacey Ruegsegger,
who were wounded but survived.[1] Yet it was the story of Cassie's
death that received the widest dissemination and initially overshad-
owed all others.

The simplest form of Cassie's story has one of the gunmen asking her, "Do you believe in God?" She answers "Yes," and is immediately shot. In other versions, she is reported to have said, "Yes, I
believe," "Yes, I do," "Yes, I believe in God," or the more emphatic
"Yes, I do believe in God" before being murdered. Sometimes the
gunman responds to this affirmation with the question "Why?" and
then pulls the trigger without giving her a chance to respond.[2] Some
who tell this story will add the theological point, as did Franklin Graham at the April 25, 1999, memorial service, "I believe that Cassie

went immediately into the presence of Almighty God."[3] Or as her father told one reporter, "We know she made her stand for God, and because of that we know exactly that she's in heaven. Without any doubt at all I know she's in heaven, she's with the Lord."[4]

Another version has Cassie taking a far less passive role. "They started shooting up the place," said a speaker at a Christian youth meeting in California. "Everybody's on the ground and he yells out, 'Anybody in here believe in God?' Cassie Bernall stands up and says, 'I do.' And he blows her away. Shoots her."[5] Another variant has the gunman yell, "Then meet him now" before pulling the trigger.[6] Still another version found on one of many "tribute" web sites has the killer asking about her belief in Jesus Christ rather than God.[7] And *Time* magazine reported this elaborate story: "A girl was asked by the gunman if she believed in God, knowing full well the safe answer. 'There is a God,' she said quietly, 'and you need to follow along God's path.' The shooter looked down at her. 'There is no God,' he said and shot her in the head."[8]

The best-selling book, *She Said Yes: The Unlikely Martyrdom of Cassie Bernall,* by Cassie's mother, Misty Bernall, relied on the testimony of Joshua Lapp, a Columbine student who had hid under a nearby table in the school library, and who says he heard the exchange between Cassie and her killer.

> One of them asked if she believed in God. She paused, like she didn't know what she was going to answer, and then she said yes. She must have been scared, but her voice didn't sound shaky. It was strong. Then they asked her why, though they didn't give her a chance to respond. They just blew her away.[9]

While, as we will see in chapter 5, Lapp's account is less reliable than it may seem, this particular version of Cassie's last moments has become in effect the "canonical" form of her martyr story. There are a number of reasons for this. Lapp's account has a special authority because it comes from someone actually present in the library, and because its authority is accepted and promoted by Cassie's mother. The fact that it has been widely disseminated in the fixed written form of *She Said Yes,* has helped to suppress word-of-mouth elaboration. And Lapp's account is simple: "Do you believe in God?" "Yes." "Why?" Bang.

The accounts of Rachel's final moments exhibit less variety, with only two basic versions. The first version has one of the gunmen asking the already wounded Rachel if she believes in God. She answers, "You know that I do." He replies, "Then go be with him now," before shooting her in the head. There are minor variations in the details. Sometimes Harris is specified as the killer. And sometimes, for an extra touch of brutality, the gunman grabs Rachel by her hair at the beginning of the exchange. There are also variations in the God question. The simplest form is: "Do you believe in God?," while other forms include: "Do you still believe in God?" and "Do you still believe in God now?" And in some versions, the killer's reply, "Then go be with him now," is omitted.[10]

In the second basic, and perhaps less common, version, Rachel replies, "Yes," "Yes, I do," "Yes, I believe," or "Yes, I believe in God." All the other details—the identification of the killer, the grabbing of her hair, the form of the God question, and the killer's reply—demonstrate the same variations as in the first version.[11] Unlike Cassie's martyr story, there does not seem to be a single "canonical" or authoritative version of Rachel's last words. Rachel's father, Darrell Scott, has used both the "You know I do" and the "Yes" versions in his various activities to spread his daughter's legacy.[12]

As in the case of Cassie, the story of Rachel's death is on occasion followed by an affirmation of her immediate heavenly reward. "And the last words she heard were 'do you believe in God?,'" Darrell Scott has said in his public presentations about his daughter, "and the next words she heard were the very voice of God Himself saying 'Well done my good and faithful servant.' Amen."[13]

While the details and usage of these accounts about both Cassie and Rachel vary, three elements remain consistent: a pointed confrontation about religious belief, an unambiguous affirmative answer, and sudden death. It was upon these elements that the popular elevation of Cassie and Rachel to the status of modern-day martyrs was founded. But what exactly is a martyr?

THE CONCEPT OF MARTYRDOM

"The badge of martyrdom," observed sociologist Samuel Z. Klausner, "is awarded by the leadership of a community to men and women who offer their lives voluntarily in solidarity with their group in conflict with another, ideologically contrasting, group."[14] The term "martyr" comes from the Christian use of the Greek word *martus,* meaning "a witness." In the early Christian community all believers were regarded as witnesses or martyrs of Christ and the Gospel. Indeed, the term martyr is often used in the New Testament, sometimes in reference to Christ himself; as historian G. W. Bowersock asserted, "but nowhere can it be shown without question to be used in any sense other than 'witness.'"[15] During the era of persecution, however, the Church came to significantly limit usage of "martyr" to those who died as Christ had. As the theologian Origen wrote in the third century, "among the brethren, inspired by their reverence for those who resisted even to death, the custom was established of calling martyrs only those who witnessed to the mystery of faith with the spilling of their blood.[16]

How and why this shift in meaning came about are matters of considerable debate among scholars. The historical relationship of the Christian form of martyrdom to similar phenomena in Judaic, Hellenic, and Roman cultures is also controversial.[17] These issues, as well as the concept of martyrdom in Islam and other major religious traditions, need not concern us here. What matters here is the Christian concept of martyrdom as it is used in the cases of Cassie and Rachel.

The earliest extant Christian account in which "martyr" meant "dying for God" is "The Martyrdom of Polycarp," a document in the form of a letter dated sometime between 155 and 177 CE.[18] This account, despite reflecting the literary and religious conventions of its own time, displays many of the basic features that characterize subsequent Christian martyr stories.

In the midst of a local persecution of Christians, Polycarp is arrested and brought before a Roman proconsul in the crowded arena of Smyrna, a city in Asia Minor. As Polycarp enters he hears a voice from heaven, "Be Strong, Polycarp, and play the man."[19] There is no particular charge announced against him, other than his being a leader of the Christians. Polycarp is repeatedly urged to save himself through swearing by the fortune of Caesar and renouncing Christ. The proconsul threatens him, "I have wild beasts; I shall throw you to them, if you do not change your mind," but Polycarp replies: "Call them."[20] The proconsul threatens again, "I shall have you consumed by fire . . . unless you change your mind." But Polycarp says: "The fire you threaten burns for but an hour and is quenched after a little time; for you do not know the fire of the coming judgment and everlasting punishment that is laid up for the impious. But why do you delay? Come, do what you will."[21] The narrator makes the point that it is not the prisoner but the judge who is distressed by this exchange. Polycarp is "inspired with courage and joy, and his face was full of grace," but the proconsul is "astonished."[22]

Finally, after Polycarp has confessed himself to be a Christian three times, the crowd "shouted with uncontrollable anger" against "the father of the Christians, the destroyer of our gods."[23] The crowd wants Polycarp burned alive, which fulfills a prophetic vision through which God had called Polycarp to martyrdom. Quickly he is placed on the pyre but, untroubled by the coming ordeal, he prays, "I bless thee because thou hast deemed me worthy of this day and hour, to take my part in the number of the martyrs, in the cup of thy Christ."[24] But when the fire is kindled, it miraculously does not burn him. In frustration, the executioner stabs him with a dagger. But in another miracle, a dove flies from the wound followed by such a profusion of blood that the fire is extinguished. "And the whole crowd marveled," the narrator observes, "that there should be such a difference between the unbelievers and the elect."[25]

Polycarp is dead but "By his patient endurance he overcame the wicked magistrate and so received the crown of immortality."[26] His bones are collected by the faithful as holy relics. Polycarp is "remembered so much the more by everyone," the narrator tells us, "that he is even spoken of by the heathen in every place. He was not only a noble teacher, but also a distinguished martyr, whose martyrdom all desire to imitate as one according to the gospel of Christ."[27] The reader is also urged to spread the story of Polycarp. "When you have informed yourself of these things, send this letter to the brethren elsewhere, in order that they too might glorify the Lord."[28]

Any reading of "The Martyrdom of Polycarp" raises the perennial question of the martyr's motive. In the case of the early Christian community, it was understood that martyrs sought the "crown of immortality" that had been bestowed upon Polycarp. This great prize was won by literally enacting Mark 8:34–35.[29] "If any man would come after me," says Christ, "let him deny himself and take up his cross and follow me. For whoever would save his life will lose it; and whoever loses his life for my sake and the gospel's will save it" (Revised Standard Version). Ignatius of Antioch was apparently taking this advice quite literally when he wrote to the Christians of Rome in 107 CE asking them not to prevent his death in the arena. "Let me be given to the wild beasts, for by their means I can attain to God."[30] By imitating the suffering death of Christ, Ignatius and later Christian martyrs hoped to participate fully and immediately in His glory. "The martyr's rewards were believed to exceed those of any other Christian overachiever," wrote historian Robin Lane Fox. "His death effaced all sin after baptism; pure and spotless, he went straight to heaven."[31]

Heaven lay beyond a dramatic public confrontation between the martyr and an agent of what Klausner calls an "ideologically contrasting" group. In this confrontation, according to sociologists Eugene and Anita Weiner, "There is generally a dissenting, deviant, non-conforming person or group, with an alternative set of convictions, and a dominant powerful person or group willing to exercise its power."[32] At issue between the two types of persons, and the groups they represent, is usually a verbal statement or symbolic action. Polycarp, for example, is told, "Take the oath and I shall release you. Curse Christ."[33] He refuses and repeatedly states that he is a

Christian. The words or actions embody the essential and absolute conflict between the groups.[34] The reader/listener would understand the conflict as one between good and evil.

The confrontation is rendered dramatic partly by what is at risk. In earthly terms, the martyr-candidate is threatened with torture and death for defiance and is promised relief or release for submission. But the Christian would also see the confrontation in light of Christ's teaching in Matthew 10:32–33. "So every one who acknowledges me before men, I also will acknowledge before my Father who is in heaven; but whoever denies me before men, I will also deny before my Father who is in heaven" (RSV). So what hangs in the balance is not only temporal life and death, but eternal salvation and damnation.[35]

It is essential that there be a clear voluntary choice between these weighty alternatives. Unlike a heroic soldier, who will accept an accidental or unavoidable death for his or her cause or community, the martyr makes a deliberate and clear choice to die an otherwise *avoidable* death. By refusing the chance to flee or rejecting the opportunity to recant, the martyr makes clear that it is a free choice to suffer and die rather than betray his or her cause or community. The reality of this choice is underlined by the narrative convention, reflecting the actual protocols of Roman magistrates, of providing the martyr with multiple opportunities, sometimes over an extended period, to avoid suffering and death.[36] The martyr is not a victim of circumstance. The martyr chooses.

Beyond the mere fact of making the choice, the martyr must capture the imagination of those hearing his or her story. As historian Lacey Baldwin Smith observed, "style remains the key to the martyr's credibility and reputation. Death, like any other human endeavor, is an art, and if martyrs are to prevail, they must die, to use Sylvia Plath's expression, 'exceptionally well.'"[37] Polycarp, for instance, always keeps the upper hand in his confrontation with the proconsul. The nameless proconsul is always kept off-balance by Polycarp's dismissive answers to the threats. "Come," says Polycarp, "do what you will." (He might well have said, "Go on. Make my day.") While Polycarp utters no especially memorable "exit line," later martyrs found a way to encapsulate the meaning of their death with a single dramatic utterance. "Be of good comfort, Master Ridley, and play the man," said Hugh Latimer to fellow Protestant Nicholas Ridley as the flames rose about them in 1655. "We shall this day light such a candle, by God's grace, in England, as I trust shall never be put out."[38]

It is likely, of course, that martyrs have had more than a little help in the artful manner of their deaths from the martyrologists, those who tell the stories of the martyrs. But a prudent skepticism of the historical accuracy of martyrology should not lead us to conclude that these accounts are total fabrications. Something about how the martyr really died may have inspired their community's martyrologists to preserve and then elaborate the memory of that death. In his comparative study of Catholic, Protestant, and Anabaptist martyrs of the Reformation era, historian Brad S. Gregory found striking evidence that the "good deaths" of the members of one community were recognized as such by their theological opponents. "Even if our evidence of martyrs' behavior relied exclusively on hostile sources, we would have to conclude that they usually died with a joyful resolve that often impressed onlookers."[39]

It should also be remembered that in many cases the martyr-to-be had time and social support to prepare for their moment of truth.[40] As Eugene and Anita Weiner observe of the preparation for martyrdom in the early church,

> It was not uncommon for fellow Christians to visit the accused in their cells and to bring food and clothing to make the imprisonment more bearable. There were even celebrations to dramatize the forthcoming test of faith. These supportive efforts both brought comfort and help in a most trying situation, and had a latent message for the martyr-designate, "what you do and say will be observed and recorded."[41]

Like anyone expected to "perform" in public, the martyrs-to-be undoubtedly considered what they would say and do. They were undoubtedly also aware of the martyr-stories of the past and thus had before them models for their own behavior.

Any preparation, whether individual or collective, will be for naught if the confrontation, the martyr's choice, and the manner of death do not take place in public, or do not become known publicly. Publicity is essential to the advancement of the martyr's cause. In the case of the early Church these things did become known. Despite the fact that only "hundreds, not thousands"[42] were martyred, the phenomenon of martyrdom, according to Bowersock, "must be reckoned the single most visible manifestation of Christianity in the pagan Roman world."[43] Tertullian, in his *Apologeticus* (197 CE) addressed to Roman officials, wrote, "Your cruelty profits you nothing, though it grows ever more ingenious; it is one of the attractions of our sect. As often you mow us down, the more numerous do we become; the blood of the Christians is the seed."[44]

Only the *public* defiance of the "ingenious" cruelties of Rome makes this paradoxical result possible. Why? "By voluntarily accepting torture and death rather than defecting," argued sociologist Rodney Stark, "a person sets the highest imaginable value upon a religion and communicates that value to others."[45] Such sacrifice provides a belief system with a plausibility and moral authority it could not gain otherwise. The martyr's sacrificial act also delegitimizes and demoralizes the opposing group.[46] Thus the martyr's suffering and death has both internal and external functions. These functions, however, can only be accomplished if both "the brethren elsewhere" and "the heathen in every place" learn of the martyr's story.

Most of the contemporary American evangelicals who have embraced Cassie and Rachel as modern-day martyrs have likely never heard of Polycarp, much less studied the many martyrologies of the early and medieval Church, or examined *Foxe's Book of Martyrs* and *The Mirror of the Martyrs.* But familiarity with this material, however enriching, is not really necessary for the recognition of modern-day martyrs. The essential pattern of the martyr story is already contained in the New Testament accounts of the life, death, and resurrection of Christ, accounts contemporary evangelicals know well. "The writers of the Gospels," write Droge and Tabor, "created a Jesus who became the prototype of the Christian martyr."[47] The Gospels present us with a figure who chooses the path of suffering death, confronts his persecutors, remains in control despite those who would control him, and dies what becomes the most widely publicized "good death" in human history. They also present the divine vindication of his suffering and death as a victory over death itself, and point toward the birth and spread of his church.

This pattern is quickly repeated in the story of Stephen. According to Acts 6, he is brought before a council of elders and priests to answer the charge of blasphemy, just as Christ had been. Stephen's defiant response in Acts 7, the accusation that his judges had "betrayed and murdered" the "Righteous One," enrages the council. And when he, "full of the Holy Spirit," tells them, "Behold, I see the heavens opened, and the Son of man standing at the right hand of the father," they put him to death. As he is stoned, Stephen prays, "Lord Jesus, receive my spirit" and asks for the forgiveness of his persecutors. The New Testament presents Stephen as the first follower of Christ to imitate his "good death."

In addition, the Christ/martyr story has been woven into any number of popular culture vehicles. Notable examples include the motion pictures *Cool Hand Luke* (1967) and *One Flew Over the Cuckoo's Nest* (1975). A more recent example is *Braveheart* (1995), often cited in the early coverage of Columbine as Cassie's favorite movie.[48] This film, a critical as well as box-office success, stars Mel Gibson as Sir William Wallace (c. 1270–1305), the leader of a Scottish rebellion against the oppressive rule of "Longshanks," the English king, Edward I (1239–1307). Wallace fights and eventually dies for his country's freedom, a sacred cause that is depicted as implicitly Christian.

At the end of the film Wallace has been captured by the English and stands before a magistrate charged with treason. As in the classic pattern, the magistrate demands a verbal statement of submission. Using the threat of torture, a magistrate tells Wallace, "Confess, and you may receive a quick death. Deny, and you must be purified by pain. Do you confess?" Wallace pointedly ignores the question and is taken back to his cell. When a visitor urges him to use a potion to dull the pain of torture, he rejects it, saying. "No. It will numb my wits, and I must have them all. For if I'm senseless or if I wail, then Longshanks will have broken me." The desire for a good death is made even more explicit. Just before being taken to his execution, a trembling Wallace prays, "I am so afraid. Give me the strength to die well."

His "purification" through torture and death takes place in public, with a large and hostile crowd. As in classic Christian martyrology, this public drama turns on a word, a speech-act symbolic of irreconcilable world-views. Throughout Wallace's tortures, the executioner urges him to say "Mercy" and his pain will be over, but Wallace remains silent. In a less-than-subtle invocation of Christ's death, Wallace is tied to a cruciform wooden block and disemboweled. Again, the executioner promises the relief of swift death for the word "Mercy." The initially hostile crowd is now moved by Wallace's suffering and cries out for him to ask for mercy. When finally it appears Wallace is trying to speak, the executioner, expecting submission, hushes the crowd, "The prisoner wishes to say a word." With great effort Wallace cries, "FREEDOM!" The executioner, recognizing defeat, has the prisoner beheaded. Wallace's prayer has been answered. He has shown the world a good death.

In the film's final scene, we see the triumph of the cause for which Wallace was martyred. The leader of a Scottish army calls out to his men, "You have bled with Wallace, now bleed with me." The Scots charge the English army. And in a final image, accompanied by Wallace's voice telling of Scottish victory, we see Wallace's sword standing in the earth like a cross with the landscape of Scotland in the background.[49]

THE MARTYRS OF COLUMBINE

There are many elements in the classic pattern of martyrdom, as well as in the Hollywood version, that are apparent in the martyr stories of Cassie and Rachel. Most obvious is the confrontation with agents of evil over the question, "Do you believe in God?" The possible answers, "yes" and "no," point to conflicting and irreconcilable worldviews. The simple answers they supposedly gave, Cassie's "Yes," and Rachel's more defiant "You know that I do," are the essence of a "good death." Although the confrontations and deaths took place in obscurity, the whole world soon learned the stories on television, through the Internet, or simply by word-of-mouth. And those who continue to tell their story stress the immediate heavenly reward enjoyed by the two girls, as well as their beneficial impact on the world. And as we will see in the chapters that follow, the families of both point to the divine calling and preparation of each for sacrifice.

In some respects, however, the martyr stories of Cassie and Rachel differ sharply from the elaborate patterns of the classic martyrologies. In contrast to the extravagant, or what Tertullian called "ingenious," cruelties visited upon the Christian martyrs of antiquity or the Reformation era, death came to Cassie and Rachel with a simple and unimaginative brutality. The sufferings of Cassie and Rachel, as terrible as they must have been, were over in minutes and not extended over hours, days, months, or even longer. Their condensed and brief exchanges with their persecutors, like Wallace's "FREEDOM!" in *Braveheart,* lack the elaborate speeches and ceremonial repetitions of older narratives. In their simplicity, brevity, and clarity, the Columbine martyr stories are well suited for the age of bumper-sticker theology, sound-bite politics, and short attention spans.

These stories also reflect their age in their avoidance of the miraculous and the fantastic. There are no voices from heaven. Doves do not fly from the bullet wounds. The bones of the two girls do not become holy relics for the faithful. (The T-shirts and other products that bear their words or pictures have a memorial rather than a sacramental function.) The supernatural only directly enters into these stories in the affirmation that Cassie and Rachel went immediately to heaven, something that science can neither confirm nor properly deny. And as the broader story of their lives is told by their respective families, the concepts of divine election, preparation, and inspiration are employed. But these concepts only pertain to the inner experiences of Cassie, Rachel, and those who mourn them. Nothing in these accounts challenges "reality" as defined by naturalistic science.

These formal differences from the classic martyrological narratives only reflect the culture in which the stories have emerged. There are less obvious but potentially more serious departures from the classic concept, however, in the Columbine martyr stories. These more essential differences become apparent if we recall Klausner's definition of martyrdom. "The badge of martyrdom is awarded by the leadership of a community to men and women who offer their lives voluntarily in solidarity with their group in conflict with another, ideologically contrasting, group."[50] In light of this definition, the Columbine martyr stories are problematic because they lack the element of voluntarism and the dimension of group/ideological conflict.

The element of voluntarism presents a problem to those who have called Cassie and Rachel martyrs. While each may have witnessed to God with her last breath, it is not clear that death was avoidable. In media interviews, Misty Bernall has referred to an unnamed girl in the library who "begged for her life and was let go."[51] Therefore, Cassie had a potential way out and voluntarily chose not to take it. But if the chronology contained in the Jefferson County *Sheriff's Report* is accurate, the "begging" exchange referred to occurred immediately *after* Cassie's death.[52] Even if it had happened before her own encounter with one of the gunmen, we have no way of knowing if Cassie was aware of that exchange. In the case of Rachel, the gunman opened fire on her without a word of warning. Thus she had already been wounded, perhaps mortally, when her God-conversation supposedly happened. The final shot to the head might have been unnecessary.

Moreover, there is no way to know if Harris or Klebold would have let Cassie or Rachel live if either had said "no" or begged for her life. By all available accounts, unlike Polycarp's judge, the teenage gunman made no such offer of mercy, at least explicitly. And without some explicit form of "if you do not change your mind," it is quite possible to argue that Cassie's and Rachel's deaths were not avoidable or voluntary, and thus they should not be considered martyrs but merely victims of murder.[53]

On a vastly larger scale, a similar difficulty has been faced by Jewish thinkers contemplating martyrdom and the Holocaust. Many previous manifestations of European anti-Semitism had offered Jews who did not simply flee, the stark choice of conversion to Christianity or death. The Nazis, however, determined to destroy everyone with Jewish blood—an involuntary condition that conversion to Christianity could not change. For this reason, theologian Richard L. Rubenstein asserted, "One of Hitler's greatest victories was that he deprived the Jews of all opportunity to be martyrs. There can be no martyrdom without free choice." He went on to observe, "the pathetic attempts of the Jewish community to see the six million as martyrs is a tragic albeit understandable misperception."[54] Is the attempt to see Cassie and Rachel as martyrs rather than as victims the same kind of misperception?

An important Jewish redefinition of martyrdom, which reintroduced choice, was rooted in the thought of Leo Baeck, the leading progressive rabbi in Germany at the time of the Holocaust. According to religious studies scholar S. Daniel Breslauer, "The choice of death" as the crucial element in martyrdom was transformed by Baeck into, "the choice of *meaning in death* given by the individual in his personal struggle for self-understanding."[55] Faced with an unavoidable death, such "martyrs" choose to defy the nihilistic despair their killers try to impose upon them, and affirm hope and meaning through their words and deeds. As one death camp survivor said of her determination, "And if I did die in Auschwitz, it would be as a human being; I would hold onto my dignity. I was not going to become the contemptible brute my enemy wanted me to be."[56] In other words, one must die a "good death"—a death that is an extension of the integrity and dignity of one's life, a death that denies the killer's power over the meaning of one's life and death.

While Cassie's and Rachel's brief confrontations with Harris or Klebold were very different from the extended and systematic degradations of Auschwitz, there is still an essential similarity. Had either lied and said, "No, I don't believe in God," or had denied God in despair, or had begged for her life, she would have become "what her enemy wanted her to be."[57] It is not hard to imagine Harris or Klebold, after hearing such denials or pleas for mercy, calling the girls hypocrites before pulling the trigger. According to the popular stories about their deaths, both gave, instead, the same affirmative answer they would have under normal circumstances. It is possible to argue that both died a good death, a martyr's death, because they chose *meaning in death.* "I know that her death was not a waste," wrote Misty Bernall, "but a triumph of honesty and courage. To me, Cassie's life says that it is better to die for what you believe, than to live a lie."[58] This reinterpretation of martyrdom as "heroic individualism" still retains the visceral power of the more traditional concept to elicit admiration, emulation, and action.[59]

The second problem with the Columbine martyr stories, stemming from Klausner's definition of martyrdom, is that of group/ideological conflict, or the political dimension of martyrdom. The martyr challenges the authority of a group or its agents to impose its definition of truth or reality. "Martyrdom," observed Klausner, "is an attempt to break through the ideological and social boundaries between the conflicting groups with hierocratic, religiously based power."[60]

Eugene and Anita Weiner suggest three kinds of circumstances in which such group conflict produces martyrs. "When a nascent group, which has been banned, attempts to form (the formative situation); when a social movement is attempting to reestablish or revitalize itself after being presumed moribund or after being banned (the reformative situation); or when existing groups are attempting to achieve hegemony over the same population (the Zero-sum competitive situation)."[61]

This typology provides a useful way of examining martyrdom as a conflict strategy in a wide variety of historical cases. Yet at first glance it is not particularly helpful in understanding the political dimension of the Columbine martyr stories. Why? The belief that Cassie and Rachel supposedly died for—belief in God—is regularly affirmed by approximately 90 percent of the U.S. population in public opinion surveys.[62] The national motto—"In God We Trust"—is embossed or imprinted on all forms of the nation's currency by an act of Congress. The "Pledge of Allegiance" that was conducted at U.S. schools on the morning of April 20, 1999, included the statement that the United States is "one nation, under God." The social landscape of America teems with voluntary religious organizations, exempted by the government from paying taxes, the vast majority of which affirm a belief in God. All this would seem to indicate that belief in God is hardly a formative or reformative social movement in America, or that theism is competing with atheism for hegemony. Generalized or nondenominational theism, "Yes, I believe in God," has been and remains dominant.

The apparent absence of a dimension of group conflict is even more pronounced when we look in vain for the "ideologically contrasting group" that Harris and Klebold represented. Much has been, and continues to be, written about the killers' possible motives, which may have been as suicidal as homicidal. And as writer A. Alvarez observed in *The Savage God,* "Suicide is a closed world with its own irresistible logic."[63] Perhaps a more complete and less speculative picture will emerge if the videotapes the two made explaining their crime are released to the public. But I find it hard to believe that we will discover in their utterances anything that could reasonably be termed a systematic or integrated program of ideas, an "ideology." Harris and Klebold seem more like Leopold and Loeb, who killed for twisted personal reasons, than Sacco and Vanzetti, who killed to advance a political cause.

As we will see in the following chapters, there is evidence that Harris and Klebold had contempt, if not hatred, for Christians.[64] This is used to assert that this hatred was the reason they killed Cassie and Rachel. Perhaps, but since their original plan was to explode a bomb in the crowded cafeteria of the school, potentially and quite indiscriminately killing hundreds, it is not obvious that "ideological" hatred of Christians, Christianity, or God was central to Harris and Klebold's motives.

Like the "tyrants" of many martyrological narratives, Harris and Klebold ruthlessly exercised the power of life and death. But unlike the magistrates who send the martyrs to the stake, the gallows, or the chopping block, Harris and Klebold did not exercise that power on behalf of any continuing empire, nation, institution, community, or cause. The so-called Trench Coat Mafia of which the two killers were supposedly "members" was at best an ephemeral school clique that ceased to exist on the day of the shooting.[65] Harris's reported desire to "kick-start a revolution"[66] through terroristic violence has led to the attempt to see the Columbine killers in the context of the American tradition of youth radicalism. In the American Studies journal *49th Parallel,* Nicholas Turse suggested that "Eric Harris and Dylan Klebold may be the Mark Rudd and Abbie Hoffman figures of today." Turse recognized that Harris and Klebold had no articulated political program, but argued, "The randomness of their 'non-campaign' may be the ultimate expression of 'rage against the machine,' ripping into the system, as it were, at its most vulnerable and fundamental level, perhaps more so than Weatherman's bombing of the U.S. Capitol."[67] Historian David Farber found Turse's description to be "ludicrous" and observed that, "It only makes sense in an academic culture in which transgression is by definition political and in which any kind of rage against society can be considered radical."[68] Whatever the relationship of Harris and Klebold to youth radicalism of the past, the more important point is that aside from a handful of copycats, now sitting in prisons, no one has joined their "revolution." Their particular community of alienated adolescents was only a nation of two, and it died with them.

Given the lack of group and ideological conflict behind these killings, it might be more accurate to regard Cassie and Rachel as victims of a crime rather than as martyrs for a cause. Like the others who died on April 20, 1999, at Columbine, and like so many others who have been killed for no reason other than the perversity of a killer, Cassie and Rachel were merely murdered not martyred.

This is clearly *not* the view of those who regard Cassie or Rachel as modern-day Christian martyrs. But Cassie and Rachel can only be martyrs if Harris and Klebold can be understood as agents or instruments of a group/ideology that is hostile to the assertion, "Yes, I believe in God." What that group/ideology might be is apparent if we remember that the community that has continued to embrace and promote Cassie and Rachel as martyrs is not the 90 percent of Americans who say they believe in God, or even the 80 percent who identify themselves as "Christian"—Roman Catholic, Protestant, or Orthodox. Instead the community whose leadership has granted the "badge of martyrdom" to Cassie and Rachel is evangelical Christianity.

So what does this tell us about the political dimension of the Columbine martyrs? A great deal. Ideological conflict has long been important to the evangelical tradition. "Distinction, engagement, and conflict vis-à-vis outsiders constitutes a crucial element of what we might call the 'cultural DNA' of American evangelicalism," observed sociologist Christian Smith. "The evangelical tradition's entire history, theology, and self-identity presupposes and reflects strong cultural boundaries with the nonevangelicals; a zealous burden to convert and transform the world outside of itself; and a keen perception of external threats and crises seen as menacing what it views to be true, good, and valuable."[69]

The nature and source of that menace has changed in the course of American history. But currently the most politicized portion of the evangelical community, religious conservatives, or the so-called Christian Right, has understood the secularization of American public life, especially in the public schools, as the essential threat to be countered. As we will see in more detail in chapter 4, secularization is understood as creating a moral vacuum in our culture and in the hearts of our children, a void that makes horrors such as Columbine not only possible but inevitable. Thus, Harris and Klebold were not really the agents of a cause or community. They were instead *symp-*

toms of a cultural pathology created by an ideological secularism and its implementation by the community of the political Left. And the dying words of the Columbine martyrs indict those responsible and challenge the legitimacy of such dangerous policies.

This argument can be, and often is, made entirely in sociological terms. There is a deeper spiritual linkage, however, between the "separation of church and state" and school shootings that makes the martyrs of Columbine powerful political as well as religious symbols for many evangelicals. The core of this linkage can be seen in the Apostle Paul's advice in Ephesians 6:11–12 (King James Version).[70] "Put on the whole armour of God, that ye may be able to stand against the wiles of the devil. For we wrestle not against flesh and blood, but against principalities, against powers, against the rulers of the darkness of this world, against spiritual wickedness in high places." Understood from this perspective, the "ideologically contrasting group" against which Cassie and Rachel stood is *spiritual:* the demonic kingdom of Satan, the adversary of God. Harris and Klebold, like all those who shed the blood of martyrs in the past, were indeed "flesh and blood," as are the secularists and leftists who created the cultural conditions for Columbine to occur. The "prince of demons" must do his work, attacking the people of God, through such fleshly instruments. The people of God must respond with similar instruments, but without forgetting the spiritual nature of the struggle and remembering who the real spiritual enemy is.

The Columbine martyrs provide a way to hold together the sociological and the spiritual, the political and the religious, in evangelicalism's ongoing argument with contemporary American culture. At least on a conceptual and symbolic level, these innocents martyred by a satanic secularism are reminiscent of Voltaire's observation, "If God did not exist, it would be necessary to invent him." The deaths of Cassie and Rachel are not inventions but hard, sad facts. The meanings derived from and given to their all-too-brief lives, however, to a degree, are works of creative and hopeful interpretation. And so we turn in the next two chapters to an examination of their lives as understood by those who believe they died as modern-day martyrs.

CHAPTER 2

CASSIE BERNALL

"Feeding the World with One Word"

Cassie's mother, Misty Bernall, in her book *She Said Yes: The Unlikely Martyrdom of Cassie Bernall,* observed, "One thing Brad [her husband] and I were totally unprepared for after Cassie's death was the extent of its impact beyond Littleton." According to Misty Bernall, letters and gifts flooded into her home from around the world. As testimony to the extent of Cassie's renown, she was even told by friends who had visited a remote village in the Sudan that people there knew of Cassie and had wanted to create a memorial to her in their church.[1]

The fact that a particular story could be spread so quickly and throughout the world should not surprise us in the age of 24–7 global media and the Internet. But why Cassie's story? Beyond the endless need of journalists to find human interest stories to fill air time and column inches, Cassie's story spread because it was so intrinsically powerful. People opened their newspapers, saw the photo of a smiling girl, read the story, and asked themselves, "Would I . . . could I . . . have done that?"

Was Cassie's story more important than that of William "Dave" Sanders, the teacher who was mortally wounded while leading students to safety? An editorial in the *Chicago Tribune* cited Sander's story and other heroic acts at Columbine. "But Cassie's is perhaps the most compelling," concluded the editorial, "because it was the simplest. She could have lied—but didn't. She could have fudged or quibbled—but didn't. She simply said 'Yes.'" The same editorial referred to this as an "example of true moral heroism" that was "humbling and awe-inspiring."[2]

As a striking example of truth-telling, Cassie's story had a certain resonance even with the most secular audience. But the real staying power of the story was rooted in its religious import. To those evangelicals for whom the public proclamation of their beliefs is essential, Cassie's last words became a rallying cry for the cause of Christ. As Reverend Dave McPherson, the youth pastor of Cassie's church, a congregation of the Evangelical Presbyterian Church, said at her funeral service, "Jesus fed 5,000 with five loaves of bread and two fish. But Cassie fed the world with one word, 'yes.'"[3] Josh McDowell, a prominent author and speaker at Christian youth events, within two weeks of the shooting predicted, "Cassie's life is going to probably have a more phenomenal impact upon young people over the next 10 years than anything I've seen in the last 10 or 15 years."[4] A cover story of *Christianity Today,* the most prominent magazine in the American evangelical community, referred to Cassie's significance with the title, "'Do You Believe in God?': How Columbine Changed America."[5]

POPULAR RESPONSES

Evidence of this elevation of Cassie within the evangelical community was anecdotal but easy to find. In the months after the massacre, for instance, she became the subject of multiple tribute web sites or pages.[6] Such sites probably did not draw many visitors and did not therefore create or form popular opinion. Instead, they may have reflected, however idiosyncratically, spontaneously generated popular sentiment about Columbine and its meaning. Varying widely in their size and degree of technical sophistication, these sites usually contained some version of the account of her martyrdom, sometimes depicting her as dying more specifically for faith in Christ, rather than simply for God.[7] These sites often featured images of Cassie, ranging from simple reproductions of her school photo or snapshots, to elaborate iconography with her smiling face superimposed over a stairway to heaven with the beckoning figure of Jesus in the background and "Yes . . . I believe!" in the foreground.[8]

A consistent theme in these tributes was the personal inspiration that Cassie's example has provided. The creator of one tribute explained, "God has put it on my heart to create a page dedicated to a very faithful Woman of God. I did not know Cassie but her story so touched me that it made me want to try for a closer relationship with the one true God and His son Jesus Christ."[9] Another such tribute site, "Cassie's Call," sponsored by a Chicago-area church, asserted, "Cassie indeed rose to the full stature of both ancient and new Christian martyrs, who received a very special baptism in the blood they shed for the sake of Christ." The site offered visitors the opportunity to take "The 'Cassie' Pledge." Those taking this pledge not only promised to become better Christians but also affirmed that "I will remember Cassie Bernall and her commitment to Christ to her very death." Visitors to this site were also offered the opportunity to make a contribution to building the "Cassie Bernall Youth Center and Gymnasium."[10]

Someone using the pen name Entropy Squared wrote, "The Temptation of Cassie Bernall," which draws a parallel with the third temptation of Christ by Satan in Matthew 4. Harris and Klebold are "Satan's minions" who have been commanded to bring to their master a "harvest of souls." Satan especially wanted "the choicest souls of all—those of Christians who had denied their faith in their Lord." The author depicts Cassie seeing another girl spared by pleading for mercy, thus offering Cassie hope of life if she will only deny belief in God. "Without words," observed the author, "Satan gave her the same temptation he gave to Jesus. 'All these things will I give thee, if thou wilt fall down and worship me.'" Like Christ's answer, "Get thee hence, Satan," her affirmation of God, the author tells us, "surely re-echoed to heaven itself." Defeated by Cassie's faith, Satan left Littleton "wailing with only his minions in tow."[11]

One of the more elaborate pieces of inspirational writing posted on the web was the text of a sermon that depicted a meeting in heaven between God and the angels held on the morning of April 20, 1999. With the hymn "Amazing Grace" playing in the background, the sermon depicts various angels reporting on their preparations. Justin, the "master angel in charge of prevention," suggests Cassie be granted "martyr status" and provided with "a special mansion in the martyr neighborhood." And in the last moments before the gunfire, God agrees, saying, "Justin, I authorize martyr status for my daughter, Cassie."[12]

The Reverend Billy Graham, perhaps the most venerable figure in the American evangelical community, paid tribute to Cassie during an April 28, 1999, interview with Larry King. After King repeated the story of Cassie's final moments, Graham said, "That's right, and how wonderful. I would like to do the same. I wish that I could die for my faith."[13] Graham also made multiple references to Columbine as an example of "spiritual warfare" in his June 5, 1999, crusade meeting in an Indianapolis, Indiana, stadium. Graham also featured the stories of both Cassie and Rachel Scott in his remarks. "Cassie and Rachel were faced with the ultimate peer pressure: the barrel of a gun," Graham told the crowd of 42,000. "Would any of you have done the same thing?" he asked.[14]

Both the religious and nonreligious press took note of how various evangelical youth ministries focused on Columbine and prominently featured Cassie's story in their literature and at events.[15] One of the largest of these events was held only five days after the shooting. Teen Mania's "Acquire the Fire" rally in a Pontiac, Michigan, stadium was attended by a reported 73,000 young people. "These school shootings are a wake-up call for our country," Teen Mania president Ron Luce told attendees. "When you leave, burn a path all the way home and start a revolution of righteousness, love and forgiveness." Speakers at the rally also frequently mentioned Cassie, who reportedly had attended a Denver-area Teen Mania event in 1998. "Her confession of faith in the face of death," stated a Teen Mania press release, "has inspired young people all around the nation to stand strong for their faith."[16]

Luce of Teen Mania also published a book, *Columbine Courage: Rock-Solid Faith,* filled with Columbine-related testimonials—many of which mentioned Cassie or Rachel—from youth pastors and teenagers. "Our youth pastor gave an amazing altar call right after the Columbine shooting happened," a student from Oklahoma named Joy reported. He talked about Cassie—"It was a large youth rally that night and over 500 kids came to the altar. It was totally a move of God!" These testimonials were grouped thematically with biblical stories about David, Elijah, Paul, Peter, Joshua, Gideon, Jeremiah, and others. The back cover bears a quotation attributed to Cassie. "I want to live completely for God. It's hard and scary but totally worth it!"[17]

A teen-led youth ministry, Revival Generation, established by coincidence in the Littleton, Colorado, area shortly before the shooting, experienced rapid growth. The ministry's leader and spokesperson, Josh Weidmann, said that before Columbine the group was receiving 5 calls a week about how to set up Bible study and prayer groups in public schools. But after the shooting, they were getting a weekly average of 100 calls.[18] A booklet produced by the group contained a tribute to Columbine's most famous victim: "Cassie would lose her life so / that others might gain theirs."[19] The *Washington Post* reported, citing Weidmann's experiences in the summer of 1999, that at "teenage revivals where survivors of Columbine speak, girls storm the stage begging for forgiveness just at the mention of Cassie's name."[20]

Billy Graham, Teen Mania, and Revival Generation were hardly the only ministries who directly used Columbine or Cassie in their evangelistic appeals. Based on reports from Doug Clark, the field director of the National Network of Youth Ministries, *Time* reported in May 1999 that there had been "hundreds of teen gatherings on the tragedy."[21] Because Columbine was so well known in the culture at large, there were innumerable sermons, prayer meetings, Bible studies, and other formal and informal gatherings and conversations, both online and offline, in which the martyr stories were repeated and reinforced in the minds of a whole generation of evangelical teenagers.

Other evangelicals have also *indirectly* tapped into the power of Columbine and Cassie's story. As part of its youth ministry, Victory Fellowship Church, a 2000-member Assemblies of God congregation in Metairie, Louisiana, created a play called "Beyond the Grave: The Class of 2000." It was meant originally to be performed twice during the 1999 Halloween weekend. By popular request, performances continued for audiences of 1000 or more. Aside from breaks for holidays and parts of the summer, "Beyond the Grave" continued to be performed every Friday evening into 2001. Dozens typically responded to an "altar call" at the end of each performance. Copies of a videotape of the play have also been distributed widely to other churches and youth ministries. The play was also taken on the road by Victory Fellowship and performed at other churches in the Southeast. This success also inspired imitation. An Assemblies of God congregation in New Jersey held their own weekly performances of "Beyond the Grave" throughout 2001–2002.[22]

"Beyond the Grave" depicts the last day in the lives of five students and one teacher who are killed in a Columbine-like shooting at "Metairie High School." We also see each victim "beyond the grave" being welcomed into heaven or dragged off to hell by demons. Their eternal destiny is based on whether they had accepted Jesus as their savior. One of the students who goes to heaven, "Liz," a Christian who wears a T-shirt with the slogan "Property of God," is obviously based on Cassie Bernall. The three gunmen, who all wear black clothing and Goth-style makeup, take over a classroom. Brian, their leader, who wears a Marilyn Manson T-shirt, rants against "Snobs, Jocks, Preps, Blacks, and Christians." Brian asks two students if they believe in Jesus, and when they say "no," he does not shoot. He then tells Liz to stand up. Menacingly cocking his gun, Brian asks, "Do you believe in Jesus?" A trembling Liz says, "I believe in Jesus with my whole heart! What about you Brian?" He responds by shooting her. This exchange is not only pivotal in dramatic terms, for the killing spree begins, but it also provides the play with its paradigmatic moment of the confrontation between spiritual good and evil. Beyond the impact on those who have had a conversion experience as a result of the play, "Beyond the Grave" has dramatically reiterated Cassie's story, and an interpretation of its meaning, to thousands without ever mentioning Columbine or her name.[23]

CASSIE'S FAMILY: KEEPERS OF THE SHRINE

Even more striking than these popular and essentially spontaneous responses to Cassie's story is the careful attempt by her parents to retain control of Cassie's image, story, and legacy. At the center of this effort is the Cassie Bernall Foundation, a nonprofit 501(c)(3) foundation established to "remember and celebrate the life of Cassie Bernall." The activities of this foundation have been variously described. On the foundation's web site, *www.cassiebernall.com,* we learn that it "will support Denver-area youth groups and administer a scholarship fund."[24] The most notable enterprise of the foundation was working with a Christian missionary organization in central Honduras to establish an orphanage, the Cassie Bernall Home for Children, dedicated on the first anniversary of her death.[25] The foundation is supported by donations from the public as well as an unspecified portion of the proceeds from a variety of projects and products described below.

A primary activity of both Brad and Misty Bernall has been a continuing series of speaking engagements at events around the country.[26] But the most successful enterprise has been Misty Bernall's book about her daughter, *She Said Yes: The Unlikely Martyrdom of Cassie Bernall.* Released in September 1999, and boosted by a national publicity campaign, *She Said Yes* appeared on several bestseller lists, including five weeks on the *New York Times* list.

By the first anniversary of the Columbine shooting in April 2000, *She Said Yes* had reportedly sold 500,000 copies. Word Publishing, a much stronger presence in the evangelical publishing industry than Plough, had released a new edition. Several foreign language editions were on the market as well as an unabridged audio version featuring the voices of the Bernall family. Simon & Schuster's Pocket Books distributed a mass-market paperback edition in the fall of 2000.[27]

There is also a series of licensed but independently produced derivative "She Said Yes" works. Each bears the phrase "She Said Yes" as well as the distinctive cover art of the book, featuring Cassie's smiling face in the cross hairs of a telescopic rifle sight. *She Said Yes: A Video Tribute to Cassie Bernall by Her Friends* was produced by West Bowles Community Church (WBCC), the church where Cassie was part of the youth group. The tape features scenes from the television coverage of students running from Columbine High, excerpts from Cassie's funeral service, as well as interviews with WBCC youth group members, friends, and the Bernalls themselves. The tape leads up to a set-to-music montage of snapshots and home video moments of Cassie smiling, fishing, rock climbing, and hanging out with her friends. It ends with an advertisement for the book, *She Said Yes,* and information on the Cassie Bernall Foundation and its web site.[28]

The "Cassie in the cross hairs" cover art also appears on other products, including *She Said Yes: A Bible Study Based on the Life of Cassie Bernall,* written by Jeff Diedrich, who explained that the Bible study was "not a chapter by chapter account of the book" but was instead intended to "pull qualities from her life and illuminate them by studying the Apostle Paul's life."[29] *Crossroads at Columbine,* a one-act play based on *She Said Yes,* was first performed at Denver's South Sheridan Baptist Church in November 1999. Rather than depicting Cassie's death, the play focuses on the events leading to her conversion to Christianity some two years earlier.[30] The author of the play is Alan Behn, a professor at Northland Baptist Bible College in Dunbar, Wisconsin. The "Proclaimers Drama Team" from that college toured churches in the Midwest and Southeast, performing the play during the spring and summer of 2000.[31] Others wishing to perform the play pay a flat fee, which covers the royalties for an unlimited number of performances, and receive copies of the script along with a CD containing a soundtrack and other materials to aid production of the play.[32] Both the Bible study and the play are distributed by Positive Action for Christ, a North Carolina-based publishing house that describes itself as "specializing in youth curriculum for fundamental churches."[33]

Rather different kinds of derivative products are available through *YesIBelieve.com*. Like the popular WWJD (What Would Jesus Do) line of apparel products for Christian teenagers, *YesIBelieve.com* offers an assortment of T-shirt, hats, and jewelry with the slogan "Yes, I believe." Copies of Misty Bernall's book, *She Said Yes*, as well as the *Video Tribute*, the *Bible Study*, and *Crossroads at Columbine* can also be purchased at this site. Started by Jason Janz, the youth pastor of South Sheridan Baptist Church where *Crossroads at Columbine* was first performed, the *YesIBelieve.com* site features the endorsement of the Bernall family "as the official line of products regarding our daughter's life and testimony." In addition to the online Yes, I Believe or YIB! Store, there is also a YIB! chat room and discussion board, and an e-mail newsletter. Visitors to this site can also "Make A Statement of Faith" by signing up for a free e-mail account (yourname@yesibelieve.com). *YesIBelieve.com* also provides online resources and literature for organizing YIB! Clubs, "non-denominational, evangelistic Bible clubs," in public schools.[34]

The Cassie Bernall Foundation also received the proceeds from *Whatever It Takes—The "She Said Yes" Music Project*, a compilation album with songs by a number of well-known Christian recording artists. Advertised with artwork used on the other *She Said Yes*-related items, the project also offers a videotape containing "interviews with Cassie's family and friends" as well as the music videos of various artists on the album.[35]

Perhaps the most popular song about Cassie was "This is Your Time," cowritten by well-known Christian recording artist Michael W. Smith after he performed at the Columbine memorial service.[36] This album does not utilize the *She Said Yes* artwork, but Smith asked for and received the Bernalls' personal approval of the song before releasing it.[37] The album on which the song appears, also called *This Is Your Time,* sold more than 120,000 copies during its first week on the market—reportedly a record for contemporary Christian musical albums.[38] A critical as well as commercial success, "This Is Your Time," was honored with a Dove Award as "Song of the Year" by the Gospel Music Association. A music video based on this song also won a Dove Award.[39] The success of these products was due in large part to Smith's long-standing popularity, but some part must undoubtedly go to their association with Cassie.

Smith also cowrote a short book entitled *This Is Your Time: Make Every Moment Count.* Combining lessons drawn from Cassie's life with those of other inspirational figures, Smith expanded on the basic theme of the song—the need to prepare for our own moment "when eternity whispers into our hearts, *This is your time.*"[40] While Smith's "This Is Your Time" products are not licensed by Plough, the Bernalls' publisher, it was evident he was operating in cooperation with them. He quoted extensively from *She Said Yes* with Plough's permission, and Smith wrote an afterword for the new edition of *She Said Yes* released in 2000 by Word Publishing.[41]

The rapidity, sophistication, and success with which the Bernalls have "marketed" their daughter's image and story have led cynics to claim that they were motivated by money. "Mommy travels on this money," read an *Amazon.com* customer review of *She Said Yes,* "she's raking it in from the book and it's [*sic*] aftermath. It is an ugly thing to make money off this, especially if you are the mother."[42] How much money the Bernalls have made from these enterprises and how much goes to their nonprofit foundation is unclear. But had the Bernalls really wanted to make money they could have gone to a major publisher rather than the small and obscure Plough Publishing House, an enterprise of the Bruderhof, a Christian communal group.[43] The Bernalls also turned down many offers for the motion picture and television rights to their daughter's story before reaching an agreement with the North American Mission Board of the Southern Baptist Convention—hardly a big-money "player" in the entertainment industry.[44]

Rather than regarding the Bernalls as exploiters of their murdered daughter it is probably better to regard them as the guardians of their daughter's memory—the keepers of her shrine. By proactively setting forth their own version of the meaning of Cassie's life and death they precluded others from promoting misconceptions and alternative meanings. Upon hearing her daughter referred to as the "martyr of Littleton," Misty Bernall recalled, "At first I didn't know what to make of it. Cassie is my daughter, I thought. You can't turn her into Joan of Arc."[45] Misty Bernall's decision to tell the story herself reflects a determination not to let others make her daughter in death something she was not in life.

It has been obvious that the Bernalls have regarded *She Said Yes* and its derivatives as part of a ministry to which they have been called by their daughter's sudden death. "We are now endeavoring," wrote the Bernalls in their endorsement of *YesIBelieve.com,* "to be responsible with the ministry that God has now given to us—to carry Cassie's message throughout the world."[46] But what is this message?

CASSIE'S MESSAGE

The most obvious meaning derived from Cassie's martyrological story was the urgency of winning converts to Christianity. Franklin Graham, after telling Cassie's story at the April 25 memorial service, said, "The gunman took her life, and I believe that Cassie went immediately into the presence of Almighty God. She was ready." Graham then asked his audience, "If, by some strange turn of events, your life came to an end this day, would you, like Cassie, be prepared to stand before a holy God?"[47] This question was, of course, a variation on evangelicalism's tried and true witnessing ploy, "If you died right now, where would you spend eternity?" Graham's nationally televised sermon was merely one of the first of many efforts by American evangelicals to use "the girl who said yes" as a powerful tool to lead others to Christ.

The usefulness of Cassie's sudden death for proselytizing was readily apparent on the grassroots level. "My unsaved friends keep asking why Cassie said yes [to the God question]," a 14-year-old from Texas told *Time*. "Sometimes if a lot of them are interested, I will get a Bible and walk them through Scripture to help them understand."[48] The unexpected nature of Cassie's death is also a reminder to share the Gospel *now,* before it is too late. As a member of Cassie's church youth group observed, "You can't hesitate in being a witness because you know how precious life is and how fast it changes."[49] And to the unsaved, one tribute web site offered this advice. "Just a little reminder, if you are ever in a situation like Cassie's, make sure that you and Jesus Christ have it all worked out."[50]

This sort of "reminder" was made even more clear by a witnessing tract, "She Said Yes: A Story of Hope From Columbine High." The cover has her smiling face floating above the famous Columbine crosses. Written as though Cassie herself was speaking from heaven, the tract presented a "first person" version of her conversion and her "moment of truth" in the Columbine library. Readers were assured by "Cassie" that she is "glad" she said "YES!" to the gunman's question. "For today, I am with God. Nothing can take that away from me!" Then "Cassie" leads readers through a series of verses from scripture, urging them to say "YES to Jesus, just as I did." And finally "Cassie" guides readers to recite the classic "sinner's prayer," which ends "Jesus, please come into my heart. Amen."[51]

Evangelicalism has always stressed the urgency of accepting and sharing the Gospel with all people at all stages in life. But evangelicals who saw Columbine as the spark for a spiritual revival seemed to concentrate particularly on teenagers. The evangelical tradition, of course, has long had a special concern with ministry to the young and their special role in the reviving work of God. As theologian Jonathan Edwards observed in his 1741 work *Some Thoughts Concerning the Revival,* "The work [of revival] has chiefly been amongst those that are young. . . . And indeed, it has commonly been so, when God has begun any great work for the revival of his church; he has taken the young people, and cast off the old and stiff-necked generation."[52]

The methods used by evangelicals to reach the young have adapted to the shifting patterns of American society and culture, especially the development of a distinctive and dynamic "youth cul-ture." These adaptations have ranged from the nineteenth-century's urban YMCA and YWCA, Billy Graham's Youth for Christ rallies in the 1940s, the long-haired street preachers and beach baptisms of the 1960s "Jesus movement," to the Christian "Heavy Metal" bands of the 1980s.[53] Continuing this tradition of pragmatic adaptation, contemporary evangelical youth ministries, "don't try to turn young people into 1950s Christians," observed historian of American reli-gion Brenda Brasher. "They try to meet young people where they are today."[54]

There is, of course, some truth in the cynical observation that evangelicals are simply trying to win the next generation of "con-sumers" to their "product" in the same way that commercial entities market to the young in order to create long-lasting brand loyalties. If appealing to the young to accept Christ using Columbine was mar-keting, it was very smart marketing. A survey about Columbine by the Pew Research Center found "public interest in the story was es-pecially high among young people, who tend to pay less attention than older Americans to most types of news." Seventy-three percent of those under 30 followed the story "very closely" compared to sixty-eight percent for the entire public.[55] For those who walk the halls of thousands of public high schools similar to Columbine, the prospect of encountering someone like Harris or Klebold may be far more real than to their elders. An *ABC News/Washington Post* poll, conducted April 22–25, 1999, asked "Can you think of any students at your own school who you think might be troubled enough to do something like this?" Some 40 percent of high school teenagers re-sponded "yes," while only 23 percent of parents of high school stu-dents gave the same answer.[56]

Over the next two years, Columbine became a favorite subject for college admission essays. While recent events are often hot topics, an admissions director of a small private college in the Northeast observed, "I've never seen the volume on a single sub-ject like this in 10 years." It is not hard to see why Columbine, a shooting at a large, middle-class, suburban high school, might have special personal resonance for those attending similar schools elsewhere. "It makes me wonder whether Columbine is this generation's Kent State," said the same admissions director. "It's really a defining moment in their teen lives."[57]

Given the "realness" of Columbine to young people, perhaps the most powerful function of Cassie was to provide an accessible model of spiritual heroism. As J. Bottum, in the conservative journal *First Things,* observed, "Cassie Bernall died a death so archetypal, it is almost an adolescent's *fantasy* of martyrdom."[58] One Internet bulletin board posting recounted Cassie's story and then asked: "DO I HAVE THAT KIND OF LOVE FOR GOD??? . . . Every time that I think of doing something that I KNOW God would not want me to do, I can think of Cassie."[59] Ben, a 15-year-old, told the *New York Times,* "She's definitely a hero. If I was ever faced with a situation like that, I hope I could do what she did."[60] "That's true faith," said an 18-year-old in *USA Today.* "I'd like to believe like that."[61] "When I heard about Columbine, and what Cassie did," read a message posted on a tribute web site by an 11-year-old girl, "I automatically wanted to grow up and be like her. She is a girls [*sic*] dream role model."[62]

Cassie was obviously accessible because of her age. One participant in a large teen ministry event, held just days after the massacre, told *Time* magazine that the most important thing for young people about Cassie's story is that "a lot of martyrs have been older, and you don't hear about teens."[63] Hearing more about teen martyrs was an important feature of *Jesus Freaks (Giving It All For Jesus),* a popular book jointly created by Voice of the Martyrs, an organization concerned with persecution of Christians around the world, and dc Talk, a recording group popular among Christian teens. Essentially a reworking and updating of the classic *Foxe's Book of Martyrs* for a contemporary youth audience, *Jesus Freaks* features the stories of many children and adolescents who are suffering for their faith today, as well as martyrological narratives from the Bible and Christian history. The book opens with a story that was clearly Cassie's, but changed so that it could be anytime, anywhere.

She was 17 years old. He stood glaring at her, his weapon before her face. "Do you believe in God?" She paused. It was a life or death decision. "Yes, I believe in God." "Why?" asked her executioner. But he never gave her the chance to respond. The teenage girl lay dead at his feet.

Readers were then told that this did not happen in ancient Rome or in a distant country. "It happened at Columbine High School in Littleton, Colorado, on April 20, 1999."[64]

Beyond the mere fact of age, Cassie was in many respects like those who came to admire her. Not particularly popular or accomplished, Cassie would have been hard to distinguish from her peers. Like so many other white, middle-class, suburban 17-year-old girls, she wore Doc Martin boots and a WWJD bracelet, struggled with her weight, and didn't have a date for the junior prom. Even within her church youth group, Cassie did not fit in particularly well.[65] In a notebook found after her death, Cassie wrote about herself. "I want to be a fun, energetic fireball who people want to be around. But I am not."[66]

Beneath her relative lack of outward distinction, a condition shared by most of her peers, Cassie's inward journey toward emotional stability and Christian commitment had been troubled— again, something many her own age may understand. This journey, which we know ends with sudden yet noble death and therefore demands the reader's sympathy, is at the heart of Misty Bernall's book about her daughter's life, *She Said Yes.* "In retrospect," wrote her mother, "Cassie's change from a trusting child to a sulking stranger was so gradual that it blindsided us."[67] This "blindsiding" is, of course, not uncommon for parents of adolescents. Teenagers often assert their independence and/or alienation by choosing music, clothing, friends, and values their parents find objectionable. Cassie's parents, however, decided to take action when they found a cache of letters from one of her friends that discussed sex, drugs, the songs of Marilyn Manson, self-mutilation, the occult, vampirism, satanic rituals, and even the murder of a teacher and their parents. "Cassie was headed toward a cliff edge," wrote her mother, "and we had to pull her back immediately. There was no choice."[68]

The Bernalls stopped all contact between Cassie and her old friends, enrolled her temporarily in a private Christian school, routinely searched her room, strictly supervised her every waking moment, and even moved to a new neighborhood. These steps were justified because, as her mother wrote, "Unfashionable as it might be to suggest it, I felt that we were engaged in a spiritual battle."[69]

Cassie's response to her parent's "tough love," according to her mother's account, was equally dramatic: fits of screaming anger, attempts to run away, and threats of suicide. While the Bernalls were able to hold their own in this battle of wills, the "spiritual battle" for her soul was only won when Cassie had a conversion experience at a church-sponsored youth retreat in the spring of 1997.

Her father, in a television interview, said she later described her conversion to him. "Dad, I felt the Lord come upon me. . . . I was filled with the Joy of the Lord and I understood where I was going, where I was then, why you did everything that you and Mom did and where I'm going now."[70] When she returned from the retreat, she told her mother, "Mom, I've changed. I've totally changed. I know you are not going to believe it, but I'll prove it to you."[71] Her father remembered, "It was as if she had been in a dark room, and somebody had turned the light on, and she could see the beauty surrounding her."[72]

Cassie's mother, however, did not make this conversion experience "the sole point of the story,"[73] but rather Cassie's subsequent struggles to grow as a person and as a Christian. Cassie was *not* turned into a plaster saint who can do no wrong. "The daughter I knew," wrote her mother, "was equally capable of being selfish and stubborn, and that sometimes she behaved like a spoiled two-year-old."[74] A school friend observed, "People can call Cassie a martyr, but they're off track if they think she was this righteous, holy person, and that all she did was read her Bible. She was just as real as anybody else."[75] This was underlined in *She Said Yes: A Bible Study.* "Though she was heroic that day," wrote the author, "she was not angelic. Cassie shared the same struggles of loneliness, anger, and depression that most teenagers have."[76] All of this only decreases the distance between Cassie and the reader and adds to the sense of recognition that says, "That could be my child," or "That could be me. I could do what she did."

This identification can be fostered by purchasing and using "Yes, I Believe" apparel or other retail merchandise described above. Many, both outside and within the evangelical community, have often ridiculed such items as "Jesus Junk" or "Christian kitsch," and have dismissed their significance except as proof of poor taste. But as historian Colleen McDannell argued in *Material Christianity,* "Christian retailing provides the visible and tactile images that help conservative Protestants create a Christian subculture." McDannell compares this to the public display of special symbols and slogans on T-shirts or bumper stickers by members of particular minority groups to "assert their special status as a community competing for social and cultural attention." The Christian teenagers who wear "Yes, I Believe" T-shirts to public school or the shopping mall are using these goods, McDannell would argue, to "create religious landscapes to tell themselves and the world around them who they are."[77] And in proclaiming their identity, they run the risk of disapproval by peers outside their Christian subculture. For the mere price of a T-shirt, such teenagers may have gained the opportunity to experience a small test of the courage of their convictions—a small, safe taste of martyrdom.

Interwoven with the theme of ordinariness and accessibility in *She Said Yes* is the theme of Cassie's preparation for her fate. "I'm not saying," wrote her mother, "she consciously prepared herself for a terrible end. . . . Yet when tragedy struck her out of the blue, she remained calm and courageous. She was ready to go. Why?"[78] Her readiness to face death is explained as the product of her daily struggle to "die to herself" in order to let Christ live in her. "The world looks at Cassie's 'yes' of April 20," asserted Dave McPherson, the Pastor of Cassie's youth group, "but we need to look at the daily 'yes' she said day after day, month after month, before giving that final answer."[79] This daily struggle, according to McPherson, is "not a question of doing great deeds, but of being selfless in the small things."[80] The ordinariness of this process of preparation, small daily struggles to think of others and Christ, permits us to consider emulating Cassie's example in daily life.

Michael W. Smith, in his book *This Is Your Time,* makes the lesson of Cassie's preparation for great things through small things even more explicit. "Most of us will never be tested to the same extent that Cassie was," Smith pointed out, "but virtually all of us are tested on a regular basis in much smaller ways." After listing examples of such tests, Smith reminds his readers, "These are the mini-martyrdoms that Christ referred to when he said we must take up our cross *daily* (Luke 9:23)."[81] These daily doses of self-denial, "a mini-death that leads to new life," asserts Smith, are God's way "to build us up into the people we'll need to be to pass the test."[82]

But Cassie, according to her mother's account, also seemed to have an extraordinary, if unconscious, sense of preparation for her destiny. On many occasions she told her parents, "I'm never going to get married. I'll never have kids."[83] Her mother later told *Christianity Today* that Cassie refused to flirt with boys and "never had a first date."[84] (Yet in *She Said Yes,* there is a passing reference to "Mike," described as "Cassie's old boyfriend."[85]) The implied motif of sexual purity, at least since her conversion, as preparation for martyrdom is reinforced by a school friend who tells us, "I think Cassie felt that only God was going to be able to fulfill her."[86] McPherson, Cassie's youth pastor, took this theme of eroticized love of God to completion when he told those at her funeral not to cry because the service was actually a celebration of her wedding that had taken place in heaven. Jesus was the groom and "on the 20th he returned for Cassie."[87]

Cassie's own words also seem to hint that she had thought about facing death. A week before her death she told her mother, "Mom, I'm not afraid to die, because I'll be in heaven."[88] A note reportedly found in her room reads in part, "I will die for my God. I will die for my faith. It's the least I can do for Christ dying for me."[89] In a book used by Cassie's youth group, *Discipleship* by Heinrich Arnold, she had underlined these passages on suffering and death: "It is important for us to decide whether we want only a nice church or the way of the cross. This must be very clear to us: Jesus' way is the way of the cross. . . . All of us should live life so as to be able to face eternity at any time."[90]

One of Cassie's poems, supposedly written just days before her death, has been read as her prophecy of what was to come. She wrote of being willing "to suffer and to Die" with Christ and pledged to do "whatever it takes."[91]

It is hardly conclusive from this that Cassie sensed her impending martyrdom. Christianity, after all, is saturated with the imagery of and calls to suffering and self-sacrificial death. But for those predisposed to believe it, Cassie's poem is powerful evidence. On a page describing Cassie's life and death at the *YesIBelieve.com* site, these lines are used to describe her as *"both martyr and prophet."*[92] After initially appearing in the *Boston Globe* on April 24, 1999, "Cassie's Poem" has been recycled endlessly on tribute web sites and pages, and in other products and/or publications discussed above.[93] The Kry, a musical group said to be one of Cassie's favorites, used parts of this poem, especially the line "whatever it takes," in "Cassie's Song."[94]

The theme of preparation was, of course, linked to ideas of some greater divine purpose that would give meaning to Cassie's death and the terrible events of April 20. For those whose loss was most personal, the need to find such a purpose is especially pressing. Cassie's mother told *Christianity Today* magazine that shortly after the massacre, "I heard him [God] say that it had to be big, because if it wasn't big, no one would listen. And that he had been grooming Cassie all along for something like this, and that he would take care of her."[95] The impact of the shooting at Columbine High School were undoubtedly "big," but what is the message to which we are to listen?

The "Bernall Family Endorsement" at *YesIBelieve.com* makes a rather sweeping declaration of this message. "This tragedy occurred to awaken people's recognition of God's good and Satan's evil and the reality of both powers. We must accept this reality and begin modeling our lives after Jesus before these things will cease. Cassie was God's tool to initiate your change."[96] Folded into this message are the obvious "get saved before it's too late" and "here's a spiritual role model for teens" messages discussed previously.

But the Bernalls have also felt called to deliver a message to the parents of teenagers—a calling entirely in line with evangelicalism's perennial anxiety about the loss of their children to worldly influences. The great nineteenth-century evangelist Dwight L. Moody spoke to this anxiety when he warned his audiences, "How many fathers and mothers, how many Christian men and women, are sleeping now while their children wander over the terrible precipice right into the bottomless pit! Father, mother, where is your boy tonight?"[97] Echoing Moody, in a statement released just days after the shooting, Brad Bernall wrote, "To all the parents across our nation I would say, 'Do you know what your kids are doing? Do you ever verify?' You should. We are the front line in all issues regarding our children."[98]

Based on their own experience with Cassie's transformation, the Bernalls offer advice to others on that "front line." Indeed, *She Said Yes* seems aimed at teaching parents how to be parents. This teaching function is made even more explicit in a video and discussion guide produced and distributed by Active Parenting Publishers. Designed for use in parent, youth, and youth leader education programs, these materials use Cassie's life story to address such questions as how to counter "unhealthy influences" on youth as well as how "a strong church youth group can help teens cope with the pressures of adolescence." Most of all, the Active Parenting guide presents the Bernall's "heroic efforts" as a blueprint for Cassie's "180-degree change on the path she was traveling."[99]

It is worth noting that the Bernalls did not turn to psychologists, but to the police, their church, and strict discipline when Cassie went out of control. They concluded they had failed as parents by failing to *be* parents, to exercise parental authority. Instead they had tried to win Cassie's friendship, which only resulted in rebellion and disrespect. "I stopped trying to please Cassie and make her like me," wrote her mother, "and I started trying to guide her more consistently. Unbelievably, instead of rebelling, she accepted the boundaries I set for her and even seemed grateful for them."[100] While the Bernalls would undoubtedly give God the ultimate credit for their daughter's transformation, the message that religious and moral discipline, not secular and relativistic psychobabble, can rescue a child from self-destruction is a potent one for those parents predisposed to accept it. As Misty Bernall wrote, "With warmth, self-sacrifice, and honesty—with the love that ultimately comes from God—every child can be guided and saved."[101]

This resembles the child-rearing wisdom made popular in the evangelical community by Dr. James Dobson in *Dare to Discipline,* and his Colorado-based ministry, Focus on the Family.[102] But unlike Dobson, and many other evangelical authors, Misty Bernall seemed unwilling to link her message to the political and public policy agenda of the Christian or Religious Right. Instead she concentrated on a religious and private response. While acknowledging the political implications of Columbine, she wrote, "we cannot forget the equally vital role of our more personal efforts to prevent tragedies like the one that claimed Cassie."[103]

Yet even the Bernalls recognize that despite all their efforts, the message that others will derive from their daughter's life and death are not fully under their control. After telling Cassie's story and her own in heart-wrenching detail, Misty Bernall concluded *She Said Yes* by observing that, "Cassie's story is not only mine and Brad's. It is yours, and what you do with it now will give it meaning."[104] Try as they might to restrict the meaning of their daughter's life and death to the religious and the personal, the Bernalls could not prevent the use of Cassie as a political and even partisan symbol.

But before I turn to that story, I must examine the phenomenon of the other Columbine martyr, Rachel Scott.

CHAPTER 3

RACHEL SCOTT

"Starting a Chain Reaction"

The day after the shooting, Rachel Scott's car, a red Acura Legend, along with the Chevy truck of John Tomlin, a 16-year-old sophomore who died in the library, became impromptu shrines in a parking lot near Columbine High School—the foci of spontaneous outpourings of grief and sympathy. Like the Vietnam Veteran's Memorial, the chain-link fence surrounding the bombing site in Oklahoma City, the gates of Kensington Palace during Princess Diana's funeral, and Union Square after the destruction of the World Trade Towers, Rachel and John's vehicles were soon laden with flowers, handwritten notes, stuffed toys, and all manner of personal mementos.[1] Images of Columbine students, praying or weeping uncontrollably, touching or even collapsed upon the vehicles, appeared in newspapers and on television screens across the nation and around the world.[2] Rachel's car and Tomlin's truck, along with the crosses set on a nearby hill, became part of the montage of grief, part of our jumbled collective memory of Columbine.

Tomlin soon became the focus of private grief alone, mourned by family and those who had known him personally. The family and friends of Rachel also grieved and mourned privately in a way that those who have never lost a child may never comprehend. Rachel, however, soon became a public figure whose image represented to many who never knew her something more than private pain.

POPULAR RESPONSES

The transformation of Rachel into a public symbol of Columbine began with her funeral service—televised live by CNN and MSNBC on April 24, the Saturday afternoon following the shooting. Darrell Scott, Rachel's father, often claims that the funeral attracted CNN's largest audience to that point in time. "CNN executives told us," reported Scott in a November 1999 speech, "four times more people watched Rachel's funeral on CNN than watched Princess Di's, or the Gulf War."[3] Even if this claim is inaccurate, it is undoubtedly true that Rachel's funeral, broadcast while public interest in Columbine was high, attracted a large viewing audience.

At the beginning of the service, Reverend Barry Palser of Orchard Road Christian Center, an Assemblies of God congregation, where Rachel participated in a youth group, stated that the primary focus of the service would be not only "celebrating Rachel's life" but also urging "the world and the nation to listen to the leadership of the church when we speak concerning the issues surrounding her tragic death." Palser referred to her as "one who has given your [sic] life for the Lord Jesus Christ, a modern-day martyr."[4] (He made no mention, nor did any other speaker, of a verbal exchange with her killers about belief in God that was later to become a standard part of Rachel's martyr story.)

Palser was followed by a long series of tearful testimonies and fond remembrances by those who had known her in church and in school. Viewers were given the impression of a Christian girl who, in the words of one mourner, "shined for God at all times"—full of life, talented, clever, confident, warm, and unfailingly kind. Several of the speakers stressed that her middle name, "Joy," described the happiness she brought to other people. A videotape montage of family photographs of the petite and pretty girl, who obviously loved the camera, set to the song "You Are So Beautiful," completed the loving portrait of Rachel Joy Scott as daughter, sister, or friend—as someone you wished you had known.[5] This wish to have known her was especially apparent in journalist Roger Rosenblatt's full-page essay, "A Note to Rachel Scott," in *Time* magazine. "I would like to have remembered it before Tuesday, April 20," concluded Rosenblatt, "when the news of the day supposedly brought you to light. Rachel, you were always in the light."[6]

This celebration of Rachel's life was followed by a sermon on, in Palser's words, "the issues surrounding her tragic death." This was supplied by Bruce Porter, the pastor of Celebration Christian Fellowship, the church attended by Rachel's mother and stepfather, Beth and Larry Nimmo. "What has happened to us as a people," asked Porter, "that this should happen to us?" His answer, reflecting the response of many religious conservatives to Columbine, was simple: "We have removed prayer from our schools and we've reaped violence, and hatred and murder. And we have the fruit of those activities before us now."

Porter pointed to Rachel as a "warrior" who carried "a torch that was stained by the blood of the martyrs from the very first day of the Church's existence in the world 2,000 years ago." And when Rachel was struck down, the torch fell from her hand. Reaching the climax of his remarks, Porter exhorted the young people in the audience, "I want to know right now who will take up that torch. Let me see you. Stand up. Who will pick up Rachel's torch? Who will do it? Hold it high!"[7] According to Porter, hundreds in the auditorium and untold thousands around the world watching on television responded to his call.[8] Regardless of the actual response, Porter's call proved the seminal moment in the transformation of Rachel into a figure of popular veneration and public meaning.

Porter's linkage of Rachel with the image of a martyr's torch figures prominently in both the organization, Torchgrab Youth Ministries, Inc., he established in May 1999 and his book, *The Martyrs' Torch*, published in February 2000.[9] The Torchgrab web site features Rachel's picture in its statement of "Vision and Purpose." She is referred to as "One of the Christian martyrs who died at Columbine High School." Based on her example, this statement goes on to say that "Torchgrab Youth Ministries is calling a generation to TAKE UP THE TORCH OF THE MARTYRS and carry it's [*sic*] brilliant light of truth in the halls of their Junior High, Senior High, and college-level schools."[10]

The intended vehicle for this is a series of "Torchgrab Youth Rallies." The first and most notable of these rallies took place August 6–7, 1999, in Littleton, Colorado, at an auditorium not far from the site of the shooting. This event featured talks by nationally known youth ministers, music and dance performances, and testimonies by members of Rachel's family. Attended by several hundred teenagers, this event attracted some local press attention and reportage in religious publications such as *Charisma*.[11] Despite the necessity of transporting a whole team of performers, Torchgrab has occasionally organized these rallies in other cities, and even overseas. Porter himself, however, is a frequent guest speaker at churches and at events organized by other ministries.[12]

Porter has had a greater impact, however, through his writing. His book, *The Martyrs' Torch,* is largely an elaboration on a series of e-mail messages that he began sending on April 21 to friends about his experiences ministering to Rachel's family. According to Porter, his dispatches from the epicenter of the tragedy were "copied, forwarded, and re-sent multiplied thousands of times around the globe!"[13] Not surprisingly, he was soon overwhelmed by phone calls and e-mail messages from concerned or moved strangers—a response that no doubt inspired his further efforts. The elaborations in *The Martyrs' Torch* take the form of "back story" or additional information, such as excerpts from Rachel's journals, that was not available when Porter first sent his e-mail messages. Several of the additional chapters are essentially expansions upon his funeral sermon's themes of national redemption, martyrdom, and the elevation of Rachel as an example of faith.

As I noted in the previous chapter, other well-established ministries, such as that of Billy Graham, have also utilized the figure of

Rachel, but usually in combination with the initially more well-known figure of Cassie Bernall. The book of Columbine-related testimonies, *Columbine Courage: Rock-Solid Faith,* by Ron Luce of Teen Mania, featured Cassie but also used Rachel as an inspirational example. "There is always more of God," observed a youth minister from Florida in one testimony. "Rachel Joy never stopped wanting more. That was shown to many thirsty souls through her life and death—something she could never have imagined God would do through her."[14]

Teen Mania, however, discovered a more direct and useful connection with Rachel. At the time of her death, she had been preparing to participate in one of Teen Mania's "Global Expeditions," a short-term mission trip to Africa during the summer of 1999. "Now Rachel will never have the opportunity herself," read a page on the Teen Mania web site that featured photos of Rachel, "We have the chance to live out the calling for which Rachel died. . . . Who will go in Rachel's place? . . . Will you?"[15] Similar to Porter's call to "pick up Rachel's torch," Luce used the question, "Who will go in her place?" at his ministry's youth events to elicit commitments to go on upcoming mission trips. Visitors to the Teen Mania web site could also download a brief video clip that demonstrates the enthusiastic response of a teen audience to the "Who will go in her place?" challenge posed by Luce.[16]

The Voice of the Martyrs, an established organization concerned with the persecution of Christians worldwide, featured Rachel's story and picture in the December 1999 issue of its magazine. The article on Rachel, part of a larger "Year in Review," begins with the speculation that, "Perhaps 1999 will go down in the history books as the year persecution came to America." After mentioning an unnamed high school girl in Littleton who was killed for belief in God and the September 1999 shooting at a Texas church, the article focuses on Rachel. "She, too," we are told, "was asked about her belief in God by one of the gunmen . . . and told him that yes, she still believed. She was then killed." After citing excerpts from her journals, the article concluded, "What America needs, now and in the future, is Christians who are ready to say, as Rachel Scott did, 'If I have to give up everything, I will.'"[17]

In addition to these more organized efforts to both elevate and use Rachel as an inspirational example, she is also the subject of multiple tribute web sites or pages. These "cyber-shrines" are similar in form and content to those dedicated to Cassie, which I examined in some detail in the previous chapter. Many of these sites merely present a photograph of Rachel, information about her life, some selections from the writings that her family has made public, and links to other Rachel-related or Columbine-related web sites.[18] Some of these simple tributes have been added to personal sites while others are part of the sites of organizations, especially youth ministries.[19] Somewhat more elaborate are those sites that add personal testimony to the inspirational influence of Rachel. "Although Rachel is gone," wrote one high school student, "I keep Rachel close to my heart by wearing a necklace I made with a cross, a chain, and Rachel's picture."[20]

More elaborate still are multipage sites that contain photographs of Rachel, the day of the shooting, the aftermath, and Rachel's funeral. Such photographs are accompanied by copied news stories about Rachel, her death, and the funeral.[21] Other sites highlight Rachel's story and example as part of commentary about Columbine. One such site, using many dramatic photographs from the day of the shooting and its aftermath, reminds its visitors that the gunmen asked many of the students about their belief in God. A typical version of Rachel's death story is then presented as an example of this. The site also asserts that what made Columbine different than other school shootings was not the number killed and wounded, or the affluence of the community in which it took place, but "that the April 20, 1999 massacre produced modern-day *Martyrs for Christ.*" Immediately below this statement is a photograph of Rachel. "Columbine has become an example," visitors are told, "of how God has taken tragedy and transformed it into a triumph! How? Through the on-going outreach of the light of Christ that continues to shine through the victims and their families. Literally thousands of teenagers across the country and around the world have come to know Christ through the testimony of Rachel Joy Scott's life, Cassie Bernall's life and many others." Visitors are then urged to become involved in this youth revival.[22]

There seemed, however, to be fewer of these tributes on the web dedicated to Rachel than to Cassie. Why? Perhaps because Cassie was the most publicized victim in the immediate aftermath, she garnered the largest spontaneous response among those inclined to create such tribute sites. Rachel's posthumous fame, in contrast, rested initially upon the funeral testimonies to her character and faith. She was proclaimed a martyr but there was not yet a compelling story of her final moments, like that of Cassie, to capture the public imagination and to make her a powerful symbol of the meaning of Columbine.

RACHEL'S FAMILY: BEARING THE TORCH

The clearest and most successful melding of a celebration of Rachel's life and an interpretation of the meaning of her death through the lens of martyrdom is to be found in the continuing efforts of the members of her own family. "Our family," asserted her mother, "was the first to respond to that challenge of picking up the torch that Rachel and the other slain Christians at Columbine carried."[23] These efforts have presented a degree of unity, at least to outside observers, that is remarkable when we remember that Rachel's parents, Darrell Scott and Beth Nimmo, had been divorced for almost a decade at the time of their daughter's death.[24]

Darrell Scott, the son of a Pentecostal minister in Shreveport, Louisiana, was the pastor of a nondenominational congregation he had started in the Denver area at the time of the separation. His former wife, Beth Nimmo, also the product of a ministerial home, had devoted herself to raising their five children, and to her role as a pastor's wife. When they separated, Darrell Scott left the ministry and Beth Nimmo was forced for the first time to work outside the home. In addition to these practical adjustments, both had been raised to believe in the sanctity of marriage and to reject the possibility of divorce. As Beth Nimmo put it in the book cowritten with her ex-husband, *Rachel's Tears*, "when Darrell and I separated in 1989, my whole world fell apart."[25]

Rachel, the third of the five children, was almost eight years old at the time of the separation. What specific effects this may have had on Rachel can't be fully known. In *Rachel's Tears*, Darrell Scott wrote of the pain in Rachel's life that her journals reveal. "Some of Rachel's pain," he observed, "was caused by the divorce Beth and I went through. She writes of the tearing that she felt, and the sense of conflicting loyalties between her mom and her dad, and the feelings of abandonment she experienced."[26] Beth Nimmo pointed to a quite different effect upon Rachel, who saw her mother's struggles. "As Rachel observed all of this transition, she started making little jokes about never getting married."[27]

Whatever the causes or effects of this divorce, Darrell Scott and Beth Nimmo shared custody of their children, and while they lived with her, the children visited him on weekends.[28] Both parents built new lives for themselves. At the time of the Columbine shooting, Darrell Scott was working as a sales manager of a food supply company and has since remarried. Beth Nimmo had married Larry Nimmo in 1995 and continued to work outside the home. Unlike many divorced parents, Beth Nimmo and Darrell Scott claim to have achieved a substantial degree of personal reconciliation. "Beth and I," wrote Darrell Scott, "were able to resolve our conflicts several years before Rachel's death."[29]

Darrell Scott and Beth Nimmo managed a notable degree of public cooperation in the aftermath of Columbine. As noted above, they coauthored, with professional writer Steve Rabey, the book *Rachel's Tears*. While the book, other than a jointly signed introduction, is divided into multiple "first-person" sections marked "Beth" or "Darrell," there is little evidence of disagreement between them about the meaning of Rachel's life and death, or about the use of Rachel's writings and drawings in publicizing that meaning. The two have also cooperated with the news media, occasionally participating in joint interviews and appearing on the same news programs.[30] They also have appeared together at Columbine-related events, most notably at a commemoration on the first anniversary of the shooting organized by Darrell Scott.[31] And both are represented, along with their second oldest daughter, Dana Scott, by the same talent agency/speakers bureau.[32]

The two also have the same publisher, Thomas Nelson, for the books each cowrote and released in 2001. These two books, however, seem to be taking the development of Rachel's legacy in different directions. Darrell Scott worked again with writer Steve Rabey on *Chain Reaction: A Call to Compassionate Revolution,* which focuses much more on the ethical, rather than the particularly Christian, import of Rachel's writings. He described the book as a memorial, "my Taj Mahal for Rachel." He explained, "I'm remembering Rachel with this book by continuing her legacy and trying—like her—to positively impact the lives of other people."[33] While *Chain Reaction* does not hide Rachel's religious commitment, it is obvious that Darrell Scott is reaching for a broader audience than the one *Rachel's Tears* found.

The Journals of Rachel Scott: A Journey of Faith at Columbine High, adapted by Beth Nimmo and professional writer Debra K. Klingsporn, is at once similar to *Rachel's Tears* and altogether unique. "So I was asked to write a first-person narrative of Rachel's life," Klingsporn explains in an introduction, "drawing extensively and freely from her journals, but not limiting what I wrote to what was available in those pages."[34] Beth Nimmo supervised this unusual adaptation, which includes previously unpublished selections from her daughter's writings. The result is as particularly Christian as *Rachel's Tears,* although it is written for a younger audience. Despite their other differences, both *Chain Reaction* and *Journals* present Rachel's martyr story in almost the same words as *Rachel's Tears.*[35]

Notwithstanding all this cooperation, there are still hints of tension and rivalry between Beth Nimmo and Darrell Scott.[36] The two have created separate, and somewhat exclusive, organizational vehicles for advancing their daughter's legacy. Beth Nimmo is on the board of directors of Porter's Torchgrab Youth Ministries, wrote the foreword to his book, and occasionally speaks at Torchgrab events.[37] Her own organization is the Rachel Joy Scott Memorial Fund. Darrell Scott's organization, which I will describe in detail shortly, is The Columbine Redemption. Each of their web sites, Beth Nimmo's *www.racheljoyscott.com,* and Darrell Scott's three sites, *www.rachelscott.com, www.columbineredemption.com,* and *www.rachelschallenge.com,* barely mentions the other parent. None of these sites even provide a link to the other parent's sites.[38]

Darrell Scott has emerged as the most active spokesperson for his daughter's legacy. In June 1999, Darrell Scott quit his job and has since devoted himself full-time to traveling and speaking. Beth Nimmo, because of her continuing responsibilities in raising her two youngest children, has been able to accept only occasional public speaking engagements. Porter, whose interpretive funeral sermon was a seminal moment for all that followed, until early 2002 remained the full-time pastor of a congregation with all the obligations that entails.[39]

Darrell Scott's primary vehicle for spreading "Rachel's message" is The Columbine Redemption, a nonprofit charitable organization incorporated in July 1999. On its 1999 tax return, the organization listed among its purposes, conducting, "Public speaking engagements before young people and their families, based on the lessons to be learned from Columbine High School, in an attempt to lessen violence and offer families a message of hope and promise." Other purposes included conducting activities for young people and using "all manner of media for the promotion of the message of redemption and forgiveness."[40]

Several versions of a "Mission Statement," or list of goals, have appeared on the Columbine Redemption web site and in literature it has distributed to the public. Goals that appeared in earlier versions— a fund for the victims of future school tragedies, and building a Columbine memorial/ministry center—disappeared entirely from a later version.[41] A monthly publication was also one of these goals, but *Rachel's Journal,* a glossy full-color magazine, filled with pictures, lasted only five issues. "Our goal," stated a page about the publication on the Columbine Redemption web site, "is to encourage young people to follow the example of Rachel who was only doing what Jesus would've done."[42] The magazine contained excerpts from Rachel's writings, tributes to other Columbine victims contributed by family and friends, and a variety of short inspirational writings by Rachel's family, Columbine survivors, and well-known Christian writers, such as Josh McDowell. *Rachel's Journal* ceased publication after the May/June 2000 issue due to, according to its editor, "the large expense and the small number of subscribers."[43]

The Mission Statement that appeared on the organization's web site in late 2000 also included entirely new programs. One program was "Adopt-a-school," meant to get members of the community and churches "involved in practical ways with their local schools." Still another new goal was "to provide education about our nation's spiritual heritage." A program called "Chain Reaction," after a phrase in one of Rachel's essays, was meant to train young people to reach out to "those in their schools who are handicapped, neglected, new to the school, and picked on by others."[44] The Chain Reaction program was relaunched in April 2001 in conjunction with the second anniversary of the shooting and the publication of Darrell Scott's book, *Chain Reaction*.[45] None of these changes conflict with spreading the "message of redemption and forgiveness," but the changes do indicate that organizationally The Columbine Redemption has been a "work-in-progress."

One goal or purpose that remains consistent, despite changes in wording, is the formation of a "ministry team who will share the message of triumph through tragedy to churches, schools, colleges and cities across America."[46] In practical terms, this has been fulfilled by Darrell Scott's extensive and ongoing public speaking engagements. He is sometimes accompanied by his wife, Sandy Scott, and/or his children. His second oldest child, Dana Scott, also speaks publicly about her sister and performs a mime, "Watch the Lamb," that Rachel once performed at Columbine High School, and that was also performed at Rachel's televised funeral service.[47]

The transformation of Darrell Scott from a private individual to public spokesperson for his daughter's legacy did not occur immediately after her death or funeral. Instead it was the result of his testimony on May 27, 1999, before a House Judiciary subcommittee hearing on new gun-control legislation. Scott dismissed the legislation as a useless attempt to scapegoat the National Rifle Association and said that it ignored the spiritual causes of the tragedy at Columbine High.[48] Darrell Scott's remarks attracted relatively little media attention, but the full text of his brief speech was rapidly spread via forwarded e-mail messages and soon appeared on multiple web sites. This led to a deluge of invitations to speak about Columbine and his daughter. He described the aftermath of his subcommittee appearance in this way: "Then doors began to fling open all over the country and I was getting 80 calls a day."[49]

Since June 1999, Darrell Scott has spoken about his daughter and Columbine before hundreds of audiences across the nation. In January 2001, he claimed that he had presented, "face-to-face," exclusive of radio and television appearances, Rachel's message to as many as one million people in the previous 18 months.[50] And the pace of his activities do not seem to have slackened. He speaks not only in churches, especially Baptist, Assemblies of God, and nondenominational congregations, but also in convention centers, sports arenas, public parks, college campuses, restaurant banquet rooms, school auditoriums and gyms, and even at the Washington, D.C., Mall. These events are sponsored by particular church congregations, youth ministries, crisis-pregnancy centers, and other community organizations. Most often these are opened free-of-charge to the public, but sometimes tickets are sold as part of an effort by a given organization to raise money. Darrell Scott's fee, once reported to be as much as $5,000 per appearance plus expenses, goes to support The Columbine Redemption. Darrell Scott also raises money by selling copies of the books *Rachel's Tears* and *Chain Reaction,* other pieces of literature, and a videotape of himself speaking, called *Untold Stories of Columbine,*[51] as well as posters, T-shirts, hats, and key chains bearing his daughter's artwork.[52]

It is not surprising that the format of Darrell Scott's presentations, like his organization, has remained a "work-in-progress." Early on he began using projected slides to show photographs of his daughter and other victims, as well as images of his daughter's artwork and passages from her diaries. More recently this has been enhanced with short videos depicting the events of April 20, 1999, home movies of Rachel, and even a montage tribute to all the victims set to a Garth Brooks song, with special lyrics written and sung by Darrell Scott himself.[53]

For a time Darrell Scott was able to incorporate in his appearances the "13 Columbine Crosses" that were originally erected on a hill near the school by carpenter Greg Zanis, and that were the focal point of much of the spontaneous public expression of grief in the days after the shooting. These crosses were carried in a climactic procession to the stage at events where Darrell Scott spoke. This procession was often combined with an "altar call," an invitation to come forward and receive Christ as one's personal savior. The magazine *Rachel's Journal* described the significance of the crosses. "They personalize the message that Darrell Scott gives. We not only hear about the victims, but they are also visually represented. We read the notes that are scrawled on them. We can see the mementos that are attached to them. We soon realize what has been lost. We are changed forever."[54]

At some point in 2000, however, Zanis and Darrell Scott parted ways. The reasons for this are not clear.[55] Even without the crosses, Darrell Scott's talks often end with a traditional invitation to surrender or rededicate one's life to Jesus. (The results of this, of course, vary, but at one event in Pensacola, Florida, I saw approximately 80, mostly teenagers, out of an audience of 600 come forward during this invitation.)

Darrell Scott always appears in casual clothing, such as jeans and open-necked shirt, never a suit or tie. His speaking style is informal and folksy, a bit rambling, with flashes of humor that offset the gravity of his central subject—the meaning and significance of his daughter's life, faith, and sudden death. He reads to his audiences many passages from her diaries and other writings, and tells stories about things she did and said, and the impact she had on others. This mixture of celebration and interpretation is interlaced with stories about Columbine as well as Darrell Scott's own insights about spiritual life, the causes of the Columbine shooting, the proper role of religion in the public schools, and the origins of the First Amendment to the U.S. Constitution.

RACHEL'S MESSAGE

In their joint introduction to *Rachel's Tears,* her parents explain their motive for writing and speaking. "We do all this because we believe that our daughter Rachel Scott has a powerful message that survives her tragic death and needs to be heard by everyone."[56] What then is "Rachel's message?"

First and foremost, Rachel's message is a call to accept salvation through Jesus Christ. As in the case of Cassie, the public attention devoted to Rachel after the shooting was seen by many as an opportunity for evangelism, especially for creating a religious revival among the young. Porter is especially clear on this point. He wrote of speaking to his church on the evening of April 21, just after Rachel's family had received official notification of her death. "When I rose to speak, I surveyed the sea of youthful faces before me, and I felt a stirring within. *Could this be the generation, Lord?* I wondered. Could this be the mighty army You promised that would come forth in the last days to carry Your banner?"[57] His remarks at Rachel's funeral service were very much his attempt to call forth that mighty army of converts with his cry of "Who will pick up Rachel's torch?" Porter made this point even more bluntly in an article for a small magazine in 1999: "Three words continually resound within me: 'Evangelization follows traumatization.'"[58]

Some were offended by the seeming opportunism of such evangelistic preaching at Columbine-related memorial services. One local minister told the *Denver Post* that he felt "hit over the head with Jesus."[59] Rachel's parents, however, were clearly not among the offended. Instead, like Porter, they saw the chance to preach to CNN's television audience as the work of God. "We know for a fact," Darrell Scott later told a youth convention, "that on her funeral day there were tens of thousands, if not hundreds of thousands, of people who gave their hearts to the Lord. Don't tell me God doesn't have a sense of humor when He can take Ted Turner's organization for three hours and allow it to preach the Gospel uninterrupted."[60] Beth Nimmo sees a similar divine purpose in her daughter's death. "I have come to the painful realization that Rachel is no longer just a part of our temporal family, but a part of God's eternal plan. It has become increasingly evident that God is honoring Rachel's dreams to reach her generation."[61]

This only superficially resembles the evangelistic efforts surrounding Cassie—which were based on the fear of Hell if one dies "unprepared" or unsaved—to gather souls for heaven. And where and when death came to Cassie—in a high school library during her lunch hour—is used to remind the unsaved that death can strike anywhere, anytime. The "Will you be ready?" appeal also fits well with the overall trajectory of Cassie's story—a troubled soul dramatically saved from destruction, who stubbornly battled back to normality, and who was ready to meet her final moment of truth with heroic faith.

In contrast, the evangelistic appeals made on behalf of Rachel utilized fear of Hell far less often, even though her death was just as sudden and unexpected as Cassie's.[62] Her appeal has been one of noble self-sacrifice. "Kids love Rachel's story," observed Robert Arnold, Executive Director of Youth For Christ, "because they want to lay their lives down; they want to be significant. People want to be called on that level."[63] The climactic question of Porter's funeral sermon, "Who will pick up Rachel's torch?" and Luce's challenge at Teen Mania events, "Who will go in her place?" were calls for idealistic dedication to Rachel's cause, the cause of Christ. Rachel's father clearly expects his daughter's generation to respond. In the congressional testimony that sparked his speaking career, he declared, "My daughter's death will not be in vain! The young people of this country will not allow that to happen!"[64]

Clearly these are appeals to do more than "get saved, get baptized, and get churched." At his numerous speaking engagements, Darrell Scott reads from an essay his daughter wrote for school on her personal code of ethics. "I have this theory," she wrote, "that if one person can go out of their way to show compassion, then it will start a chain reaction of the same." She concluded the essay with a challenge. "My codes may seem like a fantasy that can never be reached, but test them for yourself, and see the kind of effect they have in the lives of people around you. You just may start a chain reaction."[65]

Testimonies to Rachel's acts of kindness fill her father's speeches, the pages of *Rachel's Tears, Chain Reaction,* and, while it lasted, the magazine *Rachel's Journal.* These kind acts range from giving a nickel to a stranger who was five cents short at a cash register, having lunch with anxious and lonely new students on their first day at Columbine, holding an umbrella for a stranger changing a tire in the rain, and listening to the troubles of her friends late into the night. They are used to demonstrate that Rachel "walked her talk" and elicit admiration and perhaps imitation. It is apparent that Darrell Scott regards "starting a chain reaction" as the essential means through which his daughter's message will be spread. "She simply obeyed God with little acts of kindness," he told an audience in June 2000, "in simple ways letting her light shine, not realizing that that light was going to flame across this nation, that there would be hundreds of thousands of young people who picked up the torch that she dropped."[66] In the book *Chain Reaction,* Darrell Scott drew a parallel between Rachel and Anne Frank, whose diary has touched millions. "Like Rachel this young girl is someone most of us never would have heard of if it hadn't been for the way she died."[67]

As one might expect from this, Rachel's way of witnessing to non-Christians, according to her family, was not to "hit people over the head with her Bible"[68] but to demonstrate God's love through her deeds and her concern for others. In one of her many letters addressed to God, she wrote, "I want heads to turn in the halls when I walk by. I want them to stare at me, watching and wanting the light you have put in me. . . . I want you to use me to reach the un-reached."[69] But it is apparent that she could also take a far more confrontational approach as well. One piece of Rachel's artwork, which her family has reproduced on page 165 of *Rachel's Tears* as well as on clothing and other items, utilizes the classic evangelistic questions, "What if you were to die today?" and "Where will you spend your eternity?"[70] These questions are written within the stark black-and-white image of a hand that seems to confront the viewer with the message, "Stop. Consider this."

Within the classic Christian framework, however, the demon-stration of God's love inevitably involves self-sacrifice. According to her family, Rachel even tried to reach out to Harris and Klebold with whom she shared a class. Her father, based on the reports of two of Rachel's friends who overheard the conversation, claims that "She had witnessed to Eric and Dylan three weeks before they killed her."[71] Her mother also tells us that Rachel "challenged" the two boys about a violence-filled video they had created for the class, a video that did not seem to concern the teacher or draw the atten-tion of school administrators. "She wanted to help them," asserted her mother, "and possibly paid with her life for daring to do what no one else was willing to do."[72] By willingly paying such a price, her acts of kindness are thus elevated far beyond the realm of "nice-ness" to that of a martyr who demonstrated a heroic love even for her future murderers.

The dominant image that emerges from the way Rachel is de-scribed by her family and her friends is that of a spiritual and moral overachiever. "I think her passionate intimacy with God," wrote her mother, "went above and beyond what most people ever experience in their relationship with the Lord . . . she had broken through the confines that too many of us allow to hold us back."[73] The depth of this relationship with the Lord, we are led to believe, was at the root of Rachel's outpouring of loving and compassionate acts—her at-tempts to begin that chain reaction of kindness. Her moral failures are depicted as missed chances to do even more, to express God's love more fully, not as acts that were self-serving at the expense of others. In an essay, "The Gloves of Conviction," Rachel expressed her troubled conscience over failing to give food and companionship to a homeless woman who was sitting in the Subway sandwich shop in which Rachel worked. A customer instead did what Rachel had failed to do for the woman. "Convicted" by her failure she prayed and God told her, "Let this be known, child, when you do not follow through with the boldness and knowledge I have given you, more than one person is affected by it. You are as well as they."[74]

In *Rachel's Tears,* her parents found it necessary to repeatedly emphasize that Rachel was not perfect, sinless, or a saint. In a chapter entitled "Flawed But Faithful," her mother wrote, "My daughter was not a superhuman saint, and I think she probably would have been a little exasperated to be categorized that way."[75] In *The Journals of Rachel Scott,* two of the chapters are entitled, "Just a Normal Girl" and "Not Perfect—Just Forgiven."[76] In *Rachel's Tears,* her father also observed that Rachel would find being regarded as a saint "incredibly humorous."[77]

Rachel's parents generally point out her various flaws but as each is presented, they are cast in a light that minimizes or negates them. Her stubbornness, occasional disobedience, fighting with her siblings, and jealousy of someone who got the part in a play that she had wanted, are rooted in her virtues: an intense passion for life and a will to excellence. A more incongruous element was her smoking habit, which she picked up trying to be "part of the group."[78] Yet her mother only learned of this because Rachel confessed it to her and promised to give it up. And after Rachel's death, her diaries revealed that she had been tempted to go drinking with her friends—but this was a temptation, unlike smoking, she seems to have resisted. Despite this discussion of Rachel's "flaws"—mere foibles might be more accurate—her parents are really proposing their daughter's faith as a model to learn from and to emulate.

The sort of sainthood that they reject for Rachel is the "stereotypical image" of otherworldly perfection. "On the other hand," we read in *Rachel's Tears,* "if a saint is someone who is faithful to God even amid failures and doubts, then perhaps Rachel qualifies."[79]

Even the record of her failures and doubts are presented as evidence of intense spirituality. Her mother compared these passages to the Psalms of David. "David talked to God about the very issues of his heart, and he was open and passionate with the Lord in his writings." Rachel, her mother observed, had the same "passion for God" and "a transparency about her doubts and fears."[80]

Whatever her doubts and fears, we know of no great spiritual crisis in the life of Rachel. Unlike Cassie, she had no wrenching turn from the abyss of despair and self-destruction. The account of Rachel's conversion experience at age 12 is curiously devoid of crisis or drama. Rachel was a "good girl" but, her mother observed, "Outward goodness wasn't enough for her, however, and when she was quite young, she decided to go deeper in her walk with God." Attending a Pentecostal church service while visiting relatives, Rachel felt "drawn" to the altar. Once there, as she described it, "I don't remember what I said, but I will never forget the feeling I had. That night, I accepted Jesus into my heart. I was saved."[81] This does not seem to be a decisive break with the past, but the opening of a door to the future. Or, as her mother described it, "the beginning of real spiritual awareness for her."[82] Contrast this with Brad Bernall's description of the difference conversion made in Cassie, his daughter: "It was as if she had been in a dark room, and somebody had turned the light on, and she could suddenly see the beauty surrounding her."[83] Rachel, it seems, only saw that beauty more deeply than before.

Whatever the reality of Rachel's spiritual and moral life, the way she has been presented—an overachiever, a saint in all but name—creates a problem for those who wish to present her as a model for Christian teens: inaccessibility. In this, Rachel stands in contrast to Cassie, whose difficulties and outward ordinariness make it possible for her peers to feel: "If she can, I can." Rachel was the "fun, energetic fireball" that Cassie felt she was not, and that few of us ever are. The role model claims made on Cassie's behalf are also much narrower than those made for Rachel. Cassie's life as a Christian is usually understood as a quiet preparation for a single moment of truth, a final testimony to the transforming power of God. Rachel, we are told, not only faced her killers with the same faithful courage as Cassie, but the rest of her spiritual and moral life provides a model for faith and action in daily life. Rachel, who wrote on the cover of one of her diaries, "I WON'T BE LABELED AS AVERAGE," who wanted to be, and often was, the star of the show, may seem too exceptional for many to imitate.

Had Rachel's reputed "saintliness" been at all cold, aloof, or elitist, the problem of inaccessibility, especially for contemporary teenagers, would have been hard to overcome. Instead, if we can believe all that we are told, she seems to have possessed qualities—beauty, humor, generosity—that drew people to her in life, and still holds a surprising power to capture the imagination of those who know her only by the testimony of others. It is customary, of course, to speak well of the dead, but stories about Rachel's life seemed to have an unusually strong impact. Consider, for instance, the stories of how Rachel would seek out newcomers to her school. "I was miserable my first day of school," read a letter to *Rachel's Journal,* "until lunch. I was all alone, with nowhere to sit, and up walked Rachel with the biggest grin on her face. She introduced herself, sat down next to me and announced to her friends that they were going to eat lunch with me."[84] So many of us have been in that situation, "the new kid" in a cold sea of strangers, but no rescuer came. So we are, in some degree, drawn in gratitude to the person who would have helped us if only she had been there.

Not only do these testimonials to Rachel's goodness engage hopeful fantasies of gracious intervention in our lives, they typically center on meeting some concrete need—no one to eat lunch with, a nickel short at the cash register, changing a tire in the rain, being hungry or sad. The simplicity and specificity of these stories allow us to imagine, "I can do that, too." Meeting such needs can be understood, of course, as a means to the end of witnessing. As one essay in *Rachel's Journal* explained, "Showing kindness to a person consistently often breaks down walls between people and it even gives me the opportunity to share Jesus with people who might have otherwise been unreceptive."[85] Yet a simple short-term quid pro quo approach is absent from the stories about Rachel. As Lori Johnson, Rachel's youth pastor, observed, "At Columbine, she didn't preach to people; she was just Jesus to people. She defied what a lot of churches say is the right way to evangelize people."[86] Rachel's sister Dana Scott underscored Rachel's unconventional approach: "She didn't hand people watered-down, shmoopy-poopy, Bible-thumping verbal religious garbage that no one gets. She spoke in a language of honesty that anyone could interpret as *real.*"[87]

Despite the daunting image of her exceptional spirituality, Rachel's incarnational witness is a stark contrast to the narrow-minded, scripture-quoting, bully-for-Jesus stereotype that many evangelicals want to avoid. If "Saint" Rachel is not fully imitable, her manner of demonstrating her faith makes it seem possible to do so partially. "Anyone can start taking initial steps on the path of kindness by doing small, simple things," wrote Darrell Scott in *Chain Reaction.*[88] This appeal is also consistent with the "noble cause" evangelistic appeal made in her name. And if she cannot be imitated, then at least she can be admired.

Like the Bernalls, Rachel's parents present their readers with advice on parenting as part of their daughter's legacy. But their advice is very different. This is not surprising given the difference between Cassie and Rachel. Portions of *She Said Yes* describe a domestic nightmare, the pitched battle the Bernalls fought to save their daughter from self-destruction. While few parents face anything as extreme as the Bernalls did, the experience of dealing with a teen who has become a "sulking stranger" with a fiercely defended secret life is common.

Rachel's parents report they faced no such challenges in raising her. One might expect Rachel, the middle child of marriage that ended in divorce, to have developed some of the emotional/developmental problems associated with those circumstances. But her parents paint a very different picture. According to her mother, Rachel was "a very good girl who caused me very few real problems" and who "learned at a very young age how to be her own individual."[89]

Darrell Scott provided much the same picture. "Rachel was above normal," he wrote. "I have five children, and she required the least maintenance of all of them."[90] The picture of Rachel the ideal daughter is crowned by a tribute she wrote to her mother's virtues that begins, "Sacrifice should be her name. Because she has given up so much for us."[91] Understandably, Rachel's grieving mother regarded this tribute as "a priceless gift."[92]

The parenting advice that Rachel's mother and father offer is not so much based on problems with their children as it is a response to flaws in their own upbringing. The introduction to the chapter "Parenting With Grace and Love" in *Rachel's Tears* stated, "Rachel's parents were raised in homes where more emphasis was placed on fearing God than on loving God. In trying to correct that approach with their children, they believe they created an environment that helped Rachel understand God's amazing grace."[93] For Darrell Scott this means emphasizing deeper principles of maintaining a relationship with God rather than the legalistic rules. Even Rachel's smoking and temptations to drink do not disturb him. "I don't think either behavior threatened her relationship with God or her eternal life. She was exploring her freedom and testing the waters."[94] Her mother takes a similar stance in the face of her children's moral experimentation. "Instead of feeling frantic and desperate, causing myself to overreact in those situations, I let go of the rope just a bit."[95] This approach may be, of course, more workable with children who are already disposed to be faithful and good, such as Rachel reportedly was. "To let go of the rope a bit" seems the exact opposite of Misty Bernall's advice to parents.

Ultimately, however, neither of Rachel's parents claim the credit for their daughter's unusual spiritual and moral excellence. "I don't think I'm a supernatural mother, and I don't think Darrell is a supernatural father," observed her mother. "But where would a child learn about that level of supernatural insight? I think the only explanation is that God led her to be that way."[96] The notion that Rachel was divinely guided in her life is closely joined to the notion that she was divinely prepared for her death. "The ways of God are mysterious," her parents stated in their joint introduction to *Rachel's Tears,* "but we believe that God sovereignly prepared Rachel for her own death, providing her with an increasingly clear awareness that the end was near."[97]

The invocation of God's sovereignty is not casual. "If I believed for one second that God had forsaken my daughter," Darrell Scott said in November 1999, "or that he had gone to sleep or that he wasn't aware, I would be one of the angriest men in America."[98] In his public presentations, he meets the question of theodicy head-on by repeating a question a television cameraman once asked him, "Where was God when your daughter was killed?" He has told his audiences on many occasions, "I said, the same place He was at when His son was killed 2,000 years ago. And the same place He was at when He miraculously spared my son in the library." He also has often said, "God knew the day my daughter was born the day she would die."[99]

Darrell Scott has indicated, however, that this affirmation of divine sovereignty is not just a matter of theological consistency for him. He believes there is substantial evidence that God prepared his daughter's heart to be ready for the sacrifice she was called to make on April 20, 1999. "We now realize that there was a spiritual awareness on her part that time was short," he stated in *Rachel's Tears.* "She talked about the fact that she would not live long enough to get married."[100]

This is reminiscent of similar assertions that Cassie reportedly made to her parents on many occasions: "I'm never going to get married. I'll never have kids."[101] One thinks, of course, of Rachel's post-divorce "little jokes" to her mother about never getting married. We are never presented, however, with a clear statement from her writings that she seriously believed this. The evidence for this assertion is usually made in summary form—"she talked about" this with her sisters, a cousin, and her youth pastor,[102] but, interestingly, never with either of her parents. Her father infers that she must have believed it from her behavior. "She always got quiet," her father wrote, "when we talked about her having children or even getting married. I think part of that was her premonition that she wasn't going to be around long enough to be married."[103] This is underscored by an episode in *The Journals of Rachel Scott* based on an actual event. At a Goodwill store, Rachel finds "the coolest old wedding dress" and "models" it for her amused family and other Goodwill patrons. What the actual Rachel thought of the episode may or may not match what the reconstructed Rachel of *The Journals* tells us: "I think that's as close as I'll ever get to being a bride, because, you know, somehow that moment just seemed complete."[104]

As in the case of Cassie, Rachel's supposed belief that she would never be married is connected to the themes of sexual purity and an eroticized love of God. While Rachel, whom her father described as "boy crazy,"[105] did have a boyfriend for some time, she reportedly ended the relationship because it might have led to sexual immorality. "She literally walked away from the one young man she probably loved," observed her mother, "because she didn't want the relationship to turn her away from who she was called to be."[106] The diaries of adolescents are often filled with longings for love and companionship, and Rachel's parents report the same was true in her writings, but in a special way. "At times," observed her father, "it is hard to tell if the companionship Rachel cries out for is human or divine." As an illustration, he cites an undated poem/prayer in which she expresses her longing for a companion to walk with her "Through these halls of a tragedy," a companion "Who will carry your name, until the end." Read in the light of later events, the phrases "halls of a tragedy" and "carry your name, until the end" take on a special weight, but it is apparent from this passage that the human companionship she wanted was preconditioned upon a shared love of God. In her father's view, "this intimacy with God is the key that unlocks the mystery of who Rachel was."[107]

In another parallel to Cassie, Rachel's own words are used to prove she had premonitions of her early death. While this evidence is more direct than her supposed beliefs about marriage, there is still some ambiguity. A short undated poem, which begins "Just passing by," is seen as Rachel's reflection on "the brevity of her life."[108] Of course, it can also be read as a personalized meditation on the brevity of *all* life in this world compared to eternity. Less open to alternative explanations is a brief journal entry, dated May 2, 1998, which reads, "This will be my last year Lord. I have gotten what I can. Thank you."[109] Read in the light of what happened to Rachel less than twelve months later, and lacking any other information or interpretive context for "my last year," this cryptic entry carries considerable power. (Probably for this reason, it is one of the two excerpts from her writing that appear on the back cover of *Rachel's Tears*.) And for the primary audience of Rachel's message—people who tend to believe that the Bible means just what it says—this journal entry means just what it says. She knew she would die, and soon.

It is also important for Rachel's family to stress her willingness to die for God. One of Rachel's diary entries functions in much the same way as the brief note found in Cassie's room that began "I will die for my God."[110] The entry, part of which appears on the back cover of *Rachel's Tears,* is in the form of a letter to a friend. It begins by lamenting the loss of friends who apparently rejected her because of her sense of spiritual and moral dedication, or as she put it, "Now that I have begun to walk my talk, they make fun of me."[111] But she turns from lament to what is treated by her family as a ringing proclamation of spiritual obedience: "I am not going to apologize for speaking the name of Jesus. . . . If I have to sacrafice [*sic*] everything . . . I will. I will take it."[112]

This statement, dated April 20, 1998, exactly one year before her death, can be seen as the moment she volunteered to "sacrifice everything," to defy enemies to be with Jesus, and perhaps, to die a martyr's death. Her father wonders if she understood fully what was happening, but he is convinced that "Rachel Joy Scott knew God was preparing her heart for a sacrifice to be made and she expressed a willingness to make that sacrifice in her diaries."[113]

Sometimes Darrell Scott has to reassure some of the more impressionable members of his audiences that praying to be used by God doesn't mean they will be martyred like his daughter. "God has called for all of us to lay our lives down. All of us. Some of us just do it on the installment plan," he once explained. "You pay a little every day. It's little by little that you lay your life down, for Him and for others." He also assures those who still may be anxious, "If you are called to lay your life down [like Rachel], you have a loving Father who will prepare your life for that, and will prepare your family for that."[114] As proof, he points to the way his daughter and her family were prepared.

The climactic proof of Rachel's divine preparation is a complex story of two drawings she made a year apart, Darrell Scott's own sense of mission, the dream of a complete stranger, and a passage in the biblical book of Jeremiah. The first drawing, reproduced in *Rachel's Tears* on page 87, consists of many elements with a Christian theme, but includes a rose growing up out of another plant, which Rachel's family maintains is the kind of flower, a columbine, that Rachel's school was named after. The rose and the columbine are both being watered by dark droplets of liquid. On the same page, Rachel had drawn a cross with the biblical passage "Greater love hath no man than this, that a man would lay down his life for his friends." This drawing, one of many found in her room, initially held no particular significance for her family.

The second drawing is introduced by way of what seems a long digression about Darrell Scott's calling to speak about his daughter's legacy and a stranger's dream. About a month after the shooting, he awoke at 4:30 A.M. with the feeling that "God were physically in the room with me" and with two biblical passages in his mind: "I have brought you to the kingdom for such a time as this" and "I will put you before kings and leaders and you will not be afraid of what to say. I will put words in your mouth."[115] After struggling with this for days, he told God that he was willing to carry out whatever mission God gave him and within minutes he received a call from a complete stranger, a businessman named Frank Amedia, who had been wondering about the meaning of a recurring dream he had had since watching Rachel's funeral on CNN. "He dreamed," Darrell Scott wrote, "about her eyes and a flow of tears that were watering something that he couldn't quite see in the dream."[116] But the dream meant nothing to Rachel's father or other members of her family.

The meaning of the dream, however, began to be revealed a few days later when the Sheriff's office finally released the backpack Rachel had been wearing when she was shot. In the backpack Darrell Scott found his daughter's last diary. On its final page was, in her father's words, "A drawing of her eyes with a stream of tears that were watering a rose!"[117] Darrell Scott concluded that God had given Amedia, who could not possibly have seen Rachel's drawing, a vision of its contents.

The fuller meaning of the second drawing, reproduced on page 176 of *Rachel's Tears,* only became clear when it was noted that there were 13 clear tears flowing from the eyes toward the rose. These 13 tears were, of course, taken to represent the 13 victims of the shooting. Around the rose were dark droplets. These were taken to be blood. Eventually this image of a rose was connected to Rachel's similar image of a rose with dark droplets growing out of a columbine plant. This in turn was linked to the bloody redemptive self-sacrifice represented by the cross and the passage "Greater love hath no man . . ." that also appeared in that first drawing. "I knew," wrote Darrell Scott in summary, "that the columbine flower Rachel had drawn represented the tragedy out of which the youth of this generation (the rose) would emerge, anointed by the very tears of God Himself that were pictured flowing from Rachel's eyes."[118]

The power of this highly involved series of linkages between biblical texts, drawings, a dream, a calling from God, mass murder, and redemptive self-sacrifice should not be underestimated. "If they were writing a Bible today," Craig Scott once said of his sister's final drawing, "that would be in it."[119] Even the skeptically inclined can be impressed by the striking "coincidences" of the matches between the dream and the second drawing, and between the number of tears and the number of victims. And for those inclined not toward skepticism but toward the expectation of a revealed meaning, the effect can be galvanic. When Darrell Scott, after telling of the stranger's dream, projects the image of Rachel's last drawing during his talks, it is not unusual to hear some in the audience gasp and then murmur in wonder. "There are many untold spiritual stories about the Columbine tragedy," observed Darrell Scott, "but the one that has the most impact on the youth I speak to is the story of the rose."[120]

"Rachel's tears" are also given a public and political meaning by linking them to a biblical passage, Jeremiah 31:15–17 (New American Standard Bible).

> Thus says the LORD,
> "A voice is heard in Ramah,
> Lamentation and bitter weeping.
> Rachel is weeping for her children;
> She refuses to be comforted for her children,
> Because they are no more."
> Thus says the LORD,
> "Restrain your voice from weeping,
> And your eyes from tears;
> For your work shall be rewarded," declares the LORD,
> "And they shall return from the land of the enemy.
> And there is hope for your future," declares the LORD,
> "And your children shall return to their own territory."

In the videotape *Untold Stories of Columbine*, Darrell Scott reads this passage and then states, "In 1962, my generation said we don't need God where our kids are concerned anymore and we removed Him from our schools."[121] So just as the biblical Rachel weeps for her children, the Jews captive in Babylon, the tears of Rachel Scott are shed for her generation of Christian teens who also have had to dwell in "the land of the enemy," the secular public schools of America. And just as God brought His people home, so He will also return Rachel Scott's children to their own territory, schools that will once again welcome the spirit of God.

CHAPTER 4

THE POLITICS OF TRAGEDY

"I Will Heal Their Land"

On April 21, 1999, I discussed with some of my students *the* news story of the day: Columbine. We exchanged what little we knew and began to discuss the difficult questions of causes and solutions. I don't remember much of what we said, but I do recall offering this piece of advice: "You're going to hear lots of people on TV explaining why this happened and what we should do about it. These are important matters, but always ask: What is their wider social and political agenda? Answer that question before you agree with them."

I said this long before I began to study Columbine, but my experience in writing this book has convinced me that my advice was sound. The interpretations of Columbine, and the responses such interpretations imply, reflect wider understandings of American culture and society. They also reflect political understandings of how we should organize and conduct our common life and public affairs. These interpretations are used to advance particular partisan agendas. While Columbine is unique, as is each school shooting, the national discussion of Columbine largely reflects "business as usual" in American politics. The politics of tragedy is still politics.

ROUND UP THE USUAL SUSPECTS

Columbine was not by any means the first "rampage killing" or the first "senseless school shooting."[1] So when the Columbine story broke, the "cultural script" for such events was already familiar. Everyone knew who the usual suspects were and an outpouring of analysis and commentary followed.[2]

Social psychologist Elliot Aronson, in his brief and useful book *Nobody Left to Hate: Teaching Compassion After Columbine,* provides a simple way of grouping the usual suspects, the various responses to Columbine and similar events. Aronson distinguishes between "peripheral interventions," quick fixes of the manifestations of a problem, and "root cause interventions," which involve solving the underlying problem. Peripheral interventions may be useful in the short run, Aronson argues, but they simply do not provide an understanding of or engage the actual source of the problem.[3]

Among the peripheral interventions that played a large role in the post-Columbine discussion were gun control, school security, and violence in entertainment—movies, television, music, and computer games. Gun control and school security obviously deal with the means of violence, and the opportunity to use them, rather than the motives of school shooters. Discussion of the negative influence of violent imagery in entertainment, despite its psychological focus, is still also about means, not motives. Viewing Oliver Stone's film *Natural Born Killers* may have provided Eric Harris and Dylan Klebold with a vocabulary of fantasy violence to express their real urges, but this does not explain the source of those urges. Playing *Doom* may have trained the killers for what they eventually did, but it does not explain why, unlike the many million others who play such games, these two boys turned from virtual to real mayhem.[4]

While Aronson discusses these "quick fixes," *Nobody Left to Hate* is really about identifying and offering a solution to the "root cause" of school shootings. As a social psychologist with 40 years of experience, Aronson offers an examination of the "social atmosphere prevalent in most high schools in this country." While Aronson makes it clear that the actions of Harris and Klebold were "pathological," he cautions against understanding school shooters only in terms of their individual pathologies. "I would suggest," wrote Aronson, "that it is highly likely that the perpetrators were reacting in an extreme and pathological manner to a general atmosphere of exclusion."[5] This atmosphere makes schools, "highly competitive, cliquish, exclusionary places—places where you would be shunned if you were from the 'wrong' race or the 'wrong' ethnic group, came from the wrong side of the tracks, wore the wrong kind of clothes, were too short or too fat, too tall or too thin, or just 'didn't fit in.'"[6]

Aronson's description of the atmosphere of most high schools matches the negative image of the social world of Columbine High School that emerged in the aftermath of the shooting. This image involved a status hierarchy or pecking order of cliques topped by athletes, "the Jocks," who had free reign to harass those of lower status, especially those like Harris and Klebold, who found themselves, in Harris's words, "at the bottom of the ladder."[7]

"Sure, we teased them," Evan Todd, a Columbine football player and library survivor, told *Time*. "If you want to get rid of someone, usually you tease 'em. So the whole school would call them homos, and when they did something sick, we'd tell them, 'You're sick and that's wrong.'"[8] But the view from the other side was quite different. "Every day being teased and picked on," said Columbine student Brooks Brown, a friend of both killers, "pushed up against lockers— just the general feeling of fear in the school. And you either respond to a fear by having fear, or you take action and have hate. And defend yourself. And they [Harris and Klebold] chose a real disgusting way of doing that."[9]

The cumulative effect of years of such treatment, it is argued, so enraged the gunmen that it pushed them over the edge into violence.[10] "I'm going to kill you all," says Klebold in one of the videotapes he made with Harris. "You've been giving us s___ for years."[11]

This was supported by a Centers for Disease Control and Prevention study of school-associated violent deaths from 1994 to 1999 which found, "Among students, homicide perpetrators were twice as likely than homicide victims to have been bullied by peers."[12]

The "revenge of the outcasts" interpretation of Columbine has resonated with the public. A Gallup survey in March 2001 asked adults how important bullying and teasing was as a cause of school shootings. Sixty-two percent said bullying and teasing was extremely or very important. Only thirteen percent said it was not too or not at all important.[13] The revenge interpretation was supported even more strongly by young people. A nationwide survey of 2,000 students in grades 7–12 published by Alfred University in August 2001 reported that 87 percent of students agreed that the motive of school shooters was revenge, or "to get back at those who have hurt them." And 86 percent agreed that school shootings occurred because "Other kids pick on them [the shooters], make fun of them or bully them." The authors of the study concluded, "Students show a remarkable level of agreement with professionals and social commentators who have opined about this serious national issue. They agree about the revenge motive."[14]

This resonance is rooted in the realities of life in American schools. A study published in the *Journal of the American Medical Association* just after the second anniversary of Columbine reported that 30 percent of students in grades 6 to 10 said they had bullied others, been bullied, or both.[15] A study sponsored by the children's cable TV channel Nickelodeon released in March 2001 found that 74 percent of 12–15 year-olds surveyed felt "teasing and bullying" was a "very big problem" or "kind of a big problem" for people their age.[16]

The Internet provides young people with an unprecedented way of directly voicing negative experiences with the social atmosphere of schools. While this evidence is anecdotal, such material does indicate how deeply some individuals feel about their experience in contemporary schools. When the online magazine *Slashdot: News For Nerds* published an essay, "Why Kids Kill" by Jon Katz just days after the shooting, it was overwhelmed by e-mail with thousands of high school horror stories. "If Dan Rather wants to know why those guys killed those people in Littleton, Colorado, tell him for me that the kids who run the school probably drove them crazy, bit by bit," reads one response. "That doesn't mean all those kids deserved to die. But a lot of kids in America know why it happened, even if the people running the schools don't."[17]

If this survey and anecdotal evidence paints an accurate picture, why are our schools this way? In analyzing the social world of high schools, Aronson does not accept that status hierarchies, snobbery, and bullying are just the immutable tribal customs of adolescence. Instead he locates their immediate source in traditional methods of education that overemphasize competition and underemphasize cooperation in the classroom. Competition among individual students of various academic abilities means that inevitably some will be ranked as "winners," and some as "losers," with the remainder in between.

This ranking process, which has important practical consequences, also teaches a powerful social lesson—don't be a loser. "Perhaps that is why most of us tend to treat losing like a contagious disease," observed Aronson. "The winners and those in the middle ground try to differentiate themselves from the losers. They don't associate with them; they taunt them; they want the losers to just 'get lost.'"[18] Students, of course, use nonacademic criteria—athletic prowess, sex appeal, money, social skills, race—to rank their peers as winners and losers. But they learn the basic process of ranking, as well as the legitimacy and necessity of doing so, from their teachers.

The purpose of *Nobody Left to Hate,* Aronson explained, "is not simply to try to prevent pathological 'losers' from killing their fellow students. It is to create a classroom atmosphere where there *are* no losers."[19] This may sound utopian, but the bulk of Aronson's book is devoted to explaining a very concrete instructional method that he calls the "jigsaw strategy." The method requires students, initially based on their own self-interest in academic success, to work in structured teams with others whom they might otherwise avoid or even despise. It is the practical experience of interdependence in effective action, rather than mere exhortation and symbolic gestures, that builds interpersonal "empathy, compassion, and understanding."[20] While Aronson does not claim exclusive efficacy for his method, he wrote, "I am confident that, if the jigsaw strategy had been instituted a few years ago, Columbine High School would have been a happier place for all of its students and the tragedy could have been averted."[21]

Whatever the actual merits of Aronson's "jigsaw" method, it is easy enough to expand it into a much larger and very familiar sociocultural analysis. High schools are not social universes unto themselves, but can be understood as particularly intensive microcosms of contemporary America. From this point of view, the American culture of competition generates billionaire "winners" and homeless "losers," and mercilessly ranks everyone else on a slippery downward slope in between. The resulting social intolerance—"Get lost, you losers!"—is behind the multiple forms of oppression: economic exploitation, racism, sexism, and homophobia. Just as the exclusive social atmosphere of high schools results from an overemphasis on competition in the classroom, so social injustice results from an overemphasis on competition in many aspects of American life. And just as Aronson's solution to Columbine is to create a classroom in which there are no losers, the wider application of Aronson's thinking is to create a society and a culture without losers.

In presenting his educational solution, Aronson remains carefully nonpartisan. But it is not hard to see that his recommendations, and their implicit sociocultural analysis, would be more warmly received by Democrats and the Left than by Republicans and the Right. The Democratic Left has traditionally regarded itself as the champion of the exploited and the oppressed, of those at the "bottom of the ladder."

President Bill Clinton, a Democrat, for instance, in an April 22, 1999, speech on Columbine to a group of high school students, presented, and even universalized, Aronson's explanation of the root causes of violence. Clinton noted that "the young men who were involved in this horrible act apparently felt that they were subject to ridicule and ostracism." He likened their violent response to being "social outcasts" to the Serb attacks on ethnic Albanians in the Balkan region of Kosovo, which the United States was then trying to stop through bombing Serbia. "This is something you see a lot around the world and throughout human history," he observed, "that people who themselves feel they are disrespected . . . instead look for someone else to look down on." For Clinton, this cycle of disrespect, intolerance, and violence represented "a larger problem that we really have to fight."[22] This basic approach was echoed a month later at a Littleton, Colorado, school by First Lady Hillary Rodham Clinton. "We can try to bridge the differences that too often come between us. And we can look for ways at all levels of society to make the changes we know we have to make."[23]

The Clintons were not alone in this. An editorial on Columbine in the proudly leftist magazine *The Nation* made the "it's Right-wing intolerance" argument by citing Harvard psychiatrist James Gilligan's observation that the "experience of being shamed and humiliated" is the most powerful stimulant of violence. "For that reason," the editorial continued, "it is important to stand against the culture-warriors' demonization of music, video games and other pastimes of students who already feel like outcasts. For the same reason, there's no greater danger than overreacting with another round of tough juvenile-crime laws, as some Republicans are now suggesting."[24] In other words, let the "intolerant" Republicans have their way and there will be more school shootings.

In the highly polarized and politicized world of American public discourse in the late 1990s, "intolerance" also functioned as a code word for the Republicans who resisted, in the First Lady's words, "the changes we know we have to make." The Republicans' emphasis upon individualism, competitive free enterprise, and smaller government was seen as unfairly favoring social and economic winners, while fostering the continued exclusion and oppression of those branded losers: the poor, minorities, women, and gays. Even "the Jocks," the socially elite clique that reportedly tormented Harris and Klebold, were the perfect subliminal symbol of oppressive white male heterosexual privilege, poster boys for the Republican Party.

It would be easy to overstate the resemblance, and thus the linkage, between Aronson's analysis of the root cause of Columbine and the general outlook of anything as hard to define as the "political Left," or as diverse as the Democratic Party. And Aronson, let me emphasize, remains nonpartisan throughout. Yet we should not be surprised when we can recognize certain parallels, or even an alliance, between the analysis of a specific problem and a more general political agenda. Indeed, in the remainder of this chapter, we will find the same sort of alliance between the specific and the general on the other end of the political spectrum.

THE UNUSUAL SUSPECT

Along with gun control, increased school security, and limiting violence in popular culture, Aronson mentions two other peripheral or "quick fix" responses to school shootings. The first is requiring students to show respect by addressing teachers as "sir" or "ma'am." The second, and more important for the remainder of this chapter, is having prayer in public schools or posting the Ten Commandments in classrooms.[25] Unlike the other three peripheral responses, which are discussed seriously by Aronson, the function of these last two is comic relief, to elicit a knowing chuckle at the "nonsense" some people actually believe. Aronson wrote of posting the Ten Commandments, "This intervention may be politically expedient, but, as public policy, it is feeble."[26] Its inherent weakness, for Aronson, is so obvious that he seems annoyed by the necessity of having to explain.

> But anyone who knows anything about how the human mind works knows that posting the Ten Commandments would not do the trick. Students already know the Ten Commandments. Harris and Klebold were well aware of the commandment Thou shalt not kill. Tacking it up on the wall would not have deterred them from performing their outrageous action.[27]

Aronson is actually arguing against the "straw man" version of the argument for posting the Ten Commandments in public schools. The religious conservatives who favor such measures do not argue that a copy of the decalogue "tacked up" on a wall would have caused Harris and Klebold to drop their weapons.

Instead, religious conservatives are really arguing that had the public schools, and by extension American society, been consistently honoring for *decades* what the Ten Commandments represent—absolute moral laws based on transcendent authority—the Columbine school shooting would not have occurred. "At Littleton yesterday," observed political commentator and presidential candidate Pat Buchanan, "America got a glimpse of the last stop on that train to hell she boarded decades ago when we declared that God is dead, and that each of us is his or her own god who can make up the rules as we go along."[28] And Buchanan also made clear that he did not believe these decades of damage could be fixed quickly. "It's like an ocean liner," he told an interviewer a week after the shooting. "You can start turning the wheel, and it probably takes a huge arc of miles and miles and miles before you can turn it around."[29] In other words, measures such as posting the Ten Commandments and having prayer in schools are not peripheral "quick fix" responses but are based on an analysis by religious conservatives of root causes and long-term effects.

This analysis of Columbine is, of course, an extension of the now familiar argument that traces America's current social pathologies to the cultural changes that began in the 1960s. A *Wall Street Journal* editorial on Columbine entitled "No Norms" put it this way: "This country has spent about 30 years trying very hard to prove that no one, not even children, should be fettered by anyone else's idea of proper behavior. Now we have no norms. Or at least none that we hold in common. Are we happy yet?"[30] In the aftermath of Columbine, of course, the answer is no. But why? Without the restraint of strongly internalized transcendent norms, this conservative argument holds, greater external limitations become necessary to check our self-aggrandizing and destructive urges. This is hardly a new idea. Edmund Burke, the eighteenth-century English statesman and political philosopher, wrote in 1791,

> Men are qualified for civil liberty in exact proportion to their disposition to put moral chains upon their own appetites; in proportion as their love of justice is above their rapacity. . . . Society cannot exist, unless a controlling power upon will and appetite be placed somewhere; and the less of it there is within, the more there must be without.[31]

Today's conservatives would argue, as in the *Wall Street Journal* editorial quoted above, that in recent decades we have removed even the external controls upon behavior. Without God's law, and without the restraints imposed by the State, we make our own laws to suit ourselves.

A statement found on Eric Harris's web site provides an extreme example of this. "My belief is that if I say something, it goes. I am the law, if you don't like it, you die." William Kristol of the conservative *Weekly Standard* observed of this statement, "There you have it: the culmination, the end, of modernity."[32] According to Watergate figure and founder of Prison Fellowship Ministries, Charles Colson, Harris and Klebold "were only pushing to its logical conclusion the mindset of the surrounding culture."[33]

Those making this argument usually point to the Supreme Court's removal of prayer and Bible reading from public schools in 1962–1963 as the signal moment in America's turn to a secular "moral relativism." According to religious broadcaster Pat Robertson, "When we lifted the religious restraints off society in that fashion and suddenly the worship of God became unconstitutional . . . it has begun a spiral that hasn't stopped yet."[34] This was also reflected in a popular poem, "The New School Prayer," that was posted on hundreds of web sites in the aftermath of Columbine.

> Now I sit me down in school
> Where praying is against the rule

For this great nation under God
Finds mention of Him very odd.
If Scripture now the class recites,
It violates the Bill of Rights. . . .
We can get our condoms and birth controls,
Study witchcraft, vampires and totem poles.
But the Ten Commandments are not allowed,
No word of God must reach this crowd.
It's scary here I must confess,
When chaos reigns the school's a mess.
So, Lord, this silent plea I make:
Should I be shot: My soul please take!
Amen.[35]

Beyond the removal of the Bible and prayer, the influence of Darwinism on school children was also seen as contributing to Columbine. The schools, asserted Ken Ham of Answers in Genesis Ministries, are "teaching students that they are just evolved animals, and that there is no absolute authority and no such thing as sin." Ham charged that some of the students "indoctrinated" in the "bankrupt theory of evolution" will "believe that life is all about death, violence, and bloodshed because, after all, these are the processes by which they evolved."[36] Ham would argue that Harris, who wore a T-shirt bearing the words "Natural Selection" during the shooting, and Klebold were indoctrinated in this fashion.[37]

Rumors that Harris and/or Klebold were homosexual or bisexual also fit the religious conservative critique of American morals. These rumors seemed to have been based on news reports that the killers and others associated with the "Trench Coat Mafia" had been harassed with epithets such as "faggot" and "homo," and on the rather shaky assumption that the harassers actually knew what they were talking about. These rumors were spread by Internet journalist Matt Drudge, and mentioned in passing by such figures as the Reverend Jerry Falwell and conservative commentator Robert Novak in the days after the shooting. The antigay leader of the Westboro

Baptist Church in Topeka, Kansas, the Reverend Fred Phelps, allegedly issued a press release stating, "Two filthy fags slaughtered 13 people at Columbine High School."[38] But when no evidence supporting these rumors emerged, conservatives such as Falwell, who wanted to be heard in the mainstream discussion of Columbine, dropped the "gay killers" angle.

Denver-based radio talk-show host and evangelist Bob Larson brought many of these conservative accusations of cultural pathology together in his 1999 book, *Extreme Evil: Kids Killing Kids*. Larson wrote of talking to Columbine students and hearing that the "trench-coat guys" had "claimed to be vampires," were "into Wicca" or witchcraft, were regarded as homosexuals, and had used drugs. Larson admitted that all of this is hearsay but asserted, "All these elements are key to understanding the denial that took over their minds and made their actions so inhumane, so detached."[39] Larson examines other school shootings and discusses violence in movies, video games, and music as well as physical, emotional, and sexual abuse as contributing factors. But his essential argument is that Satanism is behind school shootings. His proof of Harris and Klebold's Satanism, however, is limited to the assertion that they sought out Christians, such as Cassie Bernall and Rachel Scott, and the detached and remorseless manner of the killers. "It's no accident that kids in our schools today are involved in satanism," explained Larson. "Unfortunately educators have forced Christians out, citing separation of church and state. At the same time they have allowed satanists and other cult members into the schools."[40]

The religious conservative solution to all of these problems, of course, is repentance and a return to the paths we have abandoned. The call for national repentance is often expressed with the citation of 2 Chronicles 7:14. "If my people, who are called by my name, shall humble themselves, and pray, and seek my face, and turn from their wicked ways; then I will hear from heaven, and will forgive their sin and will heal their land." But as religious conservatives such as Robertson point out, America has been unwilling to turn from "wicked ways" and remains a land in need of healing. Columbine is yet more proof of this.

If the Left laid the implicit blame for Columbine at the feet of the Right, the Right was already responding in kind, explicitly. Just as "intolerance" functioned as a code word to accuse religious conservatives and Republicans, "secularism" and "relativism" were used to lay the dead of Columbine at the feet of liberals and Democrats. Assigning such blame is, of course, a standard political tactic that is used to delegitimize, demoralize, and even demonize one's opponents. In 1995, opponents of the Speaker of the House, Newt Gingrich (R-GA), suggested that his antigovernment rhetoric had contributed to the Oklahoma City bombing.[41] Gingrich, who had left office in the fall of 1998, used Columbine for some payback. With an allusion to Émile Zola's 1898 attack on the enemies of Alfred Dreyfus, "J'Accuse!," Gingrich said in a May 12, 1999, speech, "I want to say to the elite of this country—the elite news media, the liberal academic elite, the liberal political elite—I accuse you in Littleton . . . of being afraid to talk about the mess you have made, and being afraid to take responsibility for the things you have done."[42]

House Majority Whip Tom DeLay (R-TX), in remarks on the floor of the House, made similar accusations and even managed to blame President Clinton, who had escaped removal from office just months before, for Columbine. DeLay quoted a letter to a newspaper that mocked those who were calling for gun control in the aftermath of Columbine: "It couldn't have been because we teach our children that there are no laws of morality that transcend us, that everything is relative and that actions do not have consequences. What the heck, the President gets away with it. Nah, it must have been the guns."[43]

Other religious conservatives also found in President Clinton's political survival a parable of America's moral decay that led to Columbine. Rod Martin, a columnist with the online *Vanguard Magazine,* cited President John Adams's observation that "Our Constitution was made only for a moral and religious people." Martin then told his readers, "His [Adams's] generation agreed. Ours does not. Look at its hero: Bill Clinton. Just two months ago, all we scribes were writing of the dangers of a government which no longer values or abides by the rule of law. In Littleton, we see the dangers of a people similarly debased, now for some thirty-five years."[44]

The post-Columbine religious conservative analysis also utilized the phrase "culture of death." "The kids who did this are responsible," asserted Peggy Noonan, a former speech writer for President Reagan. "But they came from a place and a time, and were yielded forth by a culture. What walked into Columbine High School Tuesday was the culture of death."[45] Originally a central concept in Pope John Paul II's 1995 encyclical *Evangelium Vitae,* "culture of death" became the shorthand to link Harris and Klebold's horrific actions with everything religious conservatives did not like about contemporary America.

In announcing his eventually unsuccessful presidential campaign, Republican Gary Bauer asserted that the culture of death is "in our movies. It's in our music. Our culture glorifies death in a thousand different ways . . . movies and music that glorify killing— that glorify killing the innocent." For Bauer, of course, the great symbol of all of this is the legalization of abortion, which "really boils down to one simple and profoundly evil idea. They [the Supreme Court] said that our unborn children have no rights that the rest of us were bound to respect."[46] In other words, *Roe v. Wade* sends the message that human life is cheap, a message reinforced by pop culture, a message Harris and Klebold took to heart and put into action.

Radio talk-show host and Republican presidential candidate Alan Keyes was typically direct in condemning "the left wing people who produce filthy music and movies that are filling the hearts of our children with the sewage that then breaks out into violence and death as a lifestyle for the young. Bill Clinton represents that kind of culture, and he is the champion of those people."[47]

By fitting their analysis of Columbine neatly into their standard interpretation of cultural decline, religious conservatives' responses naturally resembled their standard program of cultural renewal through public affirmations of traditional religion and morality. "As America struggles to understand the terrible tragedy of Littleton," stated a May 1999 Christian Coalition radio ad, "we urge all candidates for office, regardless of party, to pledge their support for putting God back in our schools, and parents back in our homes."[48]

This standard program has, despite much effort over two decades, met with only limited success. But in the aftermath of Columbine, elements of this program achieved an unexpected if temporary legislative victory. Several amendments to a juvenile justice bill (H.R. 1501) in the House of Representatives provided for: (1) the display of the Ten Commandments in public facilities; (2) a "charitable choice" provision allowing government grants to religious charities; (3) a declaration that memorials on public school campuses can contain religious speech without violating the establishment clause; (4) denying attorney's fees to those who sue public schools for violating the establishment clause by permitting religious expression. All four amendments were approved by wide margins on June 16, 1999.[49] In the first flush of success, Janet Parshall, of the religious conservative organization Family Research Council, told the *Washington Post,* "I have to tell you, it's amazing to us, there's a whole lot of us going 'Wow.' After all these school shootings we thought maybe we could get a discussion going, introduce some ideas, but this is tremendous."[50]

While none of these amendments to H.R. 1501 were enacted into law, many long-standing efforts, through both litigation and legislation, to post the Ten Commandments in schools and public buildings seemed to be reenergized in the aftermath of Columbine.[51] "From state legislators to presidential candidates, America's politicians are eagerly jumping onto the Ten Commandments bandwagon," observed Charles C. Haynes of the First Amendment Center in February 2000. "Putting the commandments on the wall of every public-school classroom seems to be a politically popular move in the post-Columbine era."[52]

CASSIE BERNALL AND THE POLITICS OF TRAGEDY

Religious conservatives, of course, have made these arguments before and about previous school shootings. After the shooting in

Jonesboro, Arkansas, in March 1998, James Dobson of Focus on the Family and Gary Bauer of the Family Research Council published a joint letter. "Jonesboro marks a point of crisis," read the letter, "but one that is hardly new or unique. What happened in this small town in Arkansas symbolizes America in moral free-fall, America on a rapidly descending spiral, America without God."[53]

The same spiritual-moral analysis has also been applied to other tragic events. In a statement on the September 11, 2001, terrorist attacks that destroyed the World Trade Center's twin towers and damaged the Pentagon, Pat Robertson reviewed the familiar litany of America's sins and concluded, "We have insulted God at the highest level of our government. Then, we say, 'Why does this happen?' It is happening because God Almighty is lifting His protection from us." Robertson's solution was equally familiar. "We must pray and ask Him for revival so that once again we will be His people, the planting of His righteousness, so that He will come to our defense and protect us as a nation."[54]

Columbine, however, provides conservatives with a unique leverage. The difference, I would argue, lies both in the character of the killers *and* in those they killed. There were other heroic victims at Columbine, such as teacher William "Dave" Sanders, who was shot while leading students out of the school. But the reported confrontation between Cassie and her killer seemed to supply a perfect dramatization of the conservative critique of American culture. As Kristol observed during the April 25, 1999, broadcast of ABC's *This Week,* "I think this episode will become a sort of famous episode in the sense that—if you have a post-Christian America, post-religious America, there's no right and wrong, there's no good and evil, you get people behaving this way and then she poses the alternative, so starkly."[55] In other words, "'Do you believe in God?' 'Yes.' Bang," was the quintessential confrontation of the culture of life and the culture of death, belief and disbelief, meaning and nihilism, good and evil. Kristol's magazine, *The Weekly Standard,* featured a photo of Cassie on the cover of its May 10, 1999, issue along with, "Do you believe in God?" "Yes."[56]

Cassie's symbolic weight is not unique in contemporary politics. *New Republic* editor Andrew Sullivan noted the "political and cultural symbolism" associated with Matthew Shepard, a gay college student murdered in Wyoming in 1998. Sullivan noted that Shepard's name was being "ritually invoked in the debate over hate-crime laws," and was often featured by gay rights organizations in their fund-raising appeals. Shepard's use as a symbol "is about the need for a victim so blameless and a crime so heinous that a story about the relationship between gay Americans and straight Americans can be told in which there are no complexities and no doubts." Sullivan also observed that Shepard's case was being used as "a kind of political blackmail," in which, "opposition to various legislative initiatives was deemed equivalent to complicity in Shepard's murder."[57]

On April 27, 1999, the conservative Republican who represented the Littleton, Colorado, area in Congress, Rep. Tom Tancredo, introduced a "sense of Congress" resolution on Columbine. Tancredo presented Cassie's martyr story with "no complexities and no doubts" in his supporting remarks.

> "Do you believe in God?" "Yes, I believe in God." Seventeen year old Cassie Bernall's life ended with that answer. Our answers to the Columbine High School murderers begin with the same question, and our answer must be the same as Cassie Bernall or the nihilistic fury unleashed by those two young murders will surely prevail. . . . Nihilism or God, that is the choice. The comfortable in-between is now gone.[58]

Cassie's martyrdom was also seen as the harbinger of a "Great Awakening," a sweeping religious revival that will transform the cultural landscape as well as the hearts of individuals. Writing in the August 1999 issue of the conservative journal *First Things,* editor J. Bottum suggested, "If the fourth Great Awakening that people have been predicting since the 1970s actually occurs, it will have begun on April 20, 1999, and Cassie Bernall will be its martyr, its catalyst and its patron saint." Bottum asserted that the impact of her goodness "may deliver a victory in the culture wars so massive that all the narrow policy wars are simply forgotten." Bottum concluded:

> To picture her standing there trembling in the school library, with a gun to her head, the question "Do you believe in God?" hanging in the air, is to believe that a change in heart is possible, that God may be loose in America again, that the pendulum may have finally begun its long arc back.[59]

1999 was, of course, a year inevitably filled with "the narrow policy wars" of presidential politics. Vice President Al Gore may have been arguing for gun control when, after telling the story of Cassie's brave answer, he asked the audience at the memorial service, "Now as we are brought to our knees in the shock of this moment, what say we? What say we into the open muzzle of this tragedy, cocked and aimed at our hearts?"[60]

Predictably, the Republican candidates drew a different lesson from Cassie's final moments. Texas Governor George W. Bush referred to her in a November 2, 1999, speech on "The True Goal of Education." She was alluded to as one of many teenagers who had demonstrated "character and courage beyond measure." Bush did not use her name but only said, "When a gun is aimed at a seventeen-year-old in Colorado—and she is shot for refusing to betray her Lord."[61]

Alan Keyes, in an April 23 radio commentary, asserted, "We should recognize in the Columbine killings the real consequences of our moral cowardice." Keyes, however, found hope in the story of the girl who said "Yes" to the gunman who demanded to know if she believed in Jesus Christ. "The martyrdom of the young lady presents to us the truth about what we should be doing to counteract this cowardice. Many guns are pointed at us, and we need to imitate her courage in facing them down."[62]

It was Gary Bauer, who launched his presidential campaign the day after the shooting, who made the most use of Columbine and Cassie in interviews and speeches.[63] On the May 9, 1999, edition of

NBC's *Meet the Press* Bauer declared, "We've created a country where it's harder and harder to make Cassies and it's easier and easier to produce people like Eric and Dylan."[64] On other occasions, Bauer used Cassie as a symbol of strength and pride for the evangelical community. When Minnesota Governor Jesse Ventura told *Playboy* magazine that "organized religion is a sham and a crutch for weak-minded people who need strength in numbers," Bauer commented that "The governor should have met Cassie Bernall.... There was nothing weak about her." Bauer further suggested that rather than "The Body," the governor should be known as "Jesse 'The Bigot' Ventura."[65]

Bauer was, of course, tying Cassie and the Columbine shooting to the theme of "anti-Christian bigotry," a theme that has long proven valuable for religious conservative organizers. "The shooting itself," observed historian of American religion Randall Balmer, "kind of symbolizes their own [evangelicals'] sense of imperilment in a larger world that is hostile to them."[66] This "sense of imperilment," or a perceived repression and opposition by a "them," helps create an "us"—a sense of common identity within an otherwise disparate constituency. It also allows the largely white, middle-class religious conservatives to claim what has been called "the moral clout that comes with victimhood"—a moral clout usually utilized by groups identified with the political Left.[67]

The deaths at Columbine of Cassie and others, such as Rachel Scott, who were identifiably religious, at Columbine helped to provide, at least in the eyes of religious conservatives themselves, that moral clout. On their home videos, Harris and Klebold displayed a marked contempt toward Christianity and Christians. Harris, for instance, said sarcastically, "Yeah, 'I love Jesus. I love Jesus.' Shut the fuck up." Klebold added an element of violence to his contempt for those wearing "What Would Jesus Do?" (WWJD) apparel. "What would Jesus do? What would I do?" He then mimicked shooting a gun at the camera. At another point Harris refers to Christ as "that asshole," and both chant "Go Romans!" referring to their role in the crucifixion.[68]

And Columbine was linked with two other violent incidents in which Christians were victims: the December 1, 1997, school shooting in West Paducah, Kentucky, in which a student, Michael Carneal, opened fire on an evangelical Christian prayer group, killing three before being apprehended; and the shooting at Wedgewood Baptist Church in Fort Worth, Texas, on September 15, 1999, in which 47-year-old Larry Ashbrook killed seven before committing suicide.[69] In the aftermath of the Forth Worth shooting, many were quick to claim that the evangelicals killed and injured in these incidents had been the victims of "hate crimes."[70] Moral Majority founder Jerry Falwell told *Time,* "Most hate crimes in America today are not directed toward African-American or Jewish people or gays or lesbians. They are directed at evangelical Christians."[71]

Like attacks on other groups, it was asserted that violence grew out of a wider social climate. Editorialist Wes Pruden of the *Washington Times* linked the Wedgewood shooting to the secularism of political liberals. He wrote, "the determination of the irreligious to destroy society's traditional respect for faith, is having a cumulative effect."[72]

There is, of course, a certain irony to religious conservatives, who have consistently opposed hate crime legislation, making use of the category of "hate crime." But religious conservatives are only following the moral logic of identity group politics. As James B. Jacobs and Kimberly Potter point out in *Hate Crimes: Criminal Law & Identity Politics,* "the greater a group's victimization, the stronger its moral claim on the larger society."[73] To be a recognized victim provides moral, and thus political, leverage.

To not have one's claim to victimhood recognized by the larger society, as is the case with white, middle-class evangelicals, is not the problem it may appear to be. Instead, a lack of recognition of victimhood makes for a claim of even greater victimization. Such unrecognized victimization can be used to strengthen group solidarity, to heighten a sense of moral entitlement within the group, and to intensify resentment against critics, competing victim groups, and the larger society. "It would seem that killing Christians is on a far lower level of seriousness than anyone else being killed," observed Dr. D. James Kennedy, a conservative religious broadcaster. "Is that where we've come to as a Christian nation?"[74]

This moral logic of victimization politics was clearly on display in "Religious Bigotry in America," a speech by House Majority Leader Dick Armey (R-TX), one of religious conservatism's most staunch allies in Congress. "We are witnessing," asserted Armey, "a rising level of bigotry against people of faith, especially Christians." Armey attacked Barry Lynn of Americans United for Separation of Church and State, a leading opponent of religious conservatism, for criticizing the popular elevation of Cassie. "I think that what we've done here is to take this one victim," said Lynn on CNN's *Crossfire,* "turned it into an example of martyrdom, and then used it to become the springboard for even more exploitation of this tragedy by people with a religious, political agenda." Armey asserted, "Such insensitivity would have been denounced if said about John F. Kennedy, Martin Luther King or even Rodney King."[75]

In the first few months after Columbine, it was Cassie's martyrdom that was cited by politicians and commentators, as well as by preachers with a political bent. With the passage of time, and the controversy that erupted in September 1999 about whether she had really said "yes" (see chapter 5), political citations of her martyrdom have become less common, but they have not disappeared. Ceremonies in Washington, D.C., celebrating the May 3, 2001, National Day of Prayer (NDP), organized by Shirley Dobson, wife of broadcaster James Dobson, were attended by Charles Colson, U.S. Senator Wayne Allard (R-CO), and U.S. Secretary of Housing and Urban Development Mel Martinez. (President George W. Bush did not attend but held a reception for NDP leaders at the White House.) This event, which so clearly blended politics and conservative religion, was closed by recording artist Michael W. Smith, who performed, "This is Your Time," his popular song about Cassie and her martyrdom.[76]

It is worth noting that Cassie's family was not present for this event. As I noted in chapter 2, her family has shown little interest in connecting Cassie to any public policy initiatives. "The more I think about it," wrote Misty Bernall, "the more certain I am that, political and public as the broader discussion might be, we cannot forget the equally vital role of our more personal efforts to prevent tragedies like the one that claimed Cassie."[77]

The central concern of *She Said Yes* is about how parents should raise their children, not what the government should be doing. The Bernalls have also lent their name to an effort by the Southern Baptist Convention to promote Internet filtering software, not government regulation of online content.[78] And the politics of Plough, the original publisher of *She Said Yes,* seem to lean to the Left rather than the Right. Rather than books by Pat Robertson, James Dobson, or Charles Colson, the Plough list has included books by Mumia Abu-Jamal, Barbara Kingsolver, Daniel Berrigan, Oscar Romero, and Dorothy Day. Other titles are strongly pacifist, anti-death penalty, and critical of the continued U.S. embargo against Iraq.[79] This does not mean the Bernalls share, or even care about, Plough's "peace and justice" politics, but simply that they were not concerned to promote a conservative political agenda with their daughter's "unlikely martyrdom."

RACHEL SCOTT AND THE POLITICS OF TRAGEDY

The relationship of the legacy of Rachel Scott, and those promoting that legacy, to politics is more complex. In the case of Cassie, it was those in politics, not those close to her, that utilized her martyrdom for political, and often narrowly partisan, purposes. In the case of Rachel, by the time her reputation as a martyr had emerged, the professional politicians had mostly decamped from Columbine and moved on. This left her family to elaborate upon the wider political import of her life and death. But these political lessons are less clear and more problematic than her family imagines.

Like Misty Bernall's emphasis on "personal efforts," much of what we learn about Rachel points away from political, constitutional, or even institutional solutions. While she wrote of carrying

God's name "Through these halls of a tragedy," one does not find in her writings complaints about how the courts removed organized prayer from the classrooms, or about the government's failure to hang the Ten Commandments in her school's "tragic hallways." Instead of an institutional-legal solution, Rachel's own writings speak only of personal initiative and interaction, not social engineering but concrete acts of self-giving. This aspect of Rachel's legacy stands in the more personal and less conventionally political tradition of evangelical Christianity—you change society by changing the hearts of individuals.

This personalistic side of Rachel's legacy is reflected in much of Darrell Scott's book *Chain Reaction,* published in April 2001. The book centers around her essay "My Ethics, My Codes of Life," from which the title phrase "chain reaction" is derived. To illustrate her ethical values, he presents a wide variety of inspirational quotations, anecdotes, and illustrations, from both Christian and non-Christian sources, as well as practical suggestions for action.

Perhaps the most striking illustration is the parallel between Rachel's "chain reaction" and the movie *Pay It Forward,* released in October 2000. In this film, based on a novel of the same name, a 12-year-old boy thinks of a way to "change the world": Do an important favor for someone else, and rather than have them pay it back, they must "pay it forward" to three other people, who in turn pay it forward, and so on. It is not difficult to see the parallel Darrell Scott is drawing, especially since the boy dies a martyr-like death, thus sanctifying the "Pay It Forward movement."[80] (Note that this fictional movement is purely personal and noninstitutional. It spreads without leadership, organization, publicity, or government sponsorship.)

While the concepts of "pay it forward" and "chain reaction" make a similar appeal to individual idealism, there are important differences. *Pay It Forward* never mentions religion, churches, God, or Christ, which, of course, the earlier book *Rachel's Tears* presents as the core and foundation of Rachel's compassion. And perhaps more important, the concept of "pay it forward" involves no moral dualism. There is no "other" who must be overcome—no ideology, structure, or agents of evil. There is no "devil," only our own imperfections, fears, and weaknesses. But *Chain Reaction* retains a clear and basic dualism. Rachel's call for a "chain reaction of compassion" is set against a statement by Harris in one of the videotapes made with Klebold. "We need a [expletive] kick start—we need to get a chain reaction going here!"[81] In other words, a chain reaction of violence.

Darrell Scott often juxtaposes these two chain reactions: "It was as though these two teenagers laid down a double challenge to their entire generation."[82] This double challenge reflects more essential and classic Christian dualities: good and evil, God and Satan, the children of light and the children of darkness, salvation and damnation. Such dualities are, of course, the structural precondition for martyrdom to have a political dimension. Martyrdom, to recall sociologist Samuel Z. Klausner words, is "an attempt to break through the ideological and social boundaries between the conflicting groups with hierocratic, religiously based power."[83]

While it might be easy to see Harris and Klebold as pure evil, as demonic agents of Satan, this would serve no ideological or social, and thus no political, function. Instead, some existing human ideology and community must be associated with their actions. The key to understanding the ideological-social dimensions of Columbine is found in the concluding line of a brief poem by Rachel, reportedly written shortly before her death: "The world you have created has lead [*sic*] to my death."[84] This could be interpreted, of course, in any number of ways. But the promoters of Rachel's legacy interpret "the world" as the secularized world of American public schools, which "you," the previous generation, created, or allowed to be created through inaction. "We are facing a moral and spiritual crisis," wrote Darrell Scott, "because of the vacuum that was created when we removed every shred of spiritual influence from our schools in the '60s."[85] Harris and Klebold were the products of that vacuum, and the Columbine shooting should awaken us to the moral-spiritual crisis.

This interpretation of Rachel's poem and of Columbine comes naturally to those already steeped in the religious conservative critique of contemporary America. Bruce Porter's funeral sermon, delivered before Rachel's writings came to light, anticipates the interpretation in full. He uses the question "How did we get here?" to present an indictment of the agents of secularization in education. He quotes the Duke of Wellington as saying, "If you divorce religion from education, you produce a race of clever devils." This divorce has three features: (1) removal of the Ten Commandments from schools, which leads to "selfish indifference and glorified hedonism"; (2) the teaching of evolution, which leads children to see "no intrinsic value to life"; and, (3) the removal of prayer from schools, which leads to "violence, hatred, and murder." Standing by Rachel's coffin, Porter adds, "And we have the fruit of those activities before us now."

The religious response to this assault by secularization's "clever devils," according to Porter, can not come from his generation, "We can't do it. We have failed." Instead it comes from Rachel's generation. "I want to say to you here today," proclaims Porter, "that prayer was established again in our public schools last Tuesday." Interrupted by applause, he continues, "What the judiciary couldn't do, what the churches couldn't do, the children did themselves." But this is not enough. He calls upon Rachel's generation to "take back" their schools: "I am hereby issuing a challenge to every student in every school across this nation. Pick up the torch that Rachel carried." Rachel's torch, Porter's favorite image, is the symbol of sacred power in the struggle against the agents of secularization. The torch is "stained by the blood of the martyrs from the very first day of the church's existence . . . nearly 2,000 years ago" and it is "a torch of the good news of Jesus Christ her Lord, of whom she was not ashamed—even in her hour of death."[86]

Porter's remarks, of course, can be read as nonpolitical, as calling upon individual teenagers to be more energetic in sharing the Gospel with their friends and classmates. But Porter's subsequent writings and statements make clear that his concerns are national and political as well as religious. Two chapters in *The Martyrs' Torch*, for instance, are entitled, "A National Emergency!" and "Retaking

Our Schools . . . Retaking Our Nation." In these chapters, Porter uses many of religious conservatism's standard phrases: "our nation's moral fabric has been systematically shredded"; "tolerance has now become a politically correct cliché"; abortion is a "holocaust"; "the popular secular mantra: 'separation of church and state'"; and, "the removal of prayer from our public schools by judicial fiat."[87] Porter's solution is also standard for religious conservatism. "We can remedy the situation and avert judgment only by repentance, prayer, and a return to the faith of our ancestors."[88]

Does Porter understand the discussion of these issues as at least partially political? Yes. At a Torchgrab rally in June 2001, Porter was presenting a series of quotations from various Founding Fathers to demonstrate the fallacy of "the separation of church and state," when he rhetorically asked his audience, "Am I making a political statement?" And his answer was, "Without apology."[89]

In an essay written in July 1999, Rachel's mother, Beth Nimmo, also blames the removal of prayer from public schools for Columbine. "This action sabotaged the safety and future well-being of generations to come," she wrote. "We have now inherited the bitter fruit." Her solution to this "grim spiritual darkness" is not surprising. "We must recapture our nation's great spiritual inheritance of Judeo-Christian values." This requires a change of heart, not legislation. Government can, however, "encourage and empower" the people to fulfill their responsibility under God.

But politicians have to do more than that. After quoting her daughter's poem, which ends, "The world you have created has led to my death," Nimmo wrote, "I plead for public repentance from our nation's leaders for removing God's influence from our schools. Please, I beg you, do not let my daughter's sacrifice be in vain."[90]

Like Porter, Nimmo sees martyrdom as essential to this transformation. "The down payment for the change we so desperately need in our nation has been paid by the blood of my daughter, Rachel, and the other precious children killed or wounded at Columbine." Despite the obvious social and political implications of "reclaiming our nation's moral heritage," Nimmo claimed this "isn't a political challenge" because it "is a job all of us should do," not just "national leaders."[91]

Whatever the accomplishments of Porter and Nimmo in this area, the politics of Rachel Scott's martyrdom have most successfully and persistently been articulated by her father. This is not surprising when we recall that Darrell Scott became a public figure through an appearance before a congressional subcommittee considering gun control legislation. In retrospect, this setting has lent a "Mr. Smith Goes to Washington" air to his remarks. Various news reports briefly mentioned his appearance in articles covering many of that day's subcommittee witnesses.[92] But the full text of his 780-word speech was rapidly spread via forwarded e-mail messages and soon appeared on hundreds of web sites. The Columbine Redemption web site asserted, "That speech became one of the most published articles on the internet, opening numerous doors of opportunity, which Darrell has used to motivate, educate, and bring positive change to many young people."[93]

What accounts for its popularity? A common version of the much-forwarded e-mail containing the speech urges the recipient to pass on the message to others. "Be courageous enough to do what the media did not—let the nation hear this man's speech. Please send this out to everyone you can!!!" This resonates with the common accusations of media bias against Christians, political conservatives, and gun-owners. The e-mail message containing the speech also reflects a deep populist suspicion of experts and elites of all kinds. "They [the Congressmen] were not prepared for what he was to say, nor was it received well. It needs to be heard by every parent, every teacher, every politician, every sociologist, every psychologist, and every so-called expert!" The e-mail continued by raising Darrell Scott to the level of a modern-day prophet. "There is no doubt that God sent this man as a voice crying in the wilderness."[94]

While members of the congressional subcommittee may have thought Darrell Scott had been invited to comment on pending firearms legislation, he announced a different purpose. "I am here today to declare that Columbine was not just a tragedy—it was a spiritual event that should be forcing us to look at where the real blame lies." And the blame lies with politicians who have permitted the prohibition of prayer in schools. "We have refused to honor God," he stated later, "and in doing so, we have opened the doors to hatred and violence."

His solution is similar to Porter's and Beth Nimmo's. "We do need a change of heart and a humble acknowledgment that this nation was founded on the principle of simple trust in God." The example of such simple trust he finds in his own son's prayers while trapped in the Columbine library. Using the same logic, and appealing to the same audience as Porter in his funeral sermon, Darrell Scott proclaimed, "I challenge every young person in America and around the world to realize that on April 20, 1999, at Columbine High School, prayer was brought back to our schools." What he calls them to do sounds something like civil disobedience. He tells them to have "a sacred disregard for legislation that violates your conscience and denies your God-given right to communicate with Him."

Throughout much of this speech, Darrell Scott does not mention his daughter and never uses the word martyr. Near the beginning he mentions her, but groups her together with the other victims. "Their blood cries out for answers," he says. But at the very conclusion, his daughter takes her singular and central place in the spiritual-civil uprising of the young for which he hopes. "My daughter's death will not be in vain. The young people of this country will not allow that to happen."[95]

Darrell Scott probably did not expect the transformation these 780 words wrought upon his life, but as the saying goes, he has taken the ball and run with it. And where he has run not only involves speaking about his daughter's spiritual and moral legacy but about the political and constitutional aspects of the causes of Columbine. As with many religious conservatives,[96] he sees the constitutional doctrine of "separation of church and state" as particularly pernicious and fallacious. He devotes a substantial amount of time during his speaking engagements to attacking this concept.

He has also developed two books, printed in a small format, making them easy to carry in a pocket or purse, which are sold at his speaking engagements. The first, *Important American Documents,* contains the Declaration of Independence, the U.S. Constitution, quotations from presidents, and Darrell Scott's own speech to the congressional subcommittee.[97] The second book, *America's Christian Roots,* is also a compilation of documents, such as the Mayflower Compact and the Gettysburg Address, as well as quotations from various Founding Fathers.[98] "As you read the proclamations, speeches, and documents contained in this small book," he wrote, "equip yourself to go out and make a difference, armed with knowledge that can help shift the balance back to our original roots."[99] This call for the restoration of "our original roots" goes beyond just reviving the strength of Christian moral principles, or even the influence of Christians upon public life. Instead, Darrell Scott is talking about a national covenant with God, America as the new world Israel. He calls it an "undeniable truth that our founders believed that this nation was birthed by God's divine election."[100]

Both books contain introductory material that conveys Darrell Scott's own views on the true meaning of the religion clauses of the First Amendment. "As a student of American history," he wrote, "I am absolutely stunned at the distortions and lies that have blinded us to the true heritage of our country."[101] The particular distortion and lie he is concerned with is, of course, the "separation of church and state." The contemporary use of this concept is exactly the opposite, he asserts, of what was originally intended.

Like many religious conservatives, he presents a litany of proof text quotations from various leaders of the colonial, revolutionary, and early national periods.[102] But his "show stopper" quotation features an oft-forgotten Massachusetts congressman and Federalist party leader, Fisher Ames (1758–1808).[103] In his public presentations, Darrell Scott asks his audiences, "Who wrote the First Amendment?" After a few in the audience guess Jefferson, Franklin, Washington, Madison, and occasionally Lincoln, he tells them it was Ames.

This is only partially correct. Ames did submit, based on James Madison's original proposal, the version of the First Amendment adopted by the House of Representatives. This went through several changes in the Senate before a House-Senate conference committee drew up the final version: "Congress shall make no law respecting an establishment of religion, or prohibiting the free exercise thereof."[104] While Darrell Scott has overstated the role of Ames as *the* author of the Amendment, as a participant, Ames can be consulted to shed light on the "original intent" of the First Amendment.[105]

Based on this premise, Darrell Scott claims Ames would have never intended the First Amendment to mean that Bible reading, and by extension organized prayer, was prohibited in public schools. The proof text is a quotation from the *Palladium* magazine, dated September 20, 1789, "one month after he wrote the 1st Amendment."[106] The quotation reads:

> We have a dangerous trend beginning to take place in our education. We're starting to put more and more textbooks into our schools—We've become accustomed of late of putting little books into the hands of children containing fables and moral lessons—We are spending less time in the classroom on the Bible, which should be the principal text in our schools—The Bible states these great moral lessons better than any other manmade books.[107]

The quotation itself may not be authentic since the publication, *The Palladium*, also known as *The New England Palladium*, did not exist in 1789.[108] But even if we leave aside the dubious character of the particular quotation, the views of Ames on the Bible or religion in "our schools" would not have involved the meaning of the First Amendment. It was not until the 1940s that the Supreme Court held that the state and local governments, through the Fourteenth Amendment (1868), were bound by the establishment and free exercise clauses.[109] For Ames, who died in 1808, the First Amendment would have applied *only* to Congress—"*Congress* shall make no law. . . ." Indeed, Ames's home state of Massachusetts retained an established church until 1833.[110] Since education in his era was a local matter conducted under the authority of the state constitutions,[111] Ames would not have seen the relevance of the First Amendment to the selection of schoolbooks. Darrell Scott's proof of the "original intent" of the First Amendment is no proof at all.

Another problem in Darrell Scott's discussion of constitutional issues is a matter of contemporary fact rather than historical evidence. He sometimes indicates that the courts have made public schools into "virtual religion-free zones."[112] In his speech to the Judiciary subcommittee he says, "As my son Craig lay under that table in the school library and saw his two friends murdered before his very eyes, he did not hesitate to pray in school. I defy any law or politician to deny him that right!" In the next sentence he asserted, "on April 20, 1999, at Columbine High School, prayer was brought back to our schools."[113] In *Important American Documents* he contends that "separation of church and state" is "used as a political blanket to eliminate anything that even hints at Christian activity where our educational system is concerned."[114]

This is not accurate. In 1995 and again in 1998, the U.S. Department of Education, in consultation with the attorney general, sent guidelines on religious activity in the public schools to every school superintendent in the nation. As one might expect, the guidelines state, "schools may not endorse religious activity or doctrine, nor may they coerce participation in religious activity. Among other things, of course, school administrators and teachers may not organize or encourage prayer exercises in the classroom."

But the Department of Education guidelines also point to a substantial sphere for *voluntary and personal* religious expression. "Schools may not forbid students acting on their own from expressing their personal religious views or beliefs solely because they are of a religious nature." And based on the Equal Access Act of 1984, the guidelines state, "Student religious activities are accorded the same access to public school facilities as are student secular activities."[115]

In other words, the law *already* protected Craig Scott's right to personal prayer in the Columbine library. Prayer, Bible study, and Christian fellowship did not have to come back to Columbine after April 20, 1999. These things were already there. And Darrell Scott should know this. In *Rachel's Tears* we read, "Like many large high schools, Columbine had an established Christian prayer group. The Columbine group organized weekly meetings at the school and participated in big annual events like See You at the Pole."[116] Every hint of Christian activity had not been eliminated from Columbine High School.

In claiming that all religious expression has been driven from the public schools, Darrell Scott is really arguing against a "straw man" version of the "separation of church and state." Why? The most obvious reason is rhetorical. Discussion of the sphere of voluntary religious expression blunts the force of the argument that secularism caused Columbine. It also lessens the moral clout that comes with Christian children being victimized by God-hating secularists. It is easier to motivate a constituency to action with the black-white image of absolute conflict between them and us, between secularists and Christians. To admit that personal and voluntary religious expression is *already* protected is to paint a wide swath of gray between the secularist black and the Christian white. These shades of gray, which hint that a workable compromise is possible, do not mix well with appeals to the spilled blood of martyrs, blood that cries out for action.

Another more practical aspect of Darrell Scott's statements on this subject, an aspect that many will find troubling, is what he does *not* say. He never discusses what will happen, in the event we return to organized prayer in public school classrooms, to students whose upbringing or personal convictions place them outside Christianity, or, more broadly, the Judeo-Christian tradition. Will they be compelled to participate in organized prayers, or will their nonparticipation be "tolerated?" Will such nonconformist students be accepted by their peers? Or will they be stigmatized and harassed as "outsiders?" How will their right to the free exercise of religion be protected? Or to ask the question more broadly: If America returns to its "Christian roots," can a non-Christian really be an American?

Darrell Scott's public silence on these sorts of questions, a silence shared by Beth Nimmo, Bruce Porter, and many religious conservatives, is not surprising. These are not the questions he gets from his predominantly evangelical audiences about the "separation of church and state," audiences that are neither equipped nor inclined to ask such critical questions. Nor are these the questions asked by reporters who write brief noncontroversial human interest stories about him, his ministry, and his daughter.

It could be that he does not think such questions need an answer because, realistically speaking, pre-1962 organized prayer will never be restored to the public schools. Perhaps he is a premillennialist, like most American evangelicals, and expects the world to become progressively godless and evil until finally Christ returns to establish a thousand-year reign of holiness, the millennium. But if this is the case, why all the fuss about separation of church and state? Isn't devoting energy to that rather like polishing the brass on a sinking ship? Wouldn't it be better to concentrate solely on getting every possible person into the lifeboat of salvation through Christ?

Yet if we take Darrell Scott at his word, with what he consistently writes and says, we have to conclude that he is optimistic about changing America. As we have seen, his speech to the Judiciary subcommittee ends with ringing confidence that the youth of America *will not let* his daughter's death be in vain. In *Important American Documents* he states, "It is time for us to stop the destruction and break the chains of bondage caused by a lack of knowledge on our part. Let's pursue the truth that will bring back the heritage and freedoms we once enjoyed as a godly nation!"[117] And in *America's Christian Roots*, he stated, "America was once a powerful Christian nation. It can be once again if each one of us simply do our part."[118] This is the language of "We have not yet begun to fight!" not "Abandon ship!"

What seems to be at work in such ringing proclamations is a deep memory of evangelicalism's lost cultural dominance. "All but the most radically alienated fundamentalists," observed historian

Grant Wacker, "have embraced the notion that Christians, especially evangelical Christians, ought to be the moral custodians of the culture."[119] This custodianship, however, for some evangelicals edges over into a sense of ownership—"America is a Christian nation!" Or more precisely, into an aggrieved sense of lost ownership—"It has been taken away from us!"—combined with a keen sense of entitlement—"It should be ours again!" This historic sense of cultural grievance and entitlement has helped energize evangelical political activists since the late 1970s. But it has not been conducive to a positive engagement with the realities of religious, cultural, and political pluralism. In other words, it inspires some people and scares the hell out of many others. It has been religious conservatism's greatest asset and its greatest liability.[120]

Considered in this wider context of grievance and entitlement, Darrell Scott's "silence" on certain school prayer questions is better understood as a "blind spot." He shows no overt hostility to faith traditions other than his own, but he simply does not seem to notice their presence at all. Deeply committed to a set of assumptions about the causes and cures of Columbine, he does not seem to see the practical difficulties or unintended consequences his solution might help create.

This apparent blindness stands in striking contrast to those aspects of Rachel Scott's legacy that emphasize sensitivity for the outsider and "welcoming the outcasts." If the picture her family has presented of her is accurate, it is not hard to imagine that her understanding of "What Jesus would do" would *not* involve requiring everyone to pray, but instead befriending the students stigmatized for *not* praying. Rather than requiring their outward compliance, or merely tolerating their noncompliance, she would try to change their hearts through a personal relationship. It is hard to reconcile the image of Rachel's expansive compassion with the potential exclusivity of a restored Christian nation. Would she approve of the political message that is being preached in her name?

What we know of Rachel, of her values and attitudes, is limited to what her family has chosen to reveal to us. This is nothing new.

Martyrs, of course, have always been at the mercy of martyrologists—those who tell, interpret, and preserve the story of the martyr. As the philosopher Albert Camus observed in his novel *The Fall,* "Martyrs, *cher ami,* must choose between being forgotten, mocked or made use of."[121] In the last three chapters, we have seen how both Cassie and Rachel have been "made use of" for a variety of causes. Would they approve or disapprove of these causes? We do not, and can not, know in any final sense. The interpretations offered by their martyrologists, the keepers of their shrines, can be accepted or challenged, but never proven or disproven. But one remaining question is open to factual proof or disproof: Were Cassie and Rachel really martyrs?

CHAPTER 5

DEFENDERS AND DEBUNKERS

"What Really Happened?"

At the heart of the entire Columbine martyrs phenomenon—both in its religious and political dimensions—are simple questions of fact. Were Cassie Bernall and Rachel Scott asked at gunpoint if they believed in God? Did each of the girls declare their faith and die a martyr's death? In short, what really happened?

These are simple questions. I cannot, however, offer simple or definitive answers given the *available* evidence. An unknown quantity of evidence collected by law enforcement agencies remains unavailable to the public. Not only are we limited by what is available, the quality of the material is uneven and often ill-suited for resolving the questions I am asking. Eyewitness accounts, upon which I must rely, are notoriously unreliable especially in complex, chaotic, and traumatic situations. The voices of other witnesses are forever stilled by death, as are the voices of the killers. Other surviving witnesses, understandably, just don't want to talk about Columbine. Journalists, working to beat a deadline or to create a particular type of story, often do not ask the questions that suit my purposes. As the multiple lawsuits by victims and their families demonstrate, serious questions have been raised about the methods and motives of the Jefferson County Sheriff's Department, which assembled much of the evidence I will use. And perhaps most important, there are a host of personal, professional, political, and ideological agendas at work, explicitly and implicitly, in all things Columbine.

Instead of definitive answers, I can only attempt to establish what probably happened to Cassie and Rachel given the publicly available evidence. (Indeed, it might be misleading to call much of this material "evidence" because much of it would be inadmissible in a court of law.) This evidence includes: (1) The statements of witnesses and law enforcement investigators to various journalists, and to myself, from the time of the shooting to date;[1] (2) the writings and other public statements of those seeking to promote the martyr stories of Cassie and Rachel, especially their families, from the time of the shooting to date;[2] (3) the conclusions and other materials presented in the *Jefferson County Sheriff's Office Report* (hereafter *Sheriff's Report*), publicly released on May 15, 2000;[3] (4) the statements of witnesses as recorded by law enforcement investigators in the weeks immediately after the shooting, publicly released under judicial order on November 21, 2000;[4] (5) other collections of evidence, such as autopsy reports, publicly released under judicial order, at various times since April 2000.[5]

As we will see below, these various types of evidence will play different roles in the examination of the two martyr stories. Moreover, each of the martyr stories poses a different evidentiary problem. In the case of Cassie's death, which took place in a large room in which dozens of persons were also trapped, there is in a sense too much information about Cassie's death. The information has been sorted out in the form of two conflicting but equally detailed accounts of her death—the martyr story and the Sheriff's "official" version, which has been embraced by "debunkers" of the Cassie martyr story. So the problem is which of the two detailed accounts is *more* credible. The Sheriff's "official account" of Rachel's death, in contrast, lacks almost any sort of specific detail. So the problem is whether there is *enough* credible evidence to support the rather detailed Rachel martyr story.

With these limitations and problems in mind, I will try to determine what really happened on April 20, 1999, to Cassie, and then to Rachel.

WHAT REALLY HAPPENED TO CASSIE BERNALL?

On September 23, 1999, only days after the release of *She Said Yes,* the online magazine *Salon.com* published "Inside the Columbine High Investigation: Everything You Know About the Littleton Killings Is Wrong," by Dave Cullen, a Denver-based journalist. The article used unnamed but "multiple sources close to the Columbine investigation" to debunk many popular notions about the massacre, including what Cullen called "the most celebrated Columbine story of all," Cassie's famous last words.

Cullen asserts that in the confusion of April 20 an exchange about God between one of the shooters and Valeen Schnurr, a student who was injured but survived the attack, had been misattributed to Cassie. Schnurr had already been shot when she was lying on the floor crying out something like "Oh my God!" One of the gunmen asked, "Do you believe in God?" After she answered "Yes," he asked, "Why?" She replied, "Because I believe and my parents brought me up that way." The gunman walked away.[6] It is not clear exactly how part of this exchange became associated with Cassie. But once it had, the story took on a life of its own. As an investigator explained to Cullen, "Students heard what other students said on TV and started repeating that as if it were true."[7]

The *Denver Rocky Mountain News,* badly scooped on a story it had apparently been sitting on, quickly published an alternative account of Cassie's death. Emily Wyant, who had been hiding under the same table as Cassie, told reporters that Cassie was praying out loud, "Dear God. Why is this happening? I just want to go home." Then Klebold slammed the top of their table, said "Peekaboo," looked underneath and shot Cassie. According to Wyant, the famous exchange about belief in God never occurred.[8] The story that Cassie may not have said "yes" was picked up, of course, by other media outlets, although it was given nowhere near the exposure of the original martyr story.[9] The *Sheriff's Report* on the shooting, released in May 2000, confirmed the version of events reported by Cullen and the *Denver Rocky Mountain News,* but identified Harris rather than Klebold as the killer.

Not surprisingly, Misty Bernall and her publisher rejected the "de-bunkers'" version of Cassie's death. Still, the publisher did anticipate some questions about the veracity of the Cassie martyr story. A special note entitled "From the Publisher," included at the beginning of the book, admitted that precisely what happened during the massacre, and exactly how Cassie died, "may never be known." The publisher's note, however, maintained that Misty Bernall's account "is based on numerous survivors of the library (the main scene of the massacre) and takes into account their varying recollections."[10] As Plough Publishing House editor Chris Zimmerman later told the *Denver Post,* "We resolved every inconsistency we came across to our satisfaction."[11] The Bernalls and Plough have continued to maintain that their multiple interviews with students who were in the library support the contention that Cassie did affirm her belief in God before her death.

An additional, and significant, "defender" of the Cassie martyr story is Wendy Murray Zoba, a senior writer with *Christianity Today* magazine and author of the book *Day of Reckoning: Columbine and the Search for America's Soul.* Zoba devotes a chapter, "Cassie's Yes: Martyrdom or Myth?" to the defense of the Cassie martyr story. "As a Christian," wrote Zoba, "I too had been inspired by the account of Cassie's confession before death; as a mother of teens, I was especially heartened to see its effect on my own sons, who were equally moved." Despite her personal reluctance to "concede that the Christian community had embraced a fabrication," as a professional journalist, Zoba told readers, "I was ready to go down that road to get to the truth about what happened to Cassie that day."[12]

Zoba's journey down that road led to a defense of the Cassie martyr story. She relied on interviews she conducted with the

Bernalls and with Jefferson County Sheriff's Department officials, statements by witnesses and other information in news reports, and, most interestingly, material prepared by the publishers of *She Said Yes,* which provides interviews with certain library witnesses and a Denver-area counselor as well as other background information.[13] When her book went to press, Zoba had access to the *Sheriff's Report,* but did not apparently utilize it in her chapter on "Cassie's Yes."[14] She, however, did not have access to the Sheriff's department materials released on and after November 21, 2000.

Certain basic facts are accepted by both debunkers and defenders of the Cassie martyr story. According to the *Sheriff's Report,* at 11:29 A.M. Eric Harris and Dylan Klebold entered the library, where students were already hiding beneath the tables. The two gunmen came in through the eastern doors, moved due west across the room, went through the western section of tables, crossed over to the eastern section, and returned to the middle section before leaving the library at 11:36. In only seven and a half minutes, Harris and Klebold killed 10 students and injured 12 more—that is, a death or injury every 20 seconds.[15]

In their crime scene diagrams, the Sheriff's Department used a system of numbering the 20 tables in the library[16] (see map). Cassie was hiding under table 19, at the far western side of the library. Schnurr was under table 2, at the far eastern side of the library. Defenders of Cassie's martyr story claim that *both* Cassie and Schnurr were asked about their belief in God by the gunmen. Debunkers of that story claim Schnurr had the *only* conversation with Harris or Klebold about God, and that this conversation was misattributed to Cassie.

We have witness statements from 46 persons about the events in the library.[17] But only 24 mentioned overhearing any statements about God, or observed interactions between either Cassie or Schnurr and either killer. Of these, 15 witnesses unambiguously reported hearing a single conversation about belief in God that occurred in the area in which Schnurr was located, or that identified Schnurr by name as the person who had this conversation. This grouping includes Schnurr herself who, of course, also reported

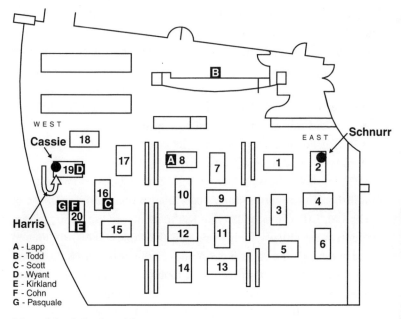

WEST

Cassie 18

A - Lapp
B - Todd
C - Scott
D - Wyant
E - Kirkland
F - Cohn
G - Pasquale

Harris

EAST

Schnurr

Map of the Columbine library

having this conversation. Both sides of the argument over Cassie's death accept that Schnurr had this conversation.

Of the remaining nine witnesses, two reported hearing someone, somewhere, say something about God, but could not or did not give additional details to investigators.

This leaves seven witnesses. Three are cited by the defenders of the martyr story, such as Zoba and Misty Bernall. The first witness is Joshua Lapp who was at table 8. In *She Said Yes,* Misty Bernall quoted Lapp's account of her daughter's death. Lapp said,

> I couldn't see anything when those guys came up to Cassie, but I could recognize her voice. I could hear everything like it was right next to me. One of them asked if she believed in God. She paused, like she didn't know what she was going to answer, and then she said yes. She must have been scared,

but her voice didn't sound shaky. It was strong. Then they asked her why, though they didn't give her a chance to respond. They just blew her away.[18]

When the controversy over Cassie's last words erupted, Lapp told the *Denver Rocky Mountain News,* "She said it. Plain and simple."[19] Beyond his steadfastness, Lapp's testimony is especially valuable to the defenders of the Cassie martyr story because he *also* claims to have heard the killer's conversation with Schnurr about God.[20] If there were two separate "God conversations," then Schnurr's could not have been misattributed to Cassie. Lapp also claimed that he recognized and could distinguish the voices of both girls.[21]

But in statements made to investigators, as well as in a narrative of April 20 written by Lapp himself and given to investigators, Lapp indicated that he heard *both* of these conversations in the section "closest the hallway," or the eastern section of the library.[22] Cassie was actually in the western section. In a television interview aired in September 1999, however, Lapp indicated that Cassie's conversation with her killer took place in "that far section by the windows," or the western section.[23]

Also in Lapp's self-composed description, we find an error in chronology. After narrating events that took place on the western section, Lapp wrote, "They [Harris and Klebold] then went in that section closest to the hallway." He then recounts the God question put to Schnurr. And then, "A little time later they asked another girl (Cassie Bernall)." Lapp then reports that the killers moved into the "middle section" before finally leaving the library.[24] The *Sheriff's Report* provides the same chronology of the killers' movements as does Lapp—western section, eastern section, middle section, and out. But this would mean that Cassie was killed in the western section *before,* not after, Schnurr's confrontation with the killers. Both errors in fact and inconsistency about those facts undermine the credibility of Lapp's testimony.

A second witness used to support the Cassie martyr story is Evan Todd, who was hiding behind the front counter. Todd told

Misty Bernall's publisher, "I heard a voice from a part of the room where I later heard Cassie was. She was talking to the gunmen. She was praying out loud and they asked her if she believed in God and she said yes. Then they shot her." He also reported that a female on the other side, or east side, of the room was screaming, "Oh my God!" but he did not hear any questions put to her.[25] This provides partial support for Lapp's "two God-conversation" testimony.

But in his May 5, 1999, interview with investigators, Todd gave a very different and, in its own way, altogether unique account. He referred to the female screaming, "Oh my God!" on the east side of the library as "Cassie." When asked why he made that identification, he reportedly admitted it was because of the news reports about her. Todd went on to recount the following exchange. One of the gunmen asked, "You believe in God?" The female who had been screaming said, "Yeah," to which the gunman replied, "God is gay." Her rejoinder was, "Go with God and you'll be saved." This was followed by multiple gunshots.[26] Todd's account to investigators made no mention of a second God-conversation. Like Lapp's, Todd's accounts are inconsistent.

A third, and controversial, witness the defenders of the Cassie martyr story have used is Craig Scott—the younger brother of Rachel Scott. (According to Zoba, Craig Scott was the first witness to tell the Bernalls of Cassie's God-conversation.[27]) He was under table 16 during the shooting. Like Lapp, Craig Scott told investigators in an April 30, 1999, interview of a girl's conversation with one of the killers. The investigator's report stated,

> Scott then heard a frantic female voice state, "oh my god, I don't want to die." This was followed by a gunman stating, "do you believe in God." Scott heard a response to the effect of "please I don't want to die." The gunman then asked again if that person believed in God. Scott heard her respond, "yes, I do." This was followed by several gunshots and Scott did not hear her voice again. At that point he could hear other female students making noises and being frantic. During this

conversation Shoels, Kechter [also under table 16] and Scott were just looking at each other in amazement.[28]

Many elements of this account support the misattribution theory advanced by the debunkers. The injured Schnurr was making the kind of spontaneous cries to God and pleas that Craig Scott describes. Defenders might point out that the gunshots *follow* the "yes, I do" and this voice is not heard again. Therefore, this could not have been Schnurr because, as Zoba wrote, "She was shot before being asked the question, answered yes, and was left alone."[29] This is less convincing than it may seem. Cassie was not killed by *several* gunshots, but by a *single* shotgun blast. Schnurr's "yes, I do" could have been followed by the sound of multiple gunshots directed at other victims. The *Sheriff's Report* places Harris's wounding of Nicole Nowlen and killing of John Tomlin, who was hit by multiple shots, at table 6 immediately after Klebold's conversation with Schnurr.[30] And Schnurr's voice was not heard again because she "'played dead' in hopes the suspects would leave her alone."[31]

The most difficult element for debunkers in Craig Scott's account is the exchange of amazed glances between Craig Scott and the other two boys hiding under the same table. This is difficult because, according to the *Sheriff's Report,* these two boys, Isaiah Shoels and Matthew Kechter, were mortally wounded or dead by the time Schnurr had her exchange with Klebold. Shoels and Kechter, however, were still uninjured when Harris killed Cassie. Looking at one another in amazement would still have been possible. It is possible to argue that Craig Scott, emotionally traumatized by his experience, has mistakenly jumbled together two real but chronologically separate memories. (Indeed, the defenders of the Cassie martyr story will make a similar psychological argument about another element in Craig Scott's testimony that weakens their case.)

A useful argument for defenders against chronological confusion can be found in Craig Scott's claim, made to a Plough editor on June 22, 1999, that, like Lapp, he had heard a second God-conversation. "She was on the other side of the room. It was louder conversation, maybe it was because my ears were ringing."[32] Once again, two God-conversations would make it impossible for Schnurr's to be misattributed to Cassie. The reference to his ears ringing would fit the Sheriff's chronology. His ears could have been ringing from the shots that killed the two boys under his table when Schnurr's God-conversation took place. But this is questionable. In his original interviews with investigators, Craig Scott, like Todd, apparently made *no* mention of a second God-conversation.

The most difficult element for defenders in Craig Scott's official testimony to investigators occurred on May 25, 1999. While revisiting the library, Craig Scott indicated to investigators that the God-conversation he had heard between Cassie and her killer had taken place at table 1 or 2, where Schnurr had been. When he was told this had not been Cassie's location, according to the investigator's report, he said, "Well she was up there then," and indicated tables 7 and 8 in the middle section of the library. When he was told this was incorrect, he became what the investigator described as "adamant." When Craig Scott was finally told that Cassie had actually been at table 19, he became upset and left the library.[33] This account of Craig Scott's confusion appeared in many of the debunking stories in the media.[34]

Zoba, who utilized the Plough Publishing research, dealt with the problem of Craig Scott's apparent disorientation by citing Dee Dee McDermott, M.Ed., L.P.C., the director of a Denver-area counseling center. Zoba tells us that McDermott, who worked with several of the Columbine library survivors, is an expert on the subject of processing psychological trauma.[35] McDermott observes that individuals vary in their ability to process information in a traumatic situation. Some do this well and can clearly recall events. "Others are so traumatized they do not have the capacity to process all the information. Those students would be the ones who would have memory blocks. They lose pieces of time." Zoba also cites McDermott's criticism of the investigators' practice of returning young witnesses, such as Craig Scott, to the library as "highly traumatic" and counterproductive. Given this, McDermott is inclined to dismiss confusion about the direction of voices as unimportant. "If Craig is firm on what he heard, I don't think the direction [of the voices] matters. The poor kid probably can't remember what direction he was facing."[36]

And Craig Scott does remain firm, and even rather defiant. Using an interview supplied by Plough Publishing, Zoba quotes Craig Scott as saying, "They can throw all this around, but I was there. Reporters can't tell me or investigators can't tell me how it went. They don't know jack. I was there. They can help somewhat to get the story together, but I heard what I heard."[37]

Anyone aware of what happened to Craig Scott on April 20, 1999, is more than willing to heed McDermott's advice and "give the poor kid a break." And if it were only his confusion where certain voices were coming from, I would also be inclined to dismiss the matter as a minor anomaly. But the investigators' reports on interviews with Lapp and Todd contain the *same* problem about what part of the library the God-conversation took place. All three of the defenders' favorite witnesses told investigators that Cassie's God-conversation occurred where Schnurr, not Cassie, was located.[38] Given this, the argument that Craig Scott was just a little confused rings hollow. It seems he was correct about the location of the voices, but incorrect about the identification of the girl who said "yes."

Aside from the apparent inconsistencies between what these three witnesses told investigators and what they have told journalists and publishers, the details each witness offers us about Cassie's final moments are not easily reconciled. (Contrast, for instance, Lapp's laconic "Yes." "Why?" exchange with Todd's didactic "God is gay." "Go with God and you'll be saved.") But perhaps the most important fact that undercuts the credibility of these three witnesses is this: All three only claim to have *heard* Cassie's God-conversation. None of them *saw* the conversation, or her death, take place.

The remaining four witnesses include those who saw as well as heard Cassie die. It is upon these witnesses that the *Sheriff's Report* bases its version of her death. "Harris walked over to table 19 where he bent down and saw two frightened girls," stated the *Sheriff's Report*. "He slapped the table top twice, said, 'Peek-a-boo,' and fired, killing Cassie Bernall."[39] A diagram in the *Sheriff's Report* indicates that Harris took a path around the west side of table 19 and was standing at its southwest corner when he shot and killed Cassie.

Wyant was under table 19 with Cassie. The report on her interview with investigators stated, "One of the gunmen came around from the southwest corner of the table, put his gun under the table and peeked at Bernall. He then shot Bernall. Wyant does not remember any conversation between Bernall and the gunman."[40] According to the report, she also made no mention of the gunman slapping the table or saying "Peek-a-boo."

Because Wyant was featured so prominently in the early debunking news stories, Zoba is particularly interested in discrediting Wyant's testimony. Her method turns on a rather minor point. The September 24, 1999, story in the *Denver Rocky Mountain News,* which first publicly presented Wyant's alternative version of Cassie's death, identified Klebold as the killer.[41] While it is not clear that it wasn't the *News* reporters who are responsible for the misidentification, Zoba asserted, "the misidentification of the killer compromises her version of events."[42] It is worth noting that in her statement to investigators, Wyant was not sure of the identity of the gunman. "She did not see his shirt or his face. She thought he may have had long hair but was not positive."[43]

The remaining three witnesses, so far as I can discover, have never been interviewed by any of the defenders of the Cassie martyr story.[44] The first of these three, Byron Kirkland, was under table 20. He provides a similar account to Wyant's of events at table 19. The investigator's report on this interview stated, "The gunman reached down under table 19 and shot one of the female students under the table. Kirkland did not recall hearing any statement by the gunman or the gunman having a conversation with the victim prior to the gunshot."[45] Kirkland, like Wyant, did not identify the gunman and made no mention of a slap to the table or "Peek-a-boo."

Aaron Cohn, also at table 20, is the least helpful of these witnesses because, as he told the investigators, he kept his eyes averted toward the nearest wall. But the report of the investigator who interviewed Cohn stated, "At one point, they went under a table and said 'Peak a boo.' Then they shot the girl."[46] One *Denver Post* article, published April 29, 1999, after the Cassie martyr story had become widely known, indicated Cohn was a witness to Cassie's death and quoted him as saying, "I heard her say yes, and then I heard a shot."[47] Cohn does not seem to have been quoted in this fashion in any other media reports, and in any case, reports on both of his interviews with investigators contain no mention of overhearing any exchanges about God.

The last and most important of these four witnesses is Bree Pasquale, whose near-hysterical live television interview immediately after the shooting has often been replayed in television pieces on Columbine. In that interview Pasquale said, "I just started screaming and crying and telling them not to shoot me, and so he shot the girl. He shot her in the head in front of me."[48] Pasquale, in any subsequent media interview I have been able to discover, has not mentioned any exchange about God she heard in the library.

Pasquale was not under a table but on the floor to the west of table 20. She therefore had the clearest view of the west end of table 19 and provided investigators with a strikingly detailed account. She said that Cassie was seated under table 19 facing east with "her hands up covering the sides of her face." Harris came to the south side of the table, "he then slapped the table twice with his left hand and stated, 'peek-a-boo.'" Harris "bent down and pointed the shotgun under the table, he then fired the weapon once."[49] It is obvious that Pasquale's account—Harris, two slaps, "peek-a-boo," a single shot, and *no* conversation about God—was accepted by the Jefferson County Sheriff's Department as what *really* happened to Cassie.

In the absence of new and compelling evidence, such as a sound recording of Cassie's conversation with Harris, I must come to the same conclusion as the *Sheriff's Report*. The testimony of the closest witnesses, especially Emily Wyant and Bree Pasquale, who *heard and saw* Cassie's death, must be trusted above that of Joshua Lapp, Craig Scott, and Evan Todd, who *only heard* from a greater distance, and who all made the same mistake about the source of that sound. The preponderance of available evidence is in favor of the debunkers, not the defenders, of the Cassie martyr story. It is more likely that Cassie was simply murdered rather than martyred.

WHAT REALLY HAPPENED TO RACHEL SCOTT?

According to the *Sheriff's Report*, Eric Harris and Dylan Klebold had planted a large propane bomb in the Columbine cafeteria. At 11:19 A.M., when the two realized the bomb was not going to work, they began shooting anyone they saw outside the building. They killed two students, injured eight others, and exchanged shots with a police officer before entering the school building at 11:24 A.M. Inside, they killed 11 and injured 13, almost all in the library. At 12:08 P.M., they committed suicide.[50]

Rachel was one of the two students killed outside. In contrast to its detailed account of Cassie's death, the *Sheriff's Report* has very little to say about Rachel's death. "The first series of gunshots, fired toward the west doors, struck Rachel Scott and Richard Castaldo, who were seated outside, eating their lunch on the north side of the library. Rachel died from the gunshot wounds. Richard was critically injured, receiving multiple gunshot wounds."[51] The crime scene diagram that accompanies this description in the *Report* shows Harris and Klebold firing at Castaldo and Rachel from at least several yards away. This account makes no mention of any conversation between Rachel and her killer, or even of the gunshot to her head. (Strictly speaking, the *Report* does not exclude the possibility that those things occurred. It simply provides no confirmation of these key elements of the Rachel martyr story.)

The reason for the lack of specifics is readily apparent if we look at the statements by witnesses to investigators. In the approximately 700 single-spaced pages of the relevant witness statements, there is little information about how Rachel or Castaldo were shot. Because this initial part of the shooting took place outdoors, almost all potential witnesses were able to flee. Witnesses running for their lives, quite naturally, did not stop to observe what was happening at the west doors. In addition, the greater distances involved made it harder to see, and impossible to hear, exactly what Harris and Klebold were doing and saying. And finally, Rachel and Castaldo's location near the west doors was only visible from a small portion of the school parking lot, and from the sports fields.

The few nearby witnesses who did see something relevant are not that helpful.

Mike Johnson, sitting in the grass across the sidewalk from Rachel and Castaldo, saw them shot. "Johnson then heard shooting," reads the investigator's report, "and he looked east and observed one person shooting two people who were sitting outside, against the library wall near the north library door and the school west door."[52]

Denny Rowe, sitting in the same area as Johnson, gave a similar account but mistakenly described Castaldo as female. "He then saw this male shoot two females," stated the investigators' report, "that were sitting against the wall outside of the west doors by the west exit door to the library. The girls immediately slumped over. He thought the two suspects were only about 10 feet away when the girls were shot."[53]

John Cook, sitting in the same area as Johnson and Rowe, saw Rachel hit but not Castaldo. Cook reported that, "The other party, who was still wearing a trench coat, then turned around and shot a girl that was sitting nearby; Rachel Scott. The girl was sitting down and fell over."[54]

What did Castaldo see and hear? He was located closer to Rachel than any other possible witness and was unable to flee due to his severe injuries. Unfortunately, the one interview he apparently had with investigators was brief and sheds little light on Rachel's final moments. The interview took place on May 4, 1999, in Castaldo's hospital room. "Castaldo advised the investigators after he had fallen over [upon being shot] he recalled hearing noises while he was laying on the ground. Castaldo advised he does not recall all the noises he heard but that it was noisy and he remembers Rachel Scott crying. . . . Castaldo advised investigators that he believed Rachel Scott had been shot also." The investigators also reported,

"Castaldo advised after he was shot he didn't see the two males for a short period of time." When the two came back, they were firing at the west entrance doors. After this, Castaldo told investigators, the gunmen disappeared from his view.[55]

This account partially confirms the Rachel martyr story. After the first burst of gunfire, Rachel was still alive because Castaldo could hear her crying. This would indicate that she had not yet been shot in the head, a wound that would have killed her instantly. Castaldo's account also states that the gunmen went away and then returned, just as the martyr stories about Rachel's death often indicate. The report on this interview with Castaldo, however, says nothing of either of the returning gunmen going to Rachel, speaking with her, grabbing her by the hair, or even shooting her in the head.

Considering the severity of Castaldo's injuries, these gaps in his account should not be surprising, or be taken as a disconfirmation of the Rachel martyr story. Either he was unable to recall these moments for physical and/or psychological reasons, or he simply lacked the strength to convey in words to the investigators what he could recall. Indeed, the investigators report that they ended the interview when they noted that Castaldo was becoming tired and "began moving his right arm around his face and neck and covering his face occasionally as if he were nervous or no longer wished to recall what had taken place."[56] Among the documents that the Jefferson County Sheriff's Department has released, there is no indication that investigators ever interviewed Castaldo again.

Given the relative lack of information from witnesses about the specifics of Rachel's death, it is therefore not surprising that the *Sheriff's Report* remains quite general.[57] What is surprising is that the popular story of Rachel's martyrdom has become so highly specific, with dramatic dialogue and striking details. The contrast between the nonspecific official account and the specific popular account compels me to ask: How do we fill in the gaps? How do we *know* Rachel died a martyr's death? What is the evidence behind the popular account?

Another potential source of useful information about Rachel's death are statements by witnesses to journalists. For instance, a June 13, 1999, article in the *Denver Post* filled in one of the gaps in Castaldo's statement to investigators. "'She was lying in the grass crying,' Castaldo later told his mother. 'They walked over to her and shot her again.'"[58] Denny Rowe, who had identified Castaldo as a female in his official statement, and the severely injured Mark Taylor, whose official statement provided almost no details, were cited by journalists as confirming that Rachel was approached by one of the gunmen and shot an additional time, or shot in the head.[59] Beyond this, a fact that could be reasonably inferred from the autopsy summary,[60] it does not seem that the army of journalists covering Columbine discovered any additional information from an *actual* witness about Rachel's final moments. So we are left with the same question: What is the evidence behind the Rachel martyr story?

The search for this evidence was one of the continuing concerns of those who came to see Rachel as a modern-day martyr. This can be seen in the e-mail messages sent by Bruce Porter, which were widely copied and re-sent in the aftermath of the shooting. In one message, dated April 22, 1999, Porter proclaimed that according to "eyewitness accounts" Rachel had said "Yes I do!!" when asked by her killer if she believed in God. He then proclaimed, "The spirit of the martyrs still lives!"[61] But in a message dated April 25—the day after he proclaimed Rachel a martyr during her funeral on CNN— Porter retracted this claim about Rachel's last words and stated that these eyewitness accounts had really been about Cassie.

Despite this setback, Porter was clearly hoping Rachel too would be confirmed as a martyr and he focused his expectations on Castaldo, the witness who had been the closest to Rachel, whose injuries were to keep him in the hospital for some four months. Porter wrote on April 25, 1999, "We are waiting for his [Richard's] account of what happened as soon as he can share it."[62] Porter's expectations were soon fulfilled. In an e-mail dated May 20, 1999, Porter proclaimed the "confirming news" that Castaldo's account established Rachel's martyrdom.

Richard Castaldo, who had been sitting outside the cafeteria with Rachel, and survived multiple wounds himself, has confirmed that Rachel answered bravely of her faith in God moments before her murderer put his gun to her head and replied: "Then go and be with Him now!"[63]

In the initial version of this message, Porter proclaims this "confirming news" without giving any details of how or to whom Castaldo provided confirmation. The reader is left to assume that the confirmation comes directly from Castaldo. When I contacted Porter about this, he admitted that the basis for this was a widely circulated rumor. "In retrospect, I should have been more restrained in my May 20 e-mail since I really didn't have clear 'confirmation' about these details at that point."[64] In *The Martyrs' Torch*, published in January 2000, a redacted version of the May 20 e-mail does not mention confirmation or Castaldo. "The family of Rachel Scott has been greatly encouraged with news that Rachel answered bravely of her faith in God moments before the gunman held his weapon to her head and said, 'Then go and be with Him now!'"[65] Porter explained to me that his publisher was responsible for this change. "They didn't want to expose themselves to potential legal entanglements by referencing Richard [Castaldo] by name since he couldn't confirm the story personally."[66] Despite this, Rachel's martyr story is presented to readers as fact.

After the "Did Cassie say 'yes'?" controversy of fall 1999, journalists raised the same issue regarding Rachel. In December 1999, Castaldo told reporters that he could not confirm that Rachel's God-conversation had take place. Given the severity of Castaldo's wounds, gaps in his memory of the attack are not surprising. "I don't remember that," Castaldo told the *Denver Post*. "I can't remember either way."[67] When informed of this, Darrell Scott, apparently relying on the "confirming news" Porter announced in May, told *Time*, "I'm surprised. If he said that, then either it didn't happen or he changed his story."[68] And Darrell Scott, who had been repeating Rachel's martyr story at speaking engagements around the country, told the *Denver Post* that he would stop telling the story, "until I'm clearer."[69]

This clarification came by way of a phone call from Connie Michalik, Castaldo's mother, to Darrell Scott. In *Rachel's Tears,* we are told that "during a January 2000 taping for a segment of NBC's *Dateline* news magazine, Richard's mother confirmed that she had heard her son describe Rachel's death in the initial days after the tragedy."[70] When the critically injured Castaldo was finally able to speak, he told his mother about what happened to Rachel. In the episode of *Dateline,* aired in July 2000, we actually hear part of Michalik's phone call: "They were yelling at her about God and, 'Do you believe in God?' And that was literally the last minute of her life."[71]

Unfortunately, the rest of Michalik's phone call is obscured by a narrative voice-over by the NBC reporter, Sara James. We don't actually hear Michalik stating that Castaldo heard Rachel give an affirmative answer to the God-question. And nowhere in the rest of this program do we hear this phone call claimed as evidence of how Rachel answered "Do you believe in God?" This omission, however, may be solely the result of *Dateline*'s editing.

In a spring 2000 interview with Zoba, Castaldo's mother confirmed that he reported hearing the killers talking to Rachel about God, but she did not say anything about Rachel's answer. "He [Richard] said they [Eric and Dylan] were being mean to her [Rachel] and teasing her about God. He could hear her crying. He said he heard 'God' several times in a taunting sarcastic tone. He said that they wanted her to say something and kept asking her questions. Then a gun went off."[72] When I contacted Zoba about the absence of Rachel's answer, she responded, "With regard to my conversation with Connie Michalik, she did not indicate, one way or the other, whether Richard heard Rachel's answer."[73]

In a December 16, 1999, *Denver Post* article, however, Kevin Simpson reported, "'Richard's memory of that day is fading,' says Castaldo's mother, Connie Michalik. 'In the beginning, he said he could hear her crying and was trying to help her. Then they came back and shot her again. Richard pretended he was dead. They said something to her, but he was too far away to know what they said.'"[74] Simpson also interviewed Michalik for an April 21, 2000, article. On this occasion, however, there seemed to be a shift in her account. She was quoted as saying that Castaldo could hear what the gunman said to Rachel. "'After he got the breathing tube out, he was crying and upset, telling me through sobs how they taunted and teased her about God,' Michalik said. 'Then he heard a shot and he didn't know what happened to her.'"[75] Later in the same article Simpson stated, "Michalik says that while Richard didn't hear Rachel's response to the gunman's taunts about God, she gathered from her son's account that Rachel probably did profess her faith."[76] I contacted Simpson and he confirmed that Michalik had told him that Castaldo was unable to hear Rachel's answer.[77]

Note Simpson's choice of words: "gathered from" and "probably." Simpson apparently felt that Michalik was unable to report Rachel's verbal affirmation of faith as a *fact*. The accuracy of Simpson's perception is implicitly supported by Zoba's interview with Michalik. Despite mentioning many details in that interview about what the killers said to Rachel, Michalik said nothing to Zoba about Rachel's last words. Even though Michalik said the killers, "wanted her [Rachel] to say something and kept asking her questions," Michalik said nothing of an answer, just, "Then a gun went off."

When I contacted Connie Michalik by telephone on June 26, 2001, however, she told me that Castaldo had indeed heard Rachel's answer. Rachel was crying, whimpering in pain, and repeatedly saying "Yes" in response to gunmen's questions and taunts about God. Given what I had read in Simpson's articles and Zoba's book, this was a surprise. When I restated my question, I got the same answer. She told me that her son had heard Rachel say "Yes." In short, Michalik confirmed an essential element of the Rachel martyr story—Rachel's affirmation of faith at gunpoint.

How do we explain this apparent change? A simple explanation would be that Simpson, Zoba, or I misquoted and/or misunderstood Michalik. Perhaps the fault is mine, but I approached Michalik with only one issue, Rachel's answer, on my mind. And Michalik gave me an answer I did not expect. I did not misunderstand her.

Did Michalik change her story? It would be hard to prove such an accusation because we lack an authoritative baseline statement of what Michalik says she heard from her son. Informal statements to journalists and scholars do not rise to that level. She has not given any sworn or otherwise legally binding testimony about this matter. And so far as I know, Michalik has not written or published a statement, in her own words, of Richard's original account.

Why would Michalik change her story? If she did, the most obvious possible motive is sympathy for Rachel's family and a desire to tell them what they wanted to hear. Michalik has consistently stated, and reiterated in my interview with her, that her son feels guilty about being unable to help Rachel.[78] He has also expressed frustration that he can no longer remember what happened to his friend. At a memorial service organized by Darrell Scott on the first anniversary of the shooting, Castaldo said, "People tell me I said she said she believed in God, and I can't remember it. Somehow, I know she did the right thing in the end."[79] While Castaldo did not specify whether his mother was one of the "people" who tell him this, it is clear that he regarded an affirmation of belief in God to have been the "right thing" for Rachel to do. Could this combination of sympathy, guilt, and frustration have moved Michalik to consciously or unconsciously change her story? Such a change, especially if done unconsciously, is entirely plausible and understandable.

But again, before we can challenge the consistency of Connie Michalik's memory, we must have proof that a change has taken place, proof that is unlikely to be forthcoming.

Is Michalik's confirmation sufficient evidence for accepting the Rachel martyr story as what *really* happened? That is a difficult question. Consider the circumstances: A critically injured and emotionally traumatized teenager, cut down by a hail of gunfire while eating lunch with a friend, whispers a fragmentary and emotional account of his friend's last moments into his mother's ear. She is the only person who can hear her son's words. With far more compelling concerns, such as her child's survival, she does not write down her son's account. *Nine months later* she calls the family of her son's friend to share his account, an account that Castaldo himself can no longer confirm because of gaps in his memory. And it is not the mother of the injured boy who tells the world, but the family of the dead friend.

It is upon this rather frail chain of transmission that we must depend for our knowledge of Rachel's final moments. At almost any point, the linkage between the story and reality could have been broken by misunderstandings and fading/shifting memories. Keeping a simple message straight as it is passed verbally from one person to the next is not easy under the best of circumstances. And the aftermath of Columbine has been anything but the best of circumstances.

Moreover, Michalik's testimony is what might be called hearsay evidence, which the *Oxford English Dictionary* defines as "evidence consisting in what the witness has heard others say, or what is commonly said, as to facts of which he has himself no original personal knowledge."[80] Hearsay is generally inadmissible as legal evidence because the person who might have original knowledge is not available to be questioned. We cannot question Castaldo because he remembers little of what happened. There are, of course, multiple exceptions to the legal presumption against the admission of hearsay evidence. It is possible that Michalik's testimony could be admitted under one of these exceptions. But the mere fact that such legal technicalities would come into play underlines my basic point: the fragility of virtually the only evidence for the martyrdom of Rachel.

The evidence of Rachel's martyrdom, however, is not being presented in a court of law. And most of the time, it is not even being presented in the general court of public opinion. Almost always, the Rachel martyr story is presented to those who are already inclined to accept it, and in a setting that encourages acceptance. The typical presentation by a member of Rachel's family, or by Porter, is sponsored by a church, often a Southern Baptist or an Assemblies of God congregation, or by an evangelical para-church group, such as Youth for Christ. These religious audiences, especially given a natural and trusting sympathy for Rachel's grieving family, are hardly inclined toward the sort of questioning I have engaged in here. (And since question-and-answer is *not* part of the format of such presentations, there is no practical outlet for the expression of doubt.) It would be reasonable to expect that most of those who purchase and read *Rachel's Tears,* and the other Rachel-books, are already inclined, religiously and emotionally, to uncritically accept the martyr story.

In addition to the willingness of typical audiences to believe, the martyr story is placed in a wider narrative context that establishes Rachel as specially called and prepared by God. Even the usual, if not unlikely, means by which the story of her "good death" comes to us, is a sort of proof that Rachel's entire story is "a God-thing." As we have seen in chapter 3, the presentation of Rachel's diary entries, writings, and drawings create the impression of a saintly, if not Christ-like, devotion to God. Since the reader/listener already knows Rachel dies, there is an inevitable expectation that this heroine die well—a death that conforms to the well-worn narrative conventions of the Christ-story and the martyrological good death. "Nobody who ever knew her would doubt her commitment," wrote her mother in *Rachel's Tears,* "and that is the main reason people accepted Richard Castaldo's account of her final moments. If you knew Rachel, her dying that way would make sense because that is the way she lived every moment of her life."[81] After hearing or reading Rachel's story, we feel we know her, and so we do not doubt.

Another element that adds to the believability of the Rachel martyr story is that of the killers' reputed animus toward Rachel because of her faith. Was this part of a wider attempt to target Christians? The evidence here is rather weak. The killers' weapon of first choice, their malfunctioning propane bomb, would have been an utterly impersonal and indiscriminate method of mass murder. When it became necessary for them to kill/injure face-to-face, hatred of Christians did not seem to have a large role. Among the dead, only Rachel and Cassie are reputed to have had a conversation with their killers about God. Other victims who have been celebrated for their faith, such as John Tomlin, who died in the library, and Mark Taylor, who was wounded outside the building, were simply shot without inquiry into their beliefs. And as I argued earlier, most of the available evidence points to the misattribution of Schnurr's God-conversation to Cassie. Schnurr's conversation with the gunmen came *after* they had already wounded her. Her affirmation and explanation of her belief in God brought neither further attack nor even further attention.

All of this makes Rachel's reported final exchange with the killers unique. But was it a *personal* matter to Harris and Klebold to confront, torment, and kill Rachel? The evidence here is stronger but still mixed. It is entirely plausible that Rachel knew the killers, especially since Klebold did technical work on the sort of stage productions in which Rachel was often involved.[82] It is quite possible that during the time she smoked cigarettes, Rachel encountered the future gunmen in the Columbine "Smokers' Pit," an area on the edge of the campus in which smoking was allowed. Columbine student Brooks Brown, a smoker and well acquainted with both Harris and Klebold, told *Rolling Stone* magazine, "Dylan knew Rachel Scott."[83]

As I noted in chapter 3, her family argues that the hostility Harris and Klebold felt for Rachel came from her reported willingness to confront them about the violent content of videos the two created for a class during the fall semester of 1998. Darrell Scott has also suggested that she witnessed to the two about accepting Christ. While this is a reasonable way of explaining a personal animus toward her, it remains unknown precisely what she said or how they responded.[84]

Evidence of this enmity was apparently found in the infamous videotapes that the two killers made in the months prior to the attack. When Darrell Scott was offered the opportunity to review these tapes, he brought along a tape recorder and soon publicly released a partial transcript of Harris's and Klebold's remarks, which he claimed mentioned his daughter.

> Harris: "Shut the f— up, Nick, you laugh too much. And those two girls sitting next to you, they probably want you to shut up, too. Rachel and Jen and whatever."

Klebold: "Stuck up little b——s, you f—ing little Christian-
ity, Godly wh——."
Harris: "Yeah, I love Jesus, I love Jesus, shut the f— up."
Klebold: "What would Jesus do? What would I do? Boosh!"
(points at camera as if holding gun).
Harris: "I would shoot you in the motherf—ing head! Go
Romans—Thank God they crucified that a———."[85]

How can Darrell Scott be sure that the "Rachel" referred to is
Rachel Scott? When asked by Zoba about this, he noted that
"Rachel" was connected to "Nick," and that his daughter's date at a
recent prom was Nick Baumgart. The mocking question "What
would Jesus do?" refers to the popular WWJD wristband that Zoba
tells us that Rachel wore. Darrell Scott told Zoba, "All of that points
to Rachel Scott."[86]

Porter also finds this transcript to be compelling evidence. "It is
beyond question that Rachel was killed because of her witness for
Christ. To those who might yet try to discredit this assertion in light
of the above empirical proof, I can only say that your failure to see
the plain truth of this fact is willful denial."[87]

Upon closer examination, this "empirical proof" is less conclusive than it seems. The first names "Nick," "Rachel," and "Jen," presumably short for Jennifer, are relatively common names. According
to the transcript, the two girls "are sitting next to" a "Nick." Since we
are dealing with students, this could be a reference to seating
arrangements in a classroom. During the Spring 1999 semester, Harris and Klebold were enrolled in a 14-student psychology class.
Among their fellow students were Nick Foss, Jennifer Grant, Rachel
Baker, and Rachael Goodwin.[88] A description by investigators of the
contents of this tape mentions that Harris and Klebold make comments about a "'Dustin Harris' or 'Dustin Harrison'" just before
they talk about "Nick." Another student enrolled in this psychology
class was Dustin Harrison.[89] It is possible, if not probable, that Harris
and Klebold were discussing persons in this class rather than Rachel
Scott.

We should also note that Harris and Klebold feel that "Rachel" shares their poor opinion of "Nick." This doesn't fit with what we know about the presumably good relationship between Rachel Scott and her prom date, Nick Baumgart. It's also worth noting that Baumgart told investigators he had known Klebold and Harris for years. Based on the same interview, investigators reported Baumgart told them, "Rachel Scott never had anything to do with Dylan and Eric, she probably did not even know them."[90] Unless Nick Baumgart was trying to mislead investigators, it is unlikely that Rachel was the disapproving "Rachel" sitting next to the "Nick" observed by Harris and Klebold.

This alternative understanding of Harris and Klebold's remarks, given the available evidence, cannot be definitively proven. We know nothing about the religiosity of the Jen/Jennifer and the Rachel/Rachael in the psychology class. It is possible that these young women wore the popular WWJD wristbands, or otherwise exhibited a Christian commitment for which Harris and Klebold had such contempt, but we simply do not know. While speculative, this alternative explanation cautions against simple acceptance of Darrell Scott's conclusion that Harris and Klebold singled out and killed his daughter because of her faith.

In addition to the reputed strength of Rachel's faith and the personal animus of the killers toward her, another element that seems to add credibility to the Rachel martyr story is its dramatic specificity. The details allow the reader/listener to imagine "what really happened" with precision and, most important, clarity of meaning. But closer and critical examination demonstrates that these dramatic details actually undermine the credibility of the Rachel martyr story.

Using the authorizing phrase, "According to Richard's earliest account," *Rachel's Tears* goes on to present the martyr story this way.

As Richard lay stunned and Rachel attempted to crawl to safety, the shooters began to walk away, only to return seconds later. At that point, Harris reportedly grabbed Rachel by her hair, held her head up, and asked her the question: "Do you believe in God?"

"You know I do," replied Rachel.

"Then go be with Him," responded Harris before shooting her in the head.[91]

A reader might assume that the details and wording of this exchange come from Castaldo, by way of his mother's call to Darrell Scott. This assumption, however, is problematic. As we have seen, the account supplied by Castaldo's mother is far more general. The question, "Do you believe in God?" did not stand alone but was part of a series of taunts and sarcastic questions. Rachel's repetition of "yes," while crying and whimpering in pain, lacks the bold clarity of "You know I do"—a more memorable response from which greater meaning can be derived. The gunman's last line—"Then go be with Him"—does not seem to be rooted in what we know of the Castaldo-Michalik account at all. It is far easier to imagine that the gunmen, tired of their sadistic "game" with Rachel and mindful of the imminent arrival of the police, simply pulled the trigger and moved on to find new victims. The line, "Then go be with Him," seems to be a dramatic closing device that provides an easy segue into the assertion that Rachel immediately went to her heavenly reward. If the killer did say anything to Rachel before shooting, I find it hard to believe it would have fit so neatly with the theological agenda of those who honor her memory.

The constructed character of the basic martyr-story phrases "You know I do" and "Then go be with Him" is apparent when we discover they were being used well *before* Connie Michalik called Darrell Scott with her son's account in January 2000. As early as April 30, 1999, an Indiana newspaper cited Rachel's maternal grandmother, Beverly Cecrle, as the source for this version of the killer's rejoinder to Rachel's declaration of faith. "'Go to him then,' the gunman said as he shot her in the temple."[92] As I noted earlier, Porter's May 20, 1999, e-mail proclaiming the confirmation of the martyr story used the phrase, "Then go and be with Him now!" In a segment of the television news magazine *48 Hours,* aired June 10, 1999, Darrell Scott said, "She was asked if she believed in God, and she said yes." Beth Nimmo adds, "And the shooters said, 'Then go be with Him.'"[93]

"God Used a Toothache," an essay by Brent High, a Tennessee youth minister, reported on a September 1999 speaking engagement by Darrell Scott. This essay, which has been copied and posted on multiple web sites, and later appeared in the short-lived magazine *Rachel's Journal,* describes what Darrell Scott said of Rachel's final moments: "One of the gunmen walked over to where Rachel lay face down, still alive. He pulled her up by the hair of her head and asked, 'Do you still believe in God?' 'You know that I do,' Rachel managed to reply. Immediately after her reply a bullet entered her temple."[94] Evangelist Bob Larson, in *Extreme Evil,* a book on school shootings published in December 1999, repeated the story of Rachel's final moments. She is asked, "Do you believe in God?" Her answer is "Yes." The killer responds, "Then go be with Him now!"[95]

In Porter's *The Martyrs' Torch,* which went to press *before* Michalik's phone call to Darrell Scott in January 2000, we find all of these elements together. "Harris then reached down, grabbed Rachel by her hair, and shouted, 'Do you still believe in your God now?' She answered, 'You know that I do.' He reportedly replied, 'Then go be with Him now!' Putting the gun to her temple, he fired. She died instantly."[96]

The use of "You know I do" and "Then go be with Him now" *before* the transmission of Castaldo's account by Michalik makes it hard to believe that these standard phrases originated with Castaldo or Michalik. Instead, Rachel's supporters have used substantial "dramatic license" to communicate to audiences what they feel is the spirit and meaning of Rachel's reported affirmation of faith at gunpoint. Much like the production of a movie "based on a true story," specific dialogue and stage directions must be created in order to convey to an audience the interpreted "truth" of the "true story." Inconvenient details and unknown information must be covered over and filled in to "make the story work." Hollywood, of course, did not invent this technique. It is as old as human storytelling. And in the

Christian tradition, it is as old as the martyrological narratives I examined in chapter 1.

It is not surprising that the promoters of Rachel's martyr story have continued to use the familiar and effective formulas they developed to tell that story before January 2000. When and how the stock phrases of this "oral tradition" developed and came into use is unknown, and probably cannot be reconstructed at present.[97] And this oral tradition may be still developing. In a videotape, *The Message of Columbine,* Porter presents the Rachel martyr story with a few interesting elaborations. The killers ask: "Where is your God now?! Do you still believe in Him?" And Rachel replies: "You know that I love Jesus."[98] Are these elaborations important? Perhaps not, but Porter's double question version, with the "now" and "still," emphasizes the killers' illusion that their actions had destroyed Rachel's faith. Her answer, of course, shatters that illusion. And more important, Rachel's new answer allows Porter to get Jesus into the story. Rather than dying for a generalized theism, Rachel is a *Christian* martyr. The last words from her lips are, "I love Jesus."

Clearly, the slender thread of available evidence does not support such elaboration. But does that evidence, such as it is, support the essential contention that Rachel died while affirming her faith?

In the case of Cassie, the problem is to determine which of the two conflicting accounts of her death was backed by more credible evidence. In the case of Rachel, the problem is to determine if there is *enough* credible evidence to support the claim of martyrdom. But how much is enough?

In law, there are three basic standards of proof: "beyond a reasonable doubt," "clear and convincing," and "preponderance of the evidence."[99] The standard used in criminal cases, and the most difficult to satisfy, "proof beyond a reasonable doubt," does not apply in this case. The available evidence I have reviewed obviously leaves much room for reasonable doubts.

The "clear and convincing proof" standard, in which there is demonstration that a particular claim is "highly probable," is less difficult to meet, but still far too demanding for this case. Hearsay testimony, about which reasonable questions of consistency can be asked, from a single witness is not enough to sustain the claim that Rachel's martyrdom was "highly probable." Possible, plausible, but not highly probable.

The least demanding standard, "preponderance of the evidence," which I use in the case of Cassie's supposed martyrdom, requires that one version of events is more likely to be true than another, or that a given claim is more probably true than untrue. This standard was helpful in Cassie's case because there were two substantial bodies of the same kind of evidence that could be compared. "Preponderance of the evidence" is difficult to apply to Rachel's supposed martyrdom because there is not really a competing or alternative account of her final moments. The *Sheriff's Report* really tells us nothing more than, "Eric Harris and Dylan Klebold shot and killed Rachel Scott." The only way, other than the martyr story, we have to deal with the concrete details of her final moments is to refuse to imagine them, to maintain that we simply do not know, to leave a blank.

While this intellectual restraint may be, given the nature of available evidence, more responsible, it is unsatisfying. We want *to know*. There is an old saying, "A little of something beats all of nothing." Thus the Rachel martyr story, even though open to question, seems more possible, more likely, more true, than any nonstory. If we follow our very natural yearning to fill in the blank space, we will find that the rhetorical burden of proof has shifted from those who claim the martyr's crown for Rachel, to those who question that claim. The issue then becomes, "Can you prove it didn't happen?" And that cannot be proven. The martyr story wins acceptance by default.

The application of legal standards to the evidence surrounding Rachel's death, as I noted earlier, is an intellectual exercise. The results of the exercise do not support the claims of martyrdom. Even the application of the least demanding standard, preponderance of the evidence, yields an inconclusive result. We cannot say that the Rachel martyr story is more likely to be true than false, because there is so little evidence, and so much of it is open to question. *We simply do not know what happened.*

Yet the "court" in which the martyr stories of Cassie and Rachel are being contested is not a court of law, or even an academic seminar. The real courtroom is the hearts and minds of those who read *She Said Yes, Rachel's Tears,* or go to hear the Bernalls, Darrell Scott, Beth Nimmo, or Bruce Porter speak. And the verdicts being delivered in those hearts and minds seem quite different from the conclusions I have reached here.

CHAPTER 6

CONCLUSIONS

"Print the Legend"

In director John Ford's 1962 Western film *The Man Who Shot Liberty Valance,* U.S. Senator Ransom Stoddard, played by James Stewart, reveals to a newspaper editor that his long and illustrious career has been built upon a lie—that he was not the man who shot a vicious outlaw, Liberty Valance. Instead, it was Tom Doniphon, played by John Wayne, who actually killed, or rather assassinated, Valance with a rifle-shot fired from the concealment of a dark alleyway. "Cold-blooded murder," Doniphon tells Stoddard, "but I can live with it." At the conclusion of Stoddard's tale, the editor explains that he won't use the story. "This is the West, sir. When the legend becomes fact, print the legend."[1]

This line, perhaps the most famous in Ford's many films, is the director's summation of the power of legend to obscure more complex and harsher historical realities. What is the legend? When forced to fight Valance, the overmatched Stoddard gets off one shot—a shot seemingly guided by the forces of justice and progress, not by skill—that apparently kills Valance. Stoddard, the champion of law and order, goes on to a distinguished political career that helps civilize the West. What are the facts? Liberty Valance was not killed by justice, but by an act of "cold-blooded murder." And Doniphon, the man who *really* shot Liberty Valance, is not honored, but forgotten. He dies a lonely pauper, buried by an undertaker who steals his boots. Civilization and progress make Stoddard, but break Doniphon. The editor cannot print the facts. To debunk Stoddard's legend is to undermine progress, the great historical imperative of turning the Western wilderness into a garden. Or perhaps the editor realizes that once legend has become fact, a fact that everyone knows, to challenge it is almost futile. People will continue to believe the legend.[2]

The lessons of Ford's *The Man Who Shot Liberty Valance* are worth keeping in mind when thinking about the meaning of Columbine as a cultural event, an event in *all* of our lives. For some, Columbine is about guns, the culture of violence, or social inequality and intolerance. Others find Columbine's meaning in Cassie Bernall and Rachel Scott. Their confessions of faith at gunpoint, like Ransom Stoddard's duel with Liberty Valance, become the twin symbols of a whole way of looking at American culture—its past, its present, and its future. The stories of Cassie and Rachel mesh seamlessly into the larger narrative of America's secular decline and the need for religious restoration. But as in Ford's *Liberty Valance,* the facts do not match the legend.

THE LEGENDS UNDER SIEGE

When *Salon.com* published Dave Cullen's "Inside the Columbine High Investigation" on September 23, 1999, the floodgates of criticism opened upon the Cassie martyr story. Given the tremendous religious, political, and cultural meanings placed upon Cassie, it is not surprising that there was a backlash, a backlash from those already skeptical of or hostile to the larger narrative in which her story seemed to be embedded. Such skepticism and hostility are not apparent in the straight news pieces, or in Cullen's original stories, but show up in interpretive feature stories and opinion pieces.

unnoticed. A handful of the customer reviews of *The Martyrs' Torch* and *Rachel's Tears* at *Amazon.com* used the *Sheriff's Report* to attack the veracity and even the integrity of the authors. One review of *The Martyrs' Torch* asserted, "Despite the fact that the witnesses, ballistics, autopsies, and sheriff [*sic*] reports all point to the fact that there were no 'Christian martyrs' at columbine [*sic*], the author [Porter] tries to get us to swallow the stories anyway, as if we have no other source for information."[18] Another customer review of *Rachel's Tears* made the same point. "She was not a martyr, noway, nohow [*sic*], so how can they justify calling her one? . . . They are calling her a martyr based on one persons [*sic*] word WHO WASN'T EVEN THERE! None of the evidence or witness statement [*sic*] back up the claim."[19]

In addition to questions about evidence, sarcasm and cynicism are common in the negative customer reviews of *Rachel's Tears*. "Lies, lies and more lies. No one at columbine [*sic*] was killed for their faith. Haven't these people made enough money yet? What, Rachels [*sic*] family didn't like seeing Cassie's family make money from the lies, they needed a piece of the pie too?"[20] It is hard to understand the bitter tone of these comments without taking into account the wider cultural politics involved in the discussion of Columbine. Just as the martyr stories were embraced by some, the debunking of such stories was celebrated by others. One is reminded of ardent spectators at a football game cheering opposing teams. What seems to matter to either side are not the facts, but the temporary advantage the use of these stories will yield.

THE LEGENDS DEFENDED

Very few who trumpeted the news of Cassie's martyrdom joined the defense of *She Said Yes*. There was little to be gained politically from such a defense. (After six months, perhaps the political "shelf life" of Cassie's story was already expiring.) Republican presidential candidates discreetly stopped mentioning her. Gary Bauer, however, continued on into at least November 1999, telling Cassie's story without mentioning the controversy over her final moments. He was also still using his comparison of Cassie and Governor Jesse Ventura. "It seemed to me that if I had to be in a foxhole with somebody," said Bauer, "I would take 17-year-old Cassie Bernall over Jesse 'The Bigot' Ventura."[21]

When Governor George W. Bush referred to her, without mentioning the controversy, in a November 2, 1999, speech,[22] few in the media noticed. *Slate.com,* an online magazine, ran an item on the speech entitled "George W., Folklorist," that reviewed the journalistic debunking of the Cassie martyr story and asserted, "It's inconceivable that Bush and his staff don't know the Bernall story has been discredited." Therefore, the "decision to use the story anyway is something a little worse than exploitative. It's immoral."[23] While it is doubtful that this criticism had much effect on the Bush campaign, when the candidate gave a speech on April 20, 2000, the first anniversary of Columbine, about character education, there were references to Columbine but none to Cassie.[24]

Commentator Richard John Neuhaus, writing in his journal *First Things: The Journal of Religion and Public Life,* came to the defense of *She Said Yes* and Misty Bernall. He observed that, "No witness to the truth goes unattacked." Neuhaus also dismissed the news reports that have "nitpicked details of the story." Neuhaus concluded by remarking upon "the determination of some, who are part of what St. Paul called the principalities and powers of the present time, to discredit the human capacity to love truth more than life."[25] This defense, however, was only one of many miscellaneous items in Neuhaus's long "The Public Square" column.

J. Bottum, who had proclaimed Cassie Bernall to be the "martyr," "catalyst," and "patron saint" of a coming Great Awakening in *First Things,* was reduced to making far more modest claims. Writing in the *Weekly Standard* in December 1999, he noted the growing confusion "though none of the sources of the original story has recanted," over whether it was Cassie and/or Valeen Schnurr and/or Rachel Scott who said "Yes." This confusion, Bottum observed, was leading to "the disappearance of the fact that *someone* said it, that at least one Colorado high school girl affirmed her faith, and was killed."[26] (Valeen Schnurr, of course, did affirm her faith, but survived.)

The primary defenders of *She Said Yes* were the Bernalls, Plough Publishing, and journalist Wendy Murray Zoba. Much of this defense was based on the evidence, such as witness accounts, which I reviewed in the previous chapter. But defenders of the Cassie martyr story also responded by questioning the motives of debunkers. "We talked to kids who were there who are 100 percent sure," said Misty Bernall, in an interview with the *Denver Post* just before the first anniversary of the shooting. "Either you believe what happened to Cassie or you don't. Some people are very cynical."[27]

Other defenders made even sharper accusations. "But the larger question is this: Why has Cullen's dubious assertion," wrote Zoba in *Christianity Today,* "based on incomplete reporting, so captured the imaginations of the media?" Zoba used Rosin's observation that "The truth is a trifle" as clear evidence that a media bias against evangelicals was at work.[28] In an April 3, 2000, article in *Christianity Today,* Zoba also took aim at the "seeming unwillingness of investigators to acknowledge the significance of anti-Christian aspects of the killings."[29]

Chris Zimmerman, spokesperson for the publisher of *She Said Yes,* struck even harder at the motives of those criticizing the grieving Misty Bernall. "Six-months [*sic*] after 'Columbine,' it is not the murderers who are standing trial (they are dead), but the mother of one of the victims." Zimmerman charged that the "real crux of the matter" was that the critics, whom he did not name, don't really care what happened on April 20, 1999. "Their discomfort lies more with her daughter's embattled legacy as a symbol of virtue in a landscape that seems increasingly dark."[30]

Although the Rachel Scott martyr story has encountered little direct criticism, the promoters of Rachel's legacy understood implicitly that they might be tarred with the same brush as the Bernalls and *She Said Yes.* Darrell Scott dealt with this potential problem by making an audio recording of a portion of Harris and Klebold's videotapes. (Whether he made the recording in response to, or in anticipation of, questions about the evidence behind Rachel's martyr story, is unclear.) As I noted in previous chapters, it is this recording that he uses to establish the killers' hatred of Christians, their animosity toward his daughter, and therefore the plausibility of her martyrdom.

This audio recording has also provided an important way of undermining the credibility of Sheriff's investigators, who failed, in Darrell Scott's view, to inform him about the content of the videotapes. "I was told specifically," he said of the investigators, "that this was not a God thing or a Christian thing. So I don't trust what I'm told."[31] If the investigators cannot be trusted on these matters, then it follows that their versions of Cassie's and Rachel's deaths, which do not confirm the martyr stories, should not be trusted, either.

In a public presentation in Pensacola, Florida, in June 2000, Darrell Scott told his audience, "Do you know that you're going to hear in the police reports things that are pure lies? I'm telling you that ahead of time. When you read the police reports about the Columbine tragedy they've omitted everything spiritual in those reports." When investigators told him that Columbine was not a "God thing," he reports that he replied, "You have to be blind, deaf, dumb, and stupid not to realize that these boys targeted Christians."

He extends the same condemnation to journalists based on his personal knowledge.

> You're going to hear the media say that nobody was asked if they believe in God. I'm going to tell you something, I've talked to the people, I talked to the kids, who heard my daughter talk. I talked to the kids who heard Cassie Bernall talk. I talked to the ones who heard Val Schnurr. And others. There were several kids asked about their belief in God.

He then reminds the audience of how his daughter was named by the killers on their videotape, and how they tormented and killed her. "So don't tell me they weren't targeting Christians."[32]

Even more important than Darrell Scott's access to the witnesses, the key to his criticism of the police-media version of Columbine is that "they've omitted everything spiritual." This is his way of saying they have missed the main point. Columbine for Darrell Scott is most essentially a spiritual event. He often tells the story of rushing to Columbine on the day of the shooting. Frightened, he prayed for his children and received an answer. "I heard these words again and again in my heart: *This is a spiritual event, a spiritual event.*"[33] Those who see that spiritual dimension, such as Darrell Scott's audiences and the readers of *Rachel's Tears,* will see the facts in their proper context. Those who omit "everything spiritual," such as members of the news media (read the *secular* news media), will be blind to the obvious, to what Darrell Scott saw from the first. "My personal opinion from the beginning," he told Zoba, "has been that these kids were targeted because they were Christians."[34]

Appeals to evidence and attacks on the credibility, motives, or world-view of the debunkers are the defenders' offensive tactics. A more defensive approach is the insistence that it really doesn't matter how Cassie or Rachel died. What matters is how they lived. "Mincing words over what was said in the library is a minor part," said Doug Clark of the National Network of Youth Ministries. "The greater part is how they lived their lives, and it's not going to change anything."[35] The title, *She Said Yes,* which at first glance seems to refer only to Cassie's last words, is reinterpreted as a broader affirmation expressed in her life. For example, one *Amazon.com* reader stated: "Whether she said yes then or not doesn't matter because every day she chose to say 'Yes, I believe in God' and it showed through her life."[36] This is also the position of the publisher. According to Zimmerman, "Questions about the particulars of what transpired in the library do not detract from the crux of Bernall's book, which is Cassie's transformation from a troubled teen who at one time entertained murderous fantasies to a young woman ready to face both life and death with confidence."[37]

In December 1999, when a few journalists asked similar questions regarding Rachel's final words, Darrell Scott offered much the same response. "It was never a major issue for me, whether Rachel said she believed in God. Her life was ample proof of that. What she did in her diaries and preceding her death is more important than the last words she may have spoken."[38]

There is a certain truth to these arguments. If the life stories and characters of these two young women did not somehow touch others, then what I've examined in this book would not have existed. But the defensive "it doesn't matter" argument is really only a tactical retreat. Those taking this position never actually concede that the martyr stories are false or unsubstantiated. By emphasizing Cassie's and Rachel's lives and not their deaths, the defenders argue that the questions raised by the debunkers are irrelevant. In other words, "Pay no attention to those people."

The message "it doesn't matter" can have a double meaning. On the one hand, it can mean "it doesn't matter if we *don't* tell the martyr stories." This is the more obvious meaning, the meaning that comes across in press releases and statements to journalists. But on the other hand, "it doesn't matter" can also mean "it doesn't matter if we *do* tell the martyr stories." This is the less obvious but more important meaning that still allows the martyr story to be told and retold. And the story of that final "yes" *must* be told to give the short lives and sudden deaths of Cassie and Rachel their fullest significance by linking them to a two-millennia-long tradition of Christian martyrdom. And the martyrdoms of these two girls offer proof that the tradition of heroic faith is not a thing of the past, or, as Bottum put it in his article on Cassie, the stories are proof "that God may be loose in America again."[39]

The bulk of *She Said Yes* is indeed concerned with the story of Cassie's spiritual transformation. But a book about this transformation may never have been published, and certainly would not have become a bestseller, if she had not been celebrated as Columbine's martyr. Think for a moment what her story would be without that triumphant exit: "Troubled teen finds God and turns her life around, but is murdered. The end." If she was murdered as the mere punchline to Harris's sick "peek-a-boo" joke, then it is very difficult to establish any meaning behind her death. All that Harris has given us—it now becomes his story—is yet another example of absurd cruelty, a grisly detail of yet another "senseless school shooting."

Because of her writings, Rachel's legacy has a broader base on which to build than Cassie's. But had Rachel lived the same life, written the same things, and yet died a more prosaic death, say an automobile accident, there would be no books and no ministries preserving or spreading her legacy. Had she simply been gunned down without the reputed conversation with her killers, Rachel may have been mourned and celebrated, as at her televised funeral, but she would be remembered, like most of the Columbine dead, only by those who knew her. It is the manner of her death, in the crucible of martyrdom, that dramatizes and clarifies the conflict between competing world-views and the conflict between good and evil.

It is their deaths that have made Cassie and Rachel objects of more than private mourning, but of public significance. Their entire lives are viewed in the context of that death. The meaning of one is inseparable from the other. And the primary spokespersons for each girl seem to know this. Cassie's mother told *Christianity Today* magazine that even before Columbine occurred she believed that the story of her daughter's transformation would have value for others. She also said that shortly after the massacre, "I heard him [God] say that it had to be big, because if it wasn't big, no one would listen."[40] In the book *Chain Reaction,* Darrell Scott draws a parallel between Rachel and Holocaust victim Anne Frank, whose diary has touched millions. "Like Rachel this young girl is someone most of us never would have heard of if it hadn't been for the way she died."[41]

THE CARAVAN MOVES ON

A final, and perhaps the most effective, way the defenders of the martyr stories overcome the debunkers is to ignore and outlast them. There is an old Arab proverb: "The dogs bark, but the caravan moves on." Now that the story has been broken, the editorials written, the political points scored, and the *Sheriff's Report* released, what else is there for the debunkers to say? Yes, news reports may make a passing reference to the controversy, but American evangelicals are used to encountering and filtering out the skepticism of the press. And if evangelicals do wonder about the evidence behind martyr stories, it is more likely they will turn to and trust *Christianity Today* and Zoba than *Salon.com* and Cullen. In contrast, the martyr stories, because of their inherent power, can be told again and again and again. In other words, keep telling the martyr stories, keep "printing the legend," and the critics will simply fade away. The dogs bark, but the caravan moves on.

There is substantial evidence that the caravan continues to move on. Despite the controversy that followed its release, *She Said Yes* sold well and continues to be popular. There were a reported one million hard- and softcover copies in print by the second anniversary of its publication. There are also several foreign-language and audio-book editions of *She Said Yes*.[42]

When Cassie or *She Said Yes* is discussed in publications with an evangelical or religious audience, with the exception of Zoba's defense articles in *Christianity Today,* there is a tendency not even to mention the controversy over Cassie's last words. This was the case in "She Lived Yes," an article in religious broadcaster James Dobson's widely distributed *Focus on the Family* magazine published in April 2000.[43] When recording artist Michael W. Smith sings his tribute to Cassie, "This is Your Time," at his sold-out concerts, no questions about her martyr story intrude. No doubts about the martyr story were apparent when the Christian musical group Jars of Clay accepted a Grammy award in February 2001. A member of the group said, "We dedicate this award to Cassie Bernall and all those standing up for truth."[44]

When the Bernalls themselves speak publicly about their daughter they apparently see no reason to mention the controversy. At an event in Lancaster, Pennsylvania, in October 2000, the Bernalls were interviewed on stage by a local minister. Cassie's martyr story was mentioned but there was no hint in either the minister's questions or the Bernall's answers that there had been any doubts about Cassie's final words. When I spoke to the minister, she told me that in preliminary discussions with the Bernalls, she had asked how she should deal with the controversy. She reported that Misty Bernall told her not to ask about it.[45] And in a new introduction to the paperback edition of *She Said Yes,* dated September 2000, Misty Bernall makes no mention of the controversy but only "the impact of Cassie's life."[46]

The Rachel Scott martyr story has been subjected to a backwash of skepticism resulting from the Cassie controversy, rather than much particular criticism. But behind the phrase, "according to Richard's earliest account," one senses a certain nervousness among the keepers of Rachel's shrine about the evidence behind, and the details of, her death. While there are few barking dogs as of yet, the Rachel caravan is most definitely moving on. There are at least four books about Rachel and her legacy in comparison to two about Cassie. These Rachel books may have not sold as well as *She Said Yes,* but *Rachel's Tears* has certainly done well.[47] Darrell Scott is almost continually traveling throughout the United States and speaking to audiences large and small. A schedule of his appearances posted on his web site shows that he is booked months in advance. While only a relative few answer the altar call, or seriously resolve to continue Rachel's "chain reaction of compassion," everywhere he goes he plants and nurtures the legend of Columbine—a spiritual event, a battleground of good and evil, a place where the blood of martyrs was spilled. And he fosters an interpretation of American culture in which secularization is destructive and traditionalist religion is the only hope of restoration.

I believe that this response—simply ignoring the debunkers and continuing to tell the martyr stories—will persist in the understanding of Columbine within the evangelical community. Dave McPherson, Cassie's youth pastor, told the *Washington Post* in October 1999, "The church is going to stick to the martyr story. It's the story they heard first, and circulated for six months uncontested. You can say it didn't happen that way, but the church won't accept it. To the church, Cassie will always say yes, period."[48] McPherson's statement leads us to think that it is only the power of familiarity, or of a first impression, that cannot be dislodged. "When the legend becomes fact, print the legend."

Familiarity is powerful, but a deeper strength of such stories is that they have the power to make sense of a senseless event. The martyrs of Columbine make it possible that what happened on April 20, 1999, was meaningful rather than meaningless. Their stories also can reveal the possibility of nobility and transcendence in the face of the problem of evil, a possibility that resides in all of us, and a problem we all ultimately face. A martyr story beckons us to defy whatever degrades us, limits us, or tempts us to despair.

In March 2001, there was a Columbine-like shooting at Santana High School in Santee, California. Charles "Andy" Williams, a 15-year-old student, killed 2 and wounded 13 before surrendering to police. Tim Eldreth, a 16-year-old Santana student, told a reporter, "As soon as I heard gunfire, I immediately thought about Columbine High School and that girl [Cassie Bernall]." It instantly occurred to Eldreth, the son of a local Southern Baptist pastor, that the shooter might be "targeting Christians." Looking back on those frightening moments, Eldreth said, "I was sitting in that classroom wondering if I would be able to stand up and say I was a believer. It sure drew a whole lot of respect for her [Bernall]."[49]

Understood in this very concrete way, the stories of Cassie and Rachel are not so much comfort as challenge. These stories can be, and are for those who honor the legacies of these two young women, a summons to heroism, not a license for complacency. This does not mean "the truth is a trifle" for those who find meaning and hope in the martyr stories of Cassie and Rachel, but for those who "stick to the martyr story" the *real* truth about Columbine will never be reducible to a mere constellation of facts.

Notes

PREFACE

1. This event was held at the Tri-County Worship Center, 1501 Schubert Road in Bethel, Pennsylvania, on October 19–20, 26–27, 2001. I attended on October 26, 2001.

2. "Hell House Outreach Kits" are produced and distributed by Abundant Life Christian Fellowship of Arvada, Colorado. See "What Is Hell House?" undated, <http://www.alccdenver.com/hh-faq.html> (October 27, 2001). [Throughout, the dates in parenthesis indicate the date the web site was accessed.] The Hell House concept predates Columbine by several years, but the school shooting scene has attracted special attention and controversy. See, for example, Pat Gordon, "Seasonal Look at Reality's Horrors: On Halloween, Texas Church Uses True Stories to Attract Teenagers," *Boston Globe,* October 31, 1999: A12; Bob Batz, Jr., "Real-Life Horrors," *Pittsburgh Post-Gazette,* October 26, 2000: D-1; Betsy Taylor, "Groups See Halloween As Opportunity To Save Souls," Associated Press, October 26, 2001.

3. Kevin Simpson, "Video's Release Outrages Kin," *Denver Post,* April 27, 2000: A1. The version that was originally released had, incredibly enough, a soundtrack with pop music. See Dave Cullen, "Images of Columbine Terror For Sale," *Salon.com,* April 27, 2000, <http://www.salon.com/news/feature/2000/04/27/columbine_video> (May 20, 2000). Jefferson County authorities soon issued a new version without the soundtrack.

4. At an event organized by Torchgrab Youth Ministries in June 2001, a portion of this tape was shown. Attendees at the "Torchgrab Youth Rally" saw the inside of the Columbine library, including closeups of the blood-stained carpet, while someone read aloud a letter from the mother of one of the victims. Beth Nimmo is a member of Torchgrab's Board of Directors, attended and spoke at this event, and she was present when the tape was played. I attended this in Myerstown,

Pennsylvania, June 22–23, 2001. Torchgrab will be described in detail in chapter 3.

INTRODUCTION

1. David J. Krajicek, "Ghoulish or Great? Columbine News Coverage," *APBnews.com,* April 18, 2000, <http://www.APBnews.com/media/mediawatch/krajicek/2000/04/18/crimebeat0418_01.html> (June 9, 2001).
2. "1999 Year End Report," *The Pew Research Center For The People & The Press,* undated, <http://www.people-press.org/yearendrpt.htm> (March 21, 2000).
3. "Attacks at Home Draw More Interest than War Abroad," *The Pew Research Center For The People & The Press,* October 22, 2001, <http://www.people-press.org/102201que.htm> (October 30, 2001).
4. "Clinton's Columbine Statement," Associated Press, April 20, 2000.
5. See the Columbine Research Task Force web site at www.columbine.n3.net. See also Holly Yettick, "Columbine Plot Theories Abound," *Denver Rocky Mountain News,* July 30, 2001: 4A.
6. Cover, *Time,* March 19, 2001.
7. See Elizabeth Bell, "High Schools React to Threats of Violence," *San Francisco Chronicle,* April 5, 2000: A15; Timothy Harper, "Shoot to Kill," *Atlantic Monthly,* October 2000: 28–33; John Cloud, "The Legacy of Columbine," *Time,* March 19, 2001: 32.

   For criticism of this response see "ACLU Challenges of Suspension of Student in Latest Example of 'Post-Columbine Hysteria,'" American Civil Liberties Union press release, November 21, 2000. Such criticism also comes from political conservatives. See Dave Kopel and Linda Gorman, "Guest Comment: Post-Columbine Syndrome," *National Review Online,* May 8, 2000, <http://nationalreview.com/comment/comment050800b.html> (September 6, 2001).
8. Quoted in Amy Wallace, "Is Hollywood Pulling Punches?" *Los Angeles Times,* December 26, 1999: 5.
9. "1999 Year End Report," *The Pew Research Center For The People & The Press,* undated, <http://www.people-press.org/yearendrpt.htm> (March 21, 2000). Columbine finished behind President Clinton's impeachment and Senate trial, which 20 percent saw as the most important story even though only 31 percent had followed it "very closely."
10. Quoted in Mark O'Keefe, "Lessons of Columbine," Newhouse News Service, April 16, 2000.
11. Mark Gillespie, "Poll Releases: One in Three Say It Is Very Likely That Columbine-Type Shootings Could Happen in Their Community," Gallup News Service, April 20, 2000. Available at <http://www.gallup.com/poll/releases/pr000420.asp>.

12. David W. Moore, "Americans Divided on Whether School Shootings Can Be Prevented, Gallup News Service, March 26, 2001. Available at <http://www.gallup.com/poll/releases/pr010326.asp>. In this poll 49 percent said they believed that school shootings could be prevented by social and governmental action, and 47 percent believed they would happen anyway. The margin of error was -/+ 3 percentage points.

13. My understanding of evangelicalism relies heavily on the work of historian George M. Marsden. See *Understanding Evangelicalism and Fundamentalism* (Grand Rapids, MI: William B. Eerdmans, 1991); "The Evangelical Denomination," in *Piety and Politics,* eds. Richard John Neuhaus and Michael Cromartie (Washington, D.C.: Ethics and Public Policy Center, 1987), 55–68.

14. Franklin Graham, Remarks at the Columbine Memorial Service, April 25, 1999, in Littleton, Colorado.

15. Bruce Porter, *The Martyrs' Torch: The Message of the Columbine Massacre* (Shippensburg, PA: Destiny Image Publishers, Inc., 1999), 53.

16. See, for instance, Misty Bernall, *She Said Yes: The Unlikely Martyrdom of Cassie Bernall* (Farmington, PA: Plough Publishing House, 1999); Beth Nimmo, Darrell Scott, and Steve Rabey, *Rachel's Tears: The Spiritual Journey of Columbine Martyr Rachel Scott* (Nashville, TN: Thomas Nelson, 2000).

17. Dave Cullen, "Inside the Columbine High Investigation," *Salon.com,* September 23, 1999, <http://www.salon.com/news/feature/1999/09/23/columbine> (July 7, 2001).

18. "Columbine's Rachel Scott May Have Said Yes," Associated Press, December 16, 1999. See also Kevin Simpson, "Apology to Rachel's Kin 'From the Heart,'" *Denver Post,* April 21, 2000: A-08.

19. Jefferson County, Colorado, Sheriff's Office, *The Jefferson County Sheriff's Office Report, Columbine High School Shootings, April 20, 1999* (Golden, CO, 2000), CD-ROM.

CHAPTER 1

1. Kenneth L. Woodward, "The Making of a Martyr," *Time,* June 14, 1999: 64. This seems to be the only time Ruegsegger was cited as having a God-conversation with the killers. She has never made such claims. See Janna L. Graber, "Kacey's Comeback," *Family Circle,* April 18, 2000: 66–70.

2. Franklin Graham, Remarks at the Columbine Memorial Service, April 25, 1999, in Littleton, Colorado; see the "Yes, I Believe" web site at <http://YesIBelieve.com>; Andrew Guy Jr., "Victims Parents Rely On Their Faith," *Denver Post,* April 24, 1999: A3; Eileen McNamara,

"A Martyr Amid the Madness," *Boston Globe,* April 24, 1999: A1; Claire Martin and Janet Bingham, "Cassie Bernall, Girl's Faith a Beacon to Those She Left," *Denver Post,* April 23, 1999: A6; Albert Gore, Remarks at the Columbine Memorial Service, April 25, 1999, in Littleton, Colorado.

3. Franklin Graham, Remarks at the Columbine Memorial Service, April 25, 1999, in Littleton, Colorado.

4. Quoted in Maria Hinojosa, "Colorado School Shooting: Cassie Bernall, a Teenager Who Simply Said 'Yes,'" *CNN Today,* Cable News Network, April 26, 1999.

5. Quoted in Larry B. Stammer, "Slain Student's Act of Faith Inspires Nation's Christians," *Los Angeles Times,* May 4, 1999: A1. On the April 21, 1999, edition of *Larry King Live* (Cable News Network), Mickie Cain, a Columbine High School student, gave essentially the same account, but she had the killers asking about "faith in Christ." Cain also said that she was not present when Cassie was killed.

    The Reverend Jerry Falwell cited Cain's account in an appearance the next day. But he changed the killer's question to "Is there a believer in Jesus Christ in this room?" Falwell reported Cassie's response as, "Yes, I'm a believer." Jerry Falwell, interview by Geraldo Rivera, *Rivera Live,* CNBC, April 22, 1999.

6. "From Tragedy Comes Faith," Copley News Service, June 10, 1999. A very similar exchange is also attributed to Rachel Scott. See Bruce Porter, *The Martyrs' Torch: The Message of the Columbine Massacre* (Shippensburg, PA: Destiny Image Publishers, Inc., 1999), 53.

7. Thomas Winters, "About Cassie," undated, <http://homepages.go.com/~thomaswinters/cassie.html> (January 30 2000).

8. Nancy Gibbs, "Special Report: The Littleton Massacre," *Time,* May 3, 1999: 25.

9. Joshua Lapp quoted in Misty Bernall, *She Said Yes: The Unlikely Martyrdom of Cassie Bernall* (Farmington, PA: Plough Publishing House, 1999), 12–13. See also Carla Crowder, "Martyr For Her Faith," *Denver Rocky Mountain News,* April 23, 1999: 5A; Eileen McNamara, "A Martyr Amid the Madness," *Boston Globe,* April 24, 1999: A1; Wendy Murray Zoba, "'Do You Believe in God?': How Columbine Changed America," *Christianity Today,* October 4, 1999: 36.

10. See Beth Nimmo, Darrell Scott, and Steve Rabey, *Rachel's Tears: The Spiritual Journey of Columbine Martyr Rachel Scott* (Nashville, TN: Thomas Nelson Publishers, 2000), 91–92; Darrell Scott and Steve Rabey, *Chain Reaction: A Call to Compassionate Revolution* (Nashville, TN: Thomas Nelson Publishers, 2001), 126; Porter, *Martyrs' Torch,* 53; Michael W. Smith and Gary Thomas, *This Is Your Time: Make Every Moment Count* (Nashville, TN: Thomas Nelson Publishers, 2000), 11–12; Darrell Scott quoted in Julia Duin, "3,100

Hear Story of Columbine," *Washington Times,* April 2, 2000: C1; Brent High, "God Used A Toothache," *Rachel's Journal,* January 2000: 11.

11. See Zoba, "Do You Believe in God?" 36; "Who Will Go In Her Place?" undated <http://www.acquirethefire.org/s2kmissions/rachel. htm> (June 24, 2000); Susanna Nikula, "Does It Echo?" *Rachel's Journal,* February/March 2000: 13; Bob Larson, *Extreme Evil: Kids Killing Kids* (Nashville, TN: Thomas Nelson Publishers, 1999), 16.

12. See *Untold Stories of Columbine,* Darrell Scott, 80 min., Gateway Films, 2000, videocassette; Darrell Scott and Beth Nimmo, interviewed by Cynthia Bowers, *48 Hours,* Columbia Broadcasting System, June 10, 1999. Until November 2000, the front page of the web site for his organization, The Columbine Redemption, presented Rachel's answer as "Yes, I believe!" to the God question. Undated, <http://thecolumbineredemption.com> (March 31, 2000). In November 2000 this was changed to "She, like others, was taunted and questioned about her faith in God. Her last words were a confirmation of the faith she lived and was willing to die for." Undated, <http://thecolumbineredemption.com> (November 5, 2000).

Ambassador Agency, a talent agency through which Darrell Scott's appearances are arranged, provides an online profile of him that is often read almost verbatim when he is introduced. The profile/introduction reports Rachel's answer as simply "YES." See "Speakers Bureau: Darrell Scott," undated, <http://www.ambassador-agency.com/Profiles.cfm?ID=77> (May 31 2001). (In chapter 5, I will return to this persistent ambiguity about her last words when I examine in detail the available evidence about her death.)

13. *Untold Stories of Columbine,* Scott.

14. Samuel Z. Klausner, *Encyclopedia of Religion* (New York: Macmillan, 1986), s.v. "Martyrdom," ed. Mircea Eliade.

15. G. W. Bowersock, *Martyrdom and Rome* (Cambridge: Cambridge University Press, 1995), 14.

16. Quoted in Leonardo Boff, "Martyrdom: An Attempt at Systematic Reflection," *Concilium* 183 (1983): 14–15.

17. W. H. C. Frend, *Martyrdom and Persecution in the Early Church: A Study of a Conflict from the Maccabees to Donatus* (Oxford: Basil Blackwell, 1965); Daniel Boyarin, *Dying for God: Martyrdom and the Making of Christianity and Judaism* (Stanford, CA: Stanford University Press, 1999); Bowersock, *Martyrdom and Rome;* and, Arthur J. Droge and James D. Tabor, *A Noble Death: Suicide and Martyrdom Among Christians and Jews in Antiquity* (San Francisco, CA: HarperSanFrancisco, 1992).

18. Droge and Tabor, *A Noble Death,* 132; Bowersock, *Martyrdom and Rome,* 13; Everett Ferguson, *Encyclopedia of Early Christianity* (New

York: Garland Publishing Inc., 1997), s.v. "Martyr, Martyrdom," and "Martyrdom of Polycarp (ca. 155/6?)," by Everett Ferguson; *New Catholic Encyclopedia* (New York: McGraw-Hill Book Company, 1967), s.v. "Martyr," by F. X. Murphy. The text is divided by chapter and verse. I have used this notation.

19. "The Martyrdom of Saint Polycarp," *The Library of Christian Classics,* Vol. I, *Early Christian Fathers,* ed. and trans. Cyril C. Richardson (Philadelphia, PA: The Westminster Press, 1953), 149–158, 9:1.

20. "The Martyrdom of Saint Polycarp," 11:1.

21. "The Martyrdom of Saint Polycarp," 11:2.

22. "The Martyrdom of Saint Polycarp," 12:1.

23. "The Martyrdom of Saint Polycarp," 12:2.

24. "The Martyrdom of Saint Polycarp," 14:2.

25. "The Martyrdom of Saint Polycarp," 16:1.

26. "The Martyrdom of Saint Polycarp," 19:2.

27. "The Martyrdom of Saint Polycarp," 19:1.

28. "The Martyrdom of Saint Polycarp," 20:1.

29. Droge and Tabor, *A Noble Death,* 126.

30. Ignatius of Antioch, "To the Romans," in *The Early Christian Fathers,* Henry Bettenson, ed. and trans. (London: Oxford University Press, 1958), 62.

31. Robin Lane Fox, *Pagans and Christians* (New York: Alfred A. Knopf, Inc., 1987), 435.

32. Eugene Weiner and Anita Weiner, *The Martyr's Conviction: A Sociological Analysis* (Atlanta, GA: Scholars Press, 1990), 10.

33. "Martyrdom of Saint Polycarp," 9:3.

34. Boyarin, *Dying for God,* 95; Ekkehard Mühlenberg, "The Martyr's Death and its Literary Presentation," *Studia Patristica* 29 (1997): 87.

35. The stakes are high for the other side as well. Rather than life and limb, it is the ideological credibility that is at risk. And the agent who makes these threats/promises may experience a threat to personal prestige and power.

36. Bowersock, *Martyrdom and Rome,* 36–37.

37. Lacey Baldwin Smith, *Fools, Martyrs, Traitors: The Story of Martyrdom in the Western World* (New York: Alfred A. Knopf, 1997), 11. The quotation is from Sylvia Plath, "Lady Lazarus," in *Ariel* (London, 1965), 17.

38. Quoted in Smith, *Fools, Martyrs, Traitors,* 204.

39. Brad S. Gregory, *Salvation at Stake: Christian Martyrdom in Early Modern Europe* (Cambridge, MA: Harvard University Press, 1999), 18.

40. Rodney Stark, *The Rise of Christianity: A Sociologist Reconsiders History* (Princeton, NJ: Princeton University Press, 1996), 180–184.

See also Donald W. Riddle, *The Martyrs, A Study in Social Control* (Chicago: University of Chicago Press, 1931).

41. Weiner and Weiner, *The Martyr's Conviction,* 80.
42. Frend, *Martyrdom and Persecution in the Early Church,* 413.
43. Bowersock, *Martyrdom and Rome,* 66.
44. Tertullian, *Apologeticus,* 50. In *The Early Christian Fathers,* Henry Bettenson, ed. and trans. (London: Oxford University Press, 1958), 230.
45. Stark, *The Rise of Christianity,* 174.
46. Weiner and Weiner, *The Martyr's Conviction,* 56–57.
47. Droge and Tabor, *A Noble Death,* 126.
48. See, for instance, Steve Lipsher and Bruce Finley, "'I Cried And Cried . . . Now I'm Dry of Tears,'" *Denver Post,* April 22, 1999: A-12.
49. *Braveheart,* prod. Alan Ladd Jr. and Mel Gibson, dir. Mel Gibson, 2 hr. 57 min., Paramount, 1995, videocassette.
50. Klausner, "Martyrdom."
51. Brad Bernall and Misty Bernall interviewed by Wendy Murray Zoba, "Tough Love Saved Cassie," *Christianity Today,* October 4, 1999: 41. See also James Langton, "Focus: The 17-Year-Old Icon," *Sunday Telegraph* (London), September 26, 1999: 28.
52. Jefferson County, Colorado, Sheriff's Office, *Jefferson County, Colorado, Sheriff's Office Report on the Columbine High School Shootings, April 20, 1999* (Golden, CO). CD-ROM.
53. Randall Balmer of Columbia University is cited as raising this possibility in Stammer, "Slain Student's Act of Faith Inspires Nation's Christians," A1.
54. Richard L. Rubenstein, "Some Perspective on Religious Faith after Auschwitz," in *Holocaust: Religious and Philosophical Implications,* John K. Roth and Michael Berenbaum, eds. (New York: Paragon House, 1989), 356–357.
55. S. Daniel Breslauer, "Martyrdom and Charisma: Leo Baeck and a New Jewish Theology," *Encounter: Creative Theological Scholarship* 42, no. 2 (Spring 1981): 138.
56. Quoted in Smith, *Fools, Martyrs, Traitors,* 314.
57. For a very different view of "What if Cassie had said no?" see Richard Roeper, "Cassie's Last 'Yes' Earns 15 Minutes of Martyrdom," *Chicago Sun Times,* June 10, 1999: 11.
58. Bernall, *She Said Yes,* 139.
59. See Smith, *Fools, Martyrs, Traitors,* 314–315.
60. Klausner, "Martyrdom."
61. Weiner and Weiner, *The Martyr's Conviction,* 78–79.
62. See, for example, George Gallup, Jr. and D. Michael Lindsay, *Surveying the Religious Landscape: Trends in U.S. Belief* (Harrisburg, PA: Morehouse Publishing, 1999), 23–25.

63. A. Alvarez, *The Savage God: A Study of Suicide* (New York: Random House, 1972), 120.

64. Steve Rabey, "Videos of Hate," *Christianity Today,* February 7, 2000: 21.

65. See Jefferson County, Colorado, Sheriff's Office, "The Trench Coat Mafia and Associates," *The Jefferson County Sheriff's Office Report, Columbine High School Shootings, April 20, 1999* (Golden, CO, 2000), CD-ROM.

66. The phrase "kick-start a revolution" comes from videotapes made by Harris and Klebold and is quoted in Nancy Gibbs and Timothy Roche, "The Columbine Tapes," *Time,* December 20, 1999: 42. By adopting the language of "revolution," Harris, whose self-adopted nickname was "Reb," short for "Rebel," was casting himself and Klebold in the role of oppressed progenitors of a nascent social movement, not the agents of an established order.

67. Nicholas Turse, "New Morning, Changing Weather: Radical Youth of the Millennial Age," *49th Parallel—An Interdisciplinary Journal of North American Studies,* Fall 1999 (Issue 4) <http://artsweb.bham.ac.uk/49thparallel/backissues/issue4/forum2.htm> (September 22, 2000).

68. David Farber, "Making No Sense of Young People Killing Other Young People," *49th Parallel—An Interdisciplinary Journal of North American Studies,* Fall 1999 (Issue 4) <http://artsweb.bham.ac.uk/49thparallel/backissues/issue4/forum2.htm> (September 22, 2000).

69. Christian Smith, *American Evangelicalism: Embattled and Thriving* (Chicago: University of Chicago Press, 1998), 121.

70. See, for instance, Porter, *The Martyrs' Torch,* 76.

CHAPTER 2

1. Misty Bernall, *She Said Yes: The Unlikely Martyrdom of Cassie Bernall* (Farmington, PA: Plough Publishing, 1999), 132; Janet Bingham, "Student's Window of Hope," *Denver Post,* May 17, 1999: B1; Hanna Rosin, "Columbine Miracle: A Matter of Belief," *Washington Post,* October 14, 1999: C1.

2. "Martyrdom at Columbine High," *Chicago Tribune,* April 28, 1999: 18.

3. Quoted in Peggy Wehmeyer, Charles Gibson, and Connie Chung, "Portrait of an Angel," *ABC News 20/20,* American Broadcasting Company, April 26, 1999.

4. Quoted in Larry B. Stammer, "Slain Student's Act of Faith Inspires Nation's Christians," *Los Angeles Times,* May 4, 1999: A1.

5. Wendy Murray Zoba, "'Do You Believe in God?': How Columbine Changed America," *Christianity Today,* October 4, 1999: 32–40.

6. See Brenda Brasher's discussion of memorial web sites devoted to Lady Diana in *Give Me That Online Religion* (San Francisco, CA: Jossey-Bass Inc., 2001), 123–128.

7. See, for example, Peggie C. Bohanon, "Cassie's Legacy—the 'Yes' Word!!," undated, <http://www.gospelcom.net/peggiesplace/words153. htm> (May 20, 2000); "I Hope You and Jesus Have It All Worked Out . . . ," undated, <http://www.geocities.com/Heartland/Flats/4229/ columbine.html> (May 20, 2000); "The Cassie Bernall Story," undated, <http://www.baptistfire.com/articles/other/cassie.html> (May 20, 2000); Kent DelHousay, "Young Christian Stood Firm," April 29, 1999, <http://www.datvis.net/fi/columbine/page10.htm> (January 30, 2000).

8. See "Cassie's Stand," undated, <http://members.aol.com/ Voice4Them/Cassie.html> (January 30, 2000). A similar image of Rachel Scott is posted next to that of Cassie. Explanatory text makes it clear that the Rachel image was added more recently.

9. Dmarie, "Cassie Bernall . . . Woman of God," undated, <http://www. angelfire.com/tx/pottslittle/cassie.html> (May 20, 2000).

10. "Cassie's Call," undated, <http://www.distributionconcepts.com/ cassieb.htm> (March 26, 2000). Information on the sponsoring church, The Lighthouse Apostolic Church of Oak Lawn, Illinois, can be found at <http://www.revdwpoc.org>.

11. Entropy Squared, "The Temptation of Cassie Bernall," undated, <http://www.sit-rep.com/arc3b.html> (May 31, 2000).

12. Chuck Wilkes, "Pre-Paration Meeting," undated, <http://www.naznet. com/~projects/classics/pre_paration.htm> (June 9, 2001). This sermon was originally given by Wilkes, the Pastor of Highland Ranch Community Fellowship in Highland Ranch, Colorado, on April 25, 1999.

13. Reverend Billy Graham, interview by Larry King, *Larry King Live,* Cable News Network, April 28, 1999.

14. "Pacers, Racers, Preacher Take Stage in Indianapolis," Billy Graham Evangelistic Association press release, June 7, 1999; Quoted in Melissa King, "Graham Taps Contemporary Christian Music As His 'Interpreter' to Reach Today's Youth," Baptist Press, June 10, 1999.

15. See Larry B. Stammer, "Slain Student's Act of Faith Inspires Nation's Christians," *Los Angeles Times,* May 4, 1999: A1; David Van Biema, "A Surge of Teen Spirit," *Time,* May 31, 1999: 58–59; Deborah Sharp, "17-Year-Old's Last Words Inspire Other Christians," *USA Today,* June 1, 1999: 3A; Sara Rimer, "Columbine Students Seek Answers in Their Faith," *New York Times,* June 6, 1999: Sect. 1, 26; Kenneth L. Woodward, "The Making of a Martyr," *Newsweek,* June 14, 1999: 64; Mary Dejevsky, "Saint Cassie of Columbine High: The Making of a Modern Martyr," *The Independent* (London) August 21, 1999: 1; Ken Walker, "Blessed Are Those Who Mourn," *Charisma,* September 1999: 38–46, 91; Kristine Vick, "Littleton Tragedy Ignites Spiritual Revival," *Christian Broadcasting Network News,* September 13, 1999, <http://www. the700club.org/newsstand/stories/990913b.asp> (June 19, 2000); Rosin, "Columbine Miracle," C1; Zoba, "'Do You Believe in God?'" 33–40.

16. "Teen Mania: Day One—Teenage Revolution," Teen Mania Ministries press release, April 25, 1999.
17. Ron Luce, *Columbine Courage: Rock-Solid Faith* (Nashville, TN: J. Countryman, 2000). The quotation from Joy is on page 46.

    The quotation from Cassie Bernall on the back cover is identified in *She Said Yes* as "a note written by Cassie the night before she was killed and handed to her friend Amanda the next morning at school." iv. The version in *She Said Yes,* however, does not end with an exclamation mark.
18. Ken Walker, "A Revival Generation," *Charisma,* September 1999: 43.
19. "Dedication: In Loving Memory of Columbine," *Revival Generation: How to Start a Prayer Ministry on Your Campus,* booklet (Englewood, CO: Revival Generation, 1999), 4. Available for download at <http://www.revivalgeneration.org>.
20. Rosin, "Columbine Miracle," C1.
21. David Van Biema, "A Surge of Teen Spirit," *Time,* May 31, 1999: 58. More information on the National Network of Youth Ministries can be found at <http://www.nnym.org>.
22. Bruce Nolan, "Columbine Cast as Morality Play; Slick Church Production Held Over for Months," *Times-Picayune* (New Orleans), February 20, 2000: A1. See also <http://www.btg2000.com>, which presents information about the "Beyond the Grave" as well as e-mailed testimonies from those who have seen the play.

    The congregation in New Jersey is Glad Tidings Assembly of God in Mt. Ephraim, New Jersey. See <http://www.gladtidingsmtephraim.org/HTML%20files/Gladtidings_Beyond_the_Grave.htm> for information. I attended a performance of the play at this location on May 25, 2001.
23. Quotations of dialogue are from *Beyond the Grave: The Class of 2000,* prod. Ty Tyler, dir. April Antonie, 1 hr. and 26 min., A Victory Fellowship Production, 2000, videocassette.

    On May 5, 2000, I attended a performance of "Beyond the Grave." I also had an opportunity to speak with Ty Tyler, the church's music minister and author of the play, and other members of the cast. Tyler told me that while he was certainly aware of the Columbine shooting, he rapidly wrote the play without doing any particular research on Columbine or Cassie Bernall.

    The Mt. Ephraim, New Jersey, congregation performing the play, however, made the connections to Columbine and Cassie Bernall explicit. The church's web site describes their version of "Beyond the Grave" as a "Powerful Drama Based in Part on Events Surrounding the Columbine High School Massacre." See "Beyond the Grave," undated, <http://www.gladtidingsmtephraim.org/HTML%20files/Gladtidings_Beyond_the_Grave.htm> (May 23, 2001). Those who respond to the altar call are given a tract that features Cassie's picture and story. I observed this during my visit on May 25, 2001.

24. "Cassie Bernall Foundation," undated, <http://www.cassiebernall. com/cassie_bernall_foundation.htm> (May 13, 2000).

25. "Coping With The Tragedy One Year Later," *YesIBelieve.com,* Newsletter # 10, April 11, 2000 <support@yesibelieve.com> (April 12, 2000). See also Susan Besze Wallace, "Voices of Columbine: The Family of Cassie Bernall," *Denver Post,* April 16, 2000: I-12; James B. Meadow, "The House That Cassie Built," *Denver Rocky Mountain News,* April 21, 2001: 1A.

26. Both Brad and Misty Bernall are available for events through *ChristianSpeakers.com,* a speakers bureau. See "Brad and Misty Bernall," undated, <http://www.ChristianSpeakers.com/speakers/bernall.htm> (May 14, 2000).

   Other speakers registered with this bureau include former football star Mike Singletary, Iran-Contra figure and talk-radio host Oliver North, college football coach Bobby Bowden, entertainer Pat Boone, former Harlem Globetrotter star Meadowlark Lemon, and former Secretary of Education William Bennett. See "Introduction," undated, <http://www.ChristianSpeakers.com/intro.htm> (May 14, 2000).

27. "One Year After Columbine, Half a Million Lives Changed for the Better," undated, <http://www.cassiebernall.org/one_year.htm> (April 30, 2000).

   The paperback edition is Misty Bernall, *She Said Yes: The Unlikely Martyrdom of Cassie Bernall* (New York: Pocket Books, 2000).

28. *She Said Yes: A Video Tribute to Cassie Bernall by Her Friends,* prod. and dir. John Burns and Dave McPherson, 25 min., West Bowles Community Church, 1999, videocassette.

29. Jeff Diedrich, *She Said Yes: A Bible Study Based on the Life of Cassie Bernall* (Rocky Mount, NC: Positive Action for Christ, 1999), 3.

30. Charlie Brennan, "Life, Death of Columbine Victim Inspire One-Act Play," *Denver Rocky Mountain News,* November 2, 1999: 22A.

31. Gretchen Murray, "'Crossroads at Columbine' Explore Teen's Faith," *Chicago Daily Herald,* March 18, 2000: F3. See also the web site of Northland Baptist Bible College, "Itineraries," undated, <http://www.nbbc.edu/College/ministries/itineraries_page.htm> (May 31, 2000).

32. Dr. Gerry Carlson <Gcarlson@pafc.com>. "Crossroads at Columbine," private e-mail message to author, May 4, 2000.

33. See the Positive Action for Christ web site, "About Us: History," undated, <http://www.pafc.org/pages/aboutus.html> (May 11, 2000).

34. Brad Bernall and Misty Bernall, "Bernall Family Endorsement," undated, <http://YesIBelieve.com/yes_endorsement.html> (March 26,

2000); "YIB! Clubs," undated, <http://YesIBelieve.com/yes_bible_clubs.html> (March 26, 2000).

See also Jody Veenker, "Retailers Marketing Martyrdom to Teens," *Christianity Today,* December 6, 1999: 22.

35. Various Artists, *Whatever It Takes—The "She Said Yes" Music Project* (Nashville, TN: New Haven Records/Franklin, TN: Provident Music Distribution, 2000), compact disc.

36. Michael W. Smith and Wes King, "This Is Your Time," *This Is Your Time* (Nashville, TN: Reunion Records, 1999), compact disc.

37. Michael W. Smith and Gary Thomas, *This Is Your Time: Make Every Moment Count* (Nashville, TN: Thomas Nelson Publishers, 2000), 24–27.

38. "Michael W. Smith's 'This Is Your Time' Makes Christian Music History," Reunion Records press release, December 1, 1999, <http://www.reunionrecords.com/news/mws_makes_history_120199.html> (June 19, 2000).

39. Michael W. Smith, *This Is Your Time,* prod. and dir. Ben Pearson and Brandon Dickerson, 3 min., Pearson-Taylor Productions, 1999, videocassette. This music video opens with a home video clip of Cassie expressing her wish "just to live for Christ." It ends with a title card bearing the words, "In Memory of Cassie Bernall."

The Dove Awards ceremony, by coincidence, was held on April 20, 2000, the first anniversary of the Columbine shooting. "Dove Awards: Winners and Nominees," April 22, 2000, <http://www.doveawards.com/categories> (April 23, 2000).

40. Smith and Thomas, *This Is Your Time,* 182.

41. Michael W. Smith, afterword to *She Said Yes: The Unlikely Martyrdom of Cassie Bernall* (Nashville, TN: Word Publishing, 2000), 160–163. Word Publishing is a division of Thomas Nelson, Inc., the publisher of Smith's book, *This Is Your Time.*

42. Jill Battles, "Yes, it Is about What She Said," customer review of *She Said Yes* by Misty Bernall, January 24, 2000 <http://www.amazon.com/exec/obidos/ASIN/0874869870/qid=961527016/sr=1–1/002–1047222–1490460> (January 30, 2000).

43. The Bruderhof are a twentieth-century offshoot of the Hutterite branch of Anabaptism, or the most radical wing of the sixteenth-century Protestant Reformation. See Benjamin Zablocki, *The Joyful Community* (Chicago: University of Chicago Press, 1980). See also <http://www.bruderhof.org>.

44. James Dotson, "New NAMB Projects to Feature Mary Lou Retton, Cassie Bernall," Baptist Press, February 10, 2000.

45. Bernall, *She Said Yes,* 115.

46. Brad Bernall and Misty Bernall, "Bernall Family Endorsement," undated, <http://YesIBelieve.com/yes_endorsement.html> (March 26, 2000).

47. Franklin Graham, Remarks at the Columbine Memorial Service, Littleton, Colorado, April 25, 1999.

48. Quoted in David Van Biema, "A Surge of Teen Spirit," *Time,* May 31, 1999: 58–59.

49. Quoted in Greg Burt, "Healing in Littleton," *Focus on the Family: Citizen,* June 1999: 16.

50. Thomas Winters, "About Cassie," undated, <http://homepages.go. com/~thomaswinters/cassie.html> (January 30, 2000).

51. "She Said Yes: A Story of Hope From Columbine High," booklet (Wheaton, IL: Good News Publishers, 1999). At the end of the tract, the new convert was urged to get more information on the Christian faith by, among other means, visiting <http://YesIBelieve. com>.

    On her personal web site, Linda Evans Sheppard claimed that she cowrote this tract with Bill Fay and Cassie's mother, Misty Bernall. See "Cassie's Story," undated, <http://www.sheppro.com/ cassie.htm> (May 30, 2000).

52. Jonathan Edwards, "Some Thoughts Concerning the Revival," in *The Great Awakening,* ed. C.C. Goen, vol. 4 of *The Works of Jonathan Edwards,* ed. John E. Smith (New Haven, CT: Yale University Press, 1972), 504.

53. Daniel G. Reid, *Dictionary of Christianity in America* (Downers Grove, IL: Intervarsity Press, 1990), s.v. "Youth Ministry/Minister," by F. W. Butin and "Jesus Movement," by R. Enroth; Bruce Shelley, "The Rise of Evangelical Youth Movements," *Fides et Historia* 18 (January 1986): 47–63; Joel A. Carpenter, *Revive Us Again: The Reawakening of American Fundamentalism* (New York: Oxford University Press, 1997), 161–176; Wendy Murray Zoba, *Generation 2K* (Downers Grove, IL: Intervarsity Press, 1999).

54. Quoted in Sara Rimer, "Columbine Students Seek Answers in Their Faith," *New York Times,* June 6, 1999: Sect 1, 26.

55. "1999 Year End Report," *The Pew Research Center For The People & The Press,* undated, <http://www.people-press.org/yearendrpt.htm> (March 21, 2000).

56. *ABC News/Washington Post* Poll, April 22–25, 1999. This was a survey of 500 high school teenagers and 522 parents of high school teenagers nationwide. "Education," April 20, 2000, <http://www.pollingreport. com/educatio.html> (June 1, 2000).

    It is worth noting, however, that 40 percent of the teenagers believed a Columbine-like incident at their school to be very or somewhat likely. But 48 percent of parents thought such an incident to be very or somewhat likely.

57. Quoted in Dave Curtin, "Columbine A Big Topic for College Applicants," *Denver Post,* November 5, 2000: B-01. See also Connie

Langland, "Columbine Is the Running Theme of College Admissions Essays," Knight Ridder/Tribune News Service, April 12, 2001.

58. J. Bottum, "Awakening at Littleton," *First Things,* August 1999: 28. Emphasis in original.

59. Message posted by marrin, "A Girl That Changed My Life," April 27, 1999, <http://christianteens.about.com/teens/christianteens/library/weekly/aa043099.htm> (May 30, 2000).

60. Quoted in Sara Rimer, "Columbine Students Seek Answers in Their Faith," *New York Times,* June 6, 1999: Sect. 1, 26.

61. Quoted in Deborah Sharp, "17-Year-Old's Last Words Inspire Other Christians," *USA Today,* June 1, 1999: 3A.

62. Hailey, untitled, January 17, 2000, <http://home.columbus.rr.com/drq/cassie/comment.html> (June 21, 2000).

63. Quoted in David Van Biema, "A Surge of Teen Spirit," *Time,* May 31, 1999: 58–59.

64. Voice of the Martyrs and dc Talk, *Jesus Freaks: Giving It All For Jesus* (Tulsa, OK: Albury Publishing, 1999), 17. Originally published in July 1999, *Jesus Freaks* had sold more than 500,000 copies in less than two years. Lauren F. Winner, "Nurturing Today's Teen Spirit," *Publishers Weekly,* March 12, 2001: 30.

65. Bernall, *She Said Yes,* 15, 96, 102–103.

66. Bernall, *She Said Yes,* 104.

67. Bernall, *She Said Yes,* 43.

68. Bernall, *She Said Yes,* 48.

69. Bernall, *She Said Yes,* 64.

70. Brad Bernall and Misty Bernall, "Modern Day Martyr," interview by Terry Meeuwsen, *The 700 Club,* Christian Broadcasting Network, September 17, 1999. Transcript available <http://www.the 700club.org/living/christianwalk/interviews/mistybernall.asp> (April 28, 2000).

71. Bernall, *She Said Yes,* 82–83.

72. Bernall, *She Said Yes,* 83.

73. Bernall, *She Said Yes,* 89.

74. Bernall, *She Said Yes,* 108.

75. Bernall, *She Said Yes,* 118.

76. Jeff Diedrich, *She Said Yes: A Bible Study* (Rocky Mount, NC: Positive Action For Christ, 1999), 38.

77. Colleen McDannell, *Material Christianity: Religion and Popular Culture in America* (New Haven, CT: Yale University Press, 1995), 272, 267–268.

78. Bernall, *She Said Yes,* 119.

79. Quoted in Bernall, *She Said Yes,* 119.

80. Quoted in Bernall, *She Said Yes,* 120.

81. Smith, *This Is Your Time,* 71. Emphasis in original.

82. Smith, *This Is Your Time,* 76, 155.

83. Bernall, *She Said Yes,* 31.
84. Brad Bernall and Misty Bernall, "Tough Love Saved Cassie," interview by Wendy Murray Zoba, *Christianity Today,* October 4, 1999: 42.
85. Bernall, *She Said Yes,* 74.
86. Bernall, *She Said Yes,* 78–79.
87. Quoted in Carla Crowder, "In Memory of Cassie Bernall," *Denver Rocky Mountain News,* April 27, 1999: 21A. See also Dave Cullen, "I Smell the Presence of Satan," *Salon.com,* May 15, 1999, <http://www.salon.com/news/feature/1999/05/15/evangelicals/index.html> (January 30, 2000).

    For a discussion of erotic elements in Jewish and Christian martyrological narratives see Daniel Boyarin, *Dying for God: Martyrdom and the Making of Christianity and Judaism* (Stanford, CA: Stanford University Press, 1999), 96, 110–111.
88. Bernall, *She Said Yes,* 122.
89. Bernall, *She Said Yes,* 122.
90. Quoted in Bernall, *She Said Yes,* 107. See also Janet Bingham, "Victim an 'Unlikely Martyr': Cassie Bernall's Faith an Example to All, Church Says " *Denver Post,* June 7, 1999: B1. Plough, the publisher of *She Said Yes,* is an enterprise of the Bruderhof community.
91. This poem, which was not used in *She Said Yes,* appeared initially in Eileen McNamara, "A Martyr Amid the Madness," *Boston Globe,* April 24, 1999: A1.
92. "Cassie Bernall," undated, <http://YesIBelieve.com/yes_about-cassie.html> (March 26, 2000). Emphasis in the original.
93. See, for instance, Thomas Winters "About Cassie," undated, <http://homepages.go.com/~thomaswinters/cassie.html> (June 19, 2000); "Cassie's Call," undated, <http://www.distributionconcepts.com/cassieb.htm> (June 19, 2000); Dmarie, "Cassie . . . Woman of God," undated, <http://www.angelfire.com/tx/pottslittle/cassie.html> (June 19, 2000).

    Ron Luce, *Columbine Courage: Rock-Solid Faith* (Nashville, TN: J. Countryman, 2000), 68–69.

    "She Said Yes: A Story of Hope From Columbine High," booklet (Wheaton, IL: Good News Publishers, 1999).
94. The Kry, "Cassie's Song," *Let Me Say* (Franklin, TN: Malaco Records, 2000), compact disc.
95. Bernall and Bernall, "Tough Love Saved Cassie," 43.
96. Brad Bernall and Misty Bernall, "Bernall Family Endorsement," undated, <http://YesIBelieve.com/yes_endorsement.html> (March 26, 2000).
97. Quoted in Mark A. Noll, *A History of Christianity in the United States and Canada* (Grand Rapids, MI: William B. Eerdman's Publishing Company, 1992), 290.

98. Quoted in Janet Bingham, "Mourning the Slain: 'Cassie Died a Mar-
     tyr's Death,'" *Denver Post,* April 27, 1999: A4.
99. Active Parenting Publishers, "Information on *She Said Yes: The Video
     Documentary* with *Discussion Guide for Faith Communities,*" un-
     dated, <http://www.activeparenting.com/ssy%20faith.htm> (April 15,
     2000).
     The 44-page *Discussion Guide* does not, however, feature the
     distinctive "Cassie in the cross hairs" cover art. Instead a photo of
     Cassie's smiling face is juxtaposed against a photo of what the viewer
     is meant to take as her gravesite. A simple wooden cross inscribed
     with "Cassie" is planted in an expanse of grass with trees and hills in
     the background. Russell G. Shinpoch, Michael H. Popkin, and Lind-
     sey Lewis, *She Said Yes: Discussion Guide for Faith Communities*
     (Marietta, GA: Active Parenting Publishers, 2000).
100. Bernall, *She Said Yes,* 71.
101. Bernall, *She Said Yes,* 131–132.
102. James C. Dobson, *Dare to Discipline* (Wheaton, IL: Tyndale House
     Publishers, 1970). This influential book has gone through multiple
     editions and remains in print. Dobson is the head of the Colorado
     Springs, Colorado-based Focus on the Family, one of the largest
     media ministries in the American evangelical community. For more
     information see <http://www.fotf.org>. See also Gustav Niebuhr,
     "Advice for Parents, and for Politicians," *New York Times,* May 30,
     1995: A12.
103. Bernall, *She Said Yes,* 139.
104. Bernall, *She Said Yes,* 140.

CHAPTER 3

1. C. Allen Haney, Christina Leimer, and Juliann Lowery, "Spontaneous
    Memorialization: Violent Death and Emerging Mourning Ritual,"
    Omega—The Journal of Death and Dying (September 1997) 35 no. 2:
    159–171.
2. Steve Caulk, "Slain Student's Car Becomes a Shrine," *Denver Rocky
    Mountain News,* April 22, 1999: 7AA; Michael Daly, "'She Had All
    That, And They Took It,'" *Daily News* (New York), April 23, 1999: 2;
    Sean Kelly, "Columbine—The Victims: John Tomlin," *Denver Post,*
    April 23, 1999: A-06; Ann Schrader, "11:21 A.M. Moment's Silence
    Speaks Volumes," *Denver Post,* April 28, 1999: A-08; Gary Massaro,
    "Mourner Finds Role at Shrine," *Denver Rocky Mountain News,*
    April 29, 1999: 36A.
3. Quoted in Wayne Tompkins, "Father Bears Message," *The Courier-
    Journal* (Louisville, KY) November 15, 1999: 1B. Bruce Porter, the
    Littleton-area minister who delivered a sermon at the funeral, and

who has started his own Columbine-related ministry, makes a some-what more modest claim. "It was later reported to us," wrote Porter in his book, *The Martyrs' Torch: The Message of the Columbine Massacre,* "that this particular event had possibly one of the largest viewing audiences ever recorded in their [CNN's] history!" Bruce Porter, *The Martyrs' Torch* (Shippensburg, PA: Destiny Image Publishers Inc., 1999), 38.

4. Reverend Barry Palser, Remarks at Funeral Service for Rachel Scott, *CNN Live Event,* Cable News Network, April 24, 1999.

5. Funeral Service for Rachel Scott, *CNN Live Event,* Cable News Network, April 24, 1999. For the impression created by the funeral service, see David Foster, "Before a Community and a Nation, A Girl's Friends Say Goodbye," Associated Press, April 24, 1999; Lisa Levitt Rickman, "In Memory of Rachel Scott: 17-Year-Old Girl 'Shined for God at all Times,'" *Denver Rocky Mountain News,* April 25, 1999: 3AA; Laura Berman, "Classmates Say Goodbye to Fun-Loving, True Friend," *Detroit News,* April 25, 1999: A5; J. Sebastian Sinisi and Julia C. Martinez, "Pastor: 'We Have Failed,'" *Denver Post,* April 25, 1999: AA-03.

6. Roger Rosenblatt, "A Note for Rachel Scott," *Time,* May 10, 1999: 102.

7. Reverend Bruce Porter, Remarks at Funeral Service for Rachel Scott, *CNN Live Event,* Cable News Network, April 24, 1999.

8. Porter, *Martyrs' Torch,* 35–40.

9. The symbolism of the torch is so important that for the first anniversary of the shooting, Porter had a gold-plated torch made and engraved with the names of the 13 victims. It is passed from hand to hand among attendees at the conclusion of Torchgrab and other events where Porter speaks. See "Teens Stand Up for the Gospel," *Religion Today,* April 14, 2000, <http://www.religiontoday.com/Archive/FeatureStory/view.cgi?file=20000414.s1.html> (December 30, 2000); Bruce Porter, "Littleton Update," February 6, 2000; Bruce Porter, "Littleton Update," September 4, 2000. Once such event was at TheCallDC, held on the Washington, D.C., Mall on September 2, 2000. Porter introduced Darrell Scott, and the torch was passed among attendees who were near the stage during Scott's remarks. I also observed this at a Torchgrab Youth rally held in Myerstown, Pennsylvania, June 22–23, 2001.

10. "What's the Vision?" undated, <http://www.torchgrab.org/Vision.htm> (September 26, 2000). Emphasis in original.

11. Porter, *Martyrs' Torch,* 83; Karen Santos, "Weekend Torchgrab Rally Begins," *Denver Post,* August 7, 1999: A-14; Greg Burt, "Teens Challenged to Take Torch From Martyrs," *Charisma,* November 1999: 19–22.

12. In a July 20, 2001, e-mail message, Porter listed 12 Torchgrab rallies held in the previous 2 years. He provided place names, but not dates or attendance figures. In regard to his other speaking engagements, he reported that "There have been scores of meetings in various forms, including student assemblies, community gatherings, rallies, Christian concerts, churches, Bible studies, etc." For obvious reasons he could not supply much specific information about such a variety of events. Bruce Porter, e-mail to author, July 20, 2001.

Porter has continued conducting Torchgrab rallies and speaking about Columbine, including a series of events during November and December 2001 in Wales and other sites in the United Kingdom. Bruce Porter, "Wales Report From Torchgrab Youth," December 3, 2001, distribution list.

In late September 2001, Porter also traveled to New York to serve as a chaplain for firefighters and rescue workers working in the wreckage at "Ground Zero," the site of the September 11 terrorist attack on the World Trade Center. Kevin Dale, "Colo. Pastor Offers Comfort to Firefighters," *Denver Post,* September 23, 2001: A-22; Bruce Porter, "New York Update," September 29, 2001, distribution list.

13. Porter, *Martyrs' Torch,* xxiii.

14. Erin, youth minister, quoted in Ron Luce, *Columbine Courage: Rock-Solid Faith* (Nashville, TN: Thomas Nelson, 2000), 32.

15. "Who Will Go In Her Place?" undated, <http://www.teenmania.org/s2kmissions/rachel.htm> (June 24, 2000).

16. "World Changer Videos," undated, <http://www.teenmania.org/GlobalExpeditions/movies.cfm> (October 8, 2000). In a customer review of *Rachel's Tears,* a book cowritten by Rachel's parents, a Canadian 16-year-old, who had just returned from a summer mission trip, reported, "Teen Mania is really 'taking up the torch,' as the book says, by telling young people about her life and her desire to go on a mission trip. SO many people decided to go this summer with Teen Mania because of the video clip they showed of her." A reader from Canada, *Amazon.com:* Customer Review of Beth Nimmo, Darrell Scott, and Steve Rabey, *Rachel's Tears: The Spiritual Journey of Columbine Martyr Rachel Scott* (Nashville, TN: Thomas Nelson Publishers, 2000), dated August 7, 2000, (January 7, 2001).

17. "USA, Rachel Scott: 'I am not going to hide the light . . . '" *The Voice of the Martyrs,* December 1999: 7. This organization was founded in 1967 by Richard Wurmbrand, a Romanian minister who spent 14 years in the communist prisons of his homeland. See Richard Wurmbrand, *Tortured for Christ* (Bartlesville, OK: Living Sacrifice Book Company, 1967).

18. See for example "Rachel Joy Scott... Remembered," undated, <http://www.geocities.com/CollegePark/Residence/7774/racheljoyscott.html> (June 27, 2000).

19. See "Remembering Rachel," undated, <http://www.lifechoicespresents.org/NEWSITE/rachel.htm> (September 30, 2000); "Living Words From a Murdered Teen-Ager," undated, <http://www.heinvites.org/story.php3/0117.html> (September 13, 2000).

20. "Remember Rachel Joy Scott," undated, <http://home.swbell.net/philmc/Rachel.html> (June 27, 2000).

21. See "Rachel Joy Scott," undated, <http://www.angelfire.com/hi2/Rachel/Rachel.html> (September 22, 2000).

22. "Columbine: Questions for the Heart," undated, <http://www.cardinalmanagement.bizland.com/HeartQuestions.html> (September 18, 2000). Emphasis in original. This site also sells a benefit CD with a song by Susan Renee entitled "Columbine." All proceeds from these CD sales go to Darrell Scott's organization, The Columbine Redemption. "Columbine Benefit CD," undated, <http://www.cardinalmanagement.bizland.com/ColumbineCD.html> (September 18, 2000).

23. Nimmo and Scott, *Rachel's Tears*, 13.

24. Information regarding their marriage, divorce, its aftermath, and effects are scattered throughout *Rachel's Tears*. Most of this is in the chapter "Finding Hope in a Broken World," 53–66. Biographical information on Darrell Scott is also found in numerous newspaper and magazine articles about his speaking activities. See for instance, Kevin Simpson, "Daughter's Death Brings Life 'Into Focus,'" *Denver Post*, October 20, 1999: A-01; S. C. Gwynne, "An Act of God?" *Time*, December 20, 1999: 58–59.

25. Nimmo and Scott, *Rachel's Tears*, 56.

26. Nimmo and Scott, *Rachel's Tears*, 36.

27. Nimmo and Scott, *Rachel's Tears*, 57.

28. Nimmo and Scott, *Rachel's Tears*, 32.

29. Nimmo and Scott, *Rachel's Tears*, 55.

30. See for example, interview with Rachel Scott's family by Kristine Vick, *The 700 Club*, Christian Broadcasting Network, April 23, 1999; Darrell Scott and Beth Nimmo, interview by Larry King, *Larry King Live*, Cable News Network, April 28, 1999; Darrell Scott, Beth Nimmo, and Larry Nimmo, interview by Katie Couric, *The Today Show*, National Broadcasting Co., Inc., April 28, 1999; "Memorial to Lives Lost in Littleton, Colorado," family members of Columbine victims, interviews by Oprah Winfrey, *Oprah: The Oprah Winfrey Show*, Harpo Productions, Inc., April 30, 1999; Cynthia Bowers, "Rachel," *48 Hours*, Columbia Broadcasting System, June 10, 1999; Sara James, "The Long Journey Back," *Dateline NBC*, National Broadcasting Co., Inc., July 21, 2000.

31. See Kevin Simpson, "Deaths Not in Vain, Speakers Conclude Victims, Kin Offer up Inspiration at Service," *Denver Post*, April 21, 2000: A-11.

32. Other speakers represented by the Ambassador Agency include Paul Harvey, Gary Bauer, Dean Jones, Tony Campolo, and Columbine survivor Heidi Johnson. See <http://www.ambassadoragency.com>.

33. Darrell Scott and Steve Rabey, *Chain Reaction: A Call to Compassionate Revolution* (Nashville, TN: Thomas Nelson Publishers, 2001), 4.

34. Beth Nimmo and Debra K. Klingsporn, *The Journals of Rachel Scott: A Journey of Faith at Columbine High* (Nashville, TN: Thomas Nelson Publishers, 2001), xi.

35. Scott and Rabey, *Chain Reaction,* 125–126; Nimmo and Klingsporn, *Journals of Rachel Scott,* 119; Nimmo and Scott, *Rachel's Tears,* 91–92.

36. These tensions may center on their fourth child, Craig Scott, who was in the Columbine library during the shooting and remains perhaps the best-known Columbine survivor. He narrowly escaped death when two other students hiding beneath the same table, on either side of him, were killed. As a July 2000 episode of NBC's *Dateline* demonstrated, Craig Scott has been traumatized deeply by his experience. He is shown joining Darrell Scott's speaking tour during the summer of 1999. The extensive travel, as well as repeatedly speaking about the shooting to crowds as large as 14,000, *Dateline* tells us, "seems to exhaust him." *Dateline* shows us Beth Nimmo saying with evident disapproval, "My son needs a rest. I don't have any intention of losing two children in this tragedy." *Dateline,* however, provides us with no response from Darrell Scott to the notion that he has endangered his son. "The Long Journey Back," NBC's *Dateline,* July 21, 2000. (One must wonder whether Craig Scott's difficulties have been heightened by the media attention such as *Dateline*'s almost voyeuristic examination of his emotional journey. See Caryn James, "Grist for TV: Family Grief Since Killings at Columbine," *New York Times,* July 20, 2000: E1.) Until Craig Scott himself elects to tell us more, we can only suppose that part of his struggle in the aftermath of Columbine may be one of conflicting loyalties to his father and to his mother, who perhaps have had different visions of how to help their son deal with his pain.

37. Porter, *Martyrs' Torch,* 88; Beth Nimmo, foreword, *Martyrs' Torch,* xv-xvi.

38. See <http://www.racheljoyscott.com>, <http://www.rachelscott.com>, and <http://www.columbineredemption.com>. Darrell Scott's site, *www.rachelscott.com,* is exclusively linked to the Columbine Redemption site, which does provide links to other Columbine-related organizations.

39. See Candice Hannigan, "Mom of Teen Victim to Be Guest Speaker," *Atlanta Journal and Constitution*, September 14, 2000: 8JG; Larry Hobbs, "Columbine Survivors Bring Spiritual Message," *Palm Beach Post*, April 21, 2001: 1B; Dan Kelly, "At Area Youth Rally, A Story About Courage at Columbine," *Eagle & Times* (Reading, PA), June 23, 2001: A1.

    Despite his Columbine-related speaking engagements and other activities, Porter remained the pastor of Celebration Church. In a January 25, 2002 e-mail message, however, Porter announced his intention to "transition as soon as possible off of church salary" and solicited financial support so he could devote more of his attention to Torchgrab. Bruce and Claudia Porter, "Compelled to Obey," January 25, 2002, distribution list.

40. The Columbine Redemption, 1999 IRS Form 990-EZ, Statement of Program Service Accomplishments.

41. "Mission Statement," undated, <http://www.thecolumbineredemption. com/mission.html> (March 31, 2000). "Columbine: May We Never Forget," pamphlet, Littleton, Colorado, 2000. The goals of the organization are listed in a section of the pamphlet entitled "About The Columbine Redemption."

42. "Rachel's Journal," undated, <http://www.thecolumbineredemption. com/RJ%20Magazine.htm> (June 24, 2000).

43. Eric Baker, "Where Do We Go From Here?" *Rachel's Journal*, May/June 2000: 13.

44. "Mission Statement," undated, <http://www.thecolumbineredemption. com/mission.html> (November 12, 2000).

45. Darrell Scott, interview by Ann Curry, *Today*, National Broadcasting Co., Inc., April 19, 2001; Darrell Scott, interview by Sean Hannity and Alan Colmes, *Hannity & Colmes*, Fox Network News, April 20, 2001.

46. "Mission Statement," undated, <http://www.thecolumbineredemption.com/mission.html> (March 31, 2000). Another and later version of this goal read, "To equip a team of people who are dedicated to carrying a message of change and triumph to cities, schools, universities, and churches everywhere." "Mission Statement," undated, <http://www.thecolumbineredemption.com/mission.html> (November 12, 2000).

47. For information on Dana Scott's presentations, see <http://www.ambassadoragency.com>.

48. Darrell Scott, "Prepared Testimony of Darrell Scott Father of Two Victims of Columbine High School Shootings Littleton, CO Before the House Judiciary Subcommittee on Crime," *Federal News Service*, May 27, 1999.

49. *Untold Stories of Columbine*, Darrell Scott, 80 min., Gateway Films, 2000, videocassette.

50. Scott made this claim at a speech on January 13, 2001, at "Excel 2001," an event sponsored by Youth For Christ and held at the Saratoga Springs (NY) City Center.

51. *Untold Stories of Columbine,* Scott. The tape shows approximately 45 minutes of Scott's appearance at Two Rivers Baptist Church in Nashville, Tennessee, on Sunday, September 19, 1999. Scott's talk is followed by approximately 30 minutes of the television coverage of his daughter's funeral service on April 24, 1999.

52. There are any number of brief journalistic accounts of Darrell Scott's public appearances. Some of the more substantial accounts include: Kevin Simpson, "Daughter's Death Brings Life 'Into Focus': Rachel Scott's Dad Delivers Message of Faith Across the U.S.," *Denver Post,* October 20, 1999: A1; S. C. Gwynne, "An Act of God?" *Time,* December 20, 1999: 58–59; Don Beideman. "Columbine Victim's Father On A Mission Of Healing," *Houston Chronicle,* January 29, 2000: 1; Julia Duin, "3,100 Hear Story of Columbine," *Washington Times,* April 2, 2000: C1; Matt Labash, "Among the Crusaders," *Weekly Standard,* April 17, 2000: 26–29. The information about Darrell Scott's fee per appearance can be found in Labash, "Among the Crusaders," 28.

    In addition to these journalistic accounts, I have personally observed a number of Darrell Scott's speaking engagements in Pensacola, Florida (June 12, 2000), Washington, D.C. (September 2, 2000), Quakertown, Pennsylvania (October 6, 2000), Souderton, Pennsylvania (October 7, 2000), Saratoga Springs, New York (January 13, 2001), and Camp Hill, Pennsylvania (April 6, 2001). My generalizations about the format and content of his speaking engagements are based on all these sources, especially my own observations.

53. I observed this at various speaking engagements by Darrell Scott in the fall of 2000 and the spring of 2001. The Garth Brooks song is "The River," from his 1991 album *Ropin' the Wind* (Capitol Records).

54. "The Crosses of the Columbine Victims," *Rachel's Journal,* April 2000: 17. Zanis and his "Columbine Crosses" are a remarkable phenomenon in their own right. See Linell Smith, "Coming to Terms with Columbine," *Baltimore Sun,* November 7, 1999: 11F.

55. Labash observed conflict over finances and over Darrell Scott's attempts to contractually secure the crosses as permanent parts of his own ministry. "I feel," wrote Labash, "as if I've stumbled onto the evangelical equivalent of Martin and Lewis's sunset years, as the act was about to unravel." See Labash, 28–29.

    Objections by the families of some Columbine victims to Zanis's practice of erecting two additional crosses for the killers may have also led Darrell Scott to disassociate himself from Zanis. See Wendy Murray Zoba, *Day of Reckoning: Columbine and the Search for America's Soul* (Grand Rapids, MI: Brazos Press, 2000), 42–55.

56. Nimmo and Scott, *Rachel's Tears,* xviii.
57. Porter, *Martyrs' Torch,* 16. Emphasis in original.
58. Bruce Porter, "Heart to Heart," *CellChurch Magazine,* Vol. 8, no. 3 (1999), <http://www.touchusa.org/cellchurch/archives/volume8/issue3.htm> (August 14, 2001).
59. Quoted in Virginia Culver, "Tone of Service Angers Some," *Denver Post,* April 29, 1999: A-08. See also Dave Cullen, "I Smell the Presence of Satan!" *Salon.com,* May 15, 1999 <http://www.salon.com/news/feature/1999/05/15/evangelicals> (May 21, 2001); Andrew Walsh, "Preaching the Word in Littleton," *Religion in the News,* Summer 1999: 4–6.
60. Darrell Scott, Remarks at Youth Alive! event, Marcus Pointe Baptist Church, Pensacola, Florida, June 12, 2000.
61. Beth Nimmo, "Foreword," *Martyrs' Torch,* xv-xvi.
62. The "Are you ready?" argument for accepting salvation now is used when Cassie and Rachel are cited together, as Billy Graham did in the summer of 1999.
63. Quoted in Duin, "3,100 Hear Story of Columbine," C1.
64. Darrell Scott, Testimony Before the Subcommittee on Crime, House Judiciary Committee, United States House of Representatives, Washington, D.C., May 27, 1999.
65. Rachel Scott, "My Code of Ethics," *Rachel's Journal,* January 2000: 22.
66. Darrell Scott, Remarks at Youth Alive! event, Marcus Pointe Baptist Church, Pensacola, Florida, June 12, 2000.
67. Scott and Rabey, *Chain Reaction,* 49–50. A comparison between Rachel's diaries and those of Anne Frank also is made in Nimmo and Klingsporn, *The Journals of Rachel Scott,* 31.
68. Nimmo and Scott, *Rachel's Tears,* xx.
69. Quoted in Nimmo and Scott, *Rachel's Tears,* 30.
70. This image is reproduced in Nimmo and Scott, *Rachel's Tears,* 165.
71. Scott, *Untold Stories of Columbine,* videocassette. In *Chain Reaction,* Darrell Scott is more indefinite. "Some people have even suggested to me that it was her outreach to Eric and Dylan that killed her. I don't know." Scott and Rabey, *Chain Reaction,* 16.
72. Nimmo and Scott, *Rachel's Tears,* 114.
73. Nimmo and Scott, *Rachel's Tears,* 31.
74. Nimmo and Scott, *Rachel's Tears,* 75. See also Scott and Rabey, *Chain Reaction,* 168–170; Nimmo and Klingsporn, *The Journals of Rachel Scott,* 100–103.
75. Nimmo and Scott, *Rachel's Tears,* 40.
76. Nimmo and Klingsporn, *The Journals of Rachel Scott,* 9–19, 23–35.
77. Nimmo and Scott, *Rachel's Tears,* 45.
78. Nimmo and Scott, *Rachel's Tears,* 44. See also Nimmo and Klingsporn, *The Journals of Rachel Scott,* 61–68.

79. Nimmo and Scott, *Rachel's Tears,* 39.
80. Nimmo and Scott, *Rachel's Tears,* 29.
81. Nimmo and Scott, *Rachel's Tears,* 27. See also Nimmo and Klingsporn, *The Journals of Rachel Scott,* 3–5.
82. Nimmo and Scott, *Rachel's Tears,* 27.
83. Quoted in Misty Bernall, *She Said Yes: The Unlikely Martyrdom of Cassie Bernall* (Farmington, PA: Plough Publishing House, 1999), 83.
84. Amberly Jackson, "Letters to the Editor," *Rachel's Journal,* January 2000: 5.
85. Lori Kauffman, "Rachel's Creed: An Example to Live By," *Rachel's Journal,* February/March 2000: 31, 33.
86. Nimmo and Scott, *Rachel's Tears,* 103.
87. Quoted in Nimmo and Scott, *Rachel's Tears,* 117. Emphasis in original.
88. Scott and Rabey, *Chain Reaction,* 186.
89. Nimmo and Scott, *Rachel's Tears,* 40.
90. Nimmo and Scott, *Rachel's Tears,* 45–46. Scott assures readers that his other children would agree with this assessment.
91. Nimmo and Scott, *Rachel's Tears,* 146.
92. Nimmo and Scott, *Rachel's Tears,* 146.
93. Nimmo and Scott, *Rachel's Tears,* 139.
94. Nimmo and Scott, *Rachel's Tears,* 143.
95. Nimmo and Scott, *Rachel's Tears,* 148.
96. Nimmo and Scott, *Rachel's Tears,* 31.
97. Nimmo and Scott, *Rachel's Tears,* xxi.
98. Quoted in Gywnne, "An Act of God?" 58.
99. Scott, *Untold Stories of Columbine,* videocassette.
100. Nimmo and Scott, *Rachel's Tears,* 51.
101. Bernall, *She Said Yes,* 31.
102. In the videotape *Untold Stories of Columbine,* her father says that Rachel made these kind of statements to her sisters, Bethanee Scott and Dana Scott, as well as a first cousin, Jeff Scott. In *Rachel's Tears,* Lori Johnson, her youth pastor, states: "On some of these rides [to church], she talked to me about the sense of foreboding she seemed to be getting from God or somewhere. She had a growing premonition that she was dying or would not be alive for very long," 130.
103. Nimmo and Scott, *Rachel's Tears,* 63.
104. Nimmo and Klingsporn, *The Journals of Rachel Scott,* 88. A picture of Rachel in the wedding gown appears on her father's web site, *www.rachelscott.com.* See "Photos: Rachel as Rachel," Undated <http://www.rachelscott.com/last%20years.htm> (January 11, 2001).
105. Scott, *Untold Stories of Columbine,* videocassette.
106. Nimmo and Scott, *Rachel's Tears,* 45.
107. Nimmo and Scott, *Rachel's Tears,* 77.
108. Nimmo and Scott, *Rachel's Tears,* 23.

109. Nimmo and Scott, *Rachel's Tears,* 23.
110. Bernall, *She Said Yes,* 122.
111. Nimmo and Scott, *Rachel's Tears,* 96. It is interesting that this entry about "walking her talk" and being rejected by old friends comes only five days after the entry in which she promises not to go drinking with her friends. See Nimmo and Scott, *Rachel's Tears,* 49–50.
112. Nimmo and Scott, *Rachel's Tears,* 97.
113. Scott, *Untold Stories of Columbine,* videocassette.
114. Scott, *Untold Stories of Columbine,* videocassette.
115. Nimmo and Scott, *Rachel's Tears,* 172.
116. Nimmo and Scott, *Rachel's Tears,* 174.
117. Nimmo and Scott, *Rachel's Tears,* 175.
118. Nimmo and Scott, *Rachel's Tears,* 179.
119. Quoted in Kevin Simpson, "Victim's Diaries Prophetic," *Denver Post,* October 20, 1999: A-10.
120. Nimmo and Scott, *Rachel's Tears,* 179.
121. Scott, *Untold Stories of Columbine,* videocassette.

CHAPTER 4

1. A series of four articles published in April 2000 by the *New York Times* examined 100 "rampage killings" from 1949 to 1999. In particular, there were a series of school shootings in 1997–1998 that brought the phenomenon to the attention of the public as never before. The first of these articles provides a statistical overview. Ford Fessenden, "They Threaten, Seethe and Unhinge, Then Kill in Quantity," *New York Times,* April 9, 2000: Sect. 1, 1.
2. A useful collection of commentary and analysis on the school shootings of the late 1990s is Denise M. Bonilla, ed., *School Violence,* The Reference Shelf, Vol. 72, no. 1 (New York: H.W. Wilson Company, 2000).
3. Elliot Aronson, *Nobody Left to Hate: Teaching Compassion After Columbine* (New York: W.H. Freeman and Company, 2000), 10.
4. Aronson, *Nobody Left to Hate,* 45–67.
5. Aronson, *Nobody Left to Hate,* 13.
6. Aronson, *Nobody Left to Hate,* 16.
7. Quoted in Nancy Gibbs and Timothy Roche, "The Columbine Tapes," *Time,* December 20, 1999: 44. See Frank Kogan, "School's Been Blown to Pieces," *Village Voice,* April 28–May 4, 1999: 40–44; Jerry Adler, "The Truth About High School," *Newsweek,* May 10, 1999: 56.
8. Quoted in Gibbs and Roche, "The Columbine Tapes," 50–51.
9. Peter Wilkinson and Matt Hendrickson, "Humiliation and Revenge: The Story of Reb and VoDkA," *Rolling Stone,* June 18, 1999: 141.
10. See, for instance, Kogan, "School's Been Blown to Pieces," *Village Voice,* 40–44; Adler, "The Truth About High School," 56.

11. Quoted in Gibbs and Roche, "The Columbine Tapes," 44.

12. Centers for Disease Control, National Center for Injury Prevention and Control, "Study Finds School-Associated Deaths Rare, Fewer Events But More Deaths Per Event," press release, December 4, 2001, <http://www.cdc.gov/od/oc/media/pressrel/r011204.htm> (December 10, 2001). See M. Anderson, J. Kaufman, T. R. Simon, L. Barrios, L. Paulozzi, G. Ryan, R. Hammond, W. Modzeleski, T. Feucht, L. Potter, "School-Associated Violent Deaths in the United States, 1994–1999," *Journal of the American Medical Association,* December 5, 2001: 2695–2702.

13. Frank Newport, "Americans Say the Family Is the Starting Point for Preventing Another Columbine," Gallup News Service, April 20, 2001, <http://www.gallup.com/poll/releases/pr010420.asp> (July 24, 2001). It is worth noting that 92 percent of those surveyed felt home life and relationship to parents was an extremely or very important cause of school shooting.

14. Edward Gaughan, Jay D. Cerio, and Robert A. Myers, *Lethal Violence In Schools: A National Study* (Alfred, NY: Alfred University, 2001), 5, 34. Available online at <www.alfred.edu/teenviolence>.

15. T. Nansel, M. Overpeck, R. Pilla, W. Ruan, B. Simons-Morton, P. Scheidt, "Bullying Behaviors Among U.S. Youth: Prevalence and Association with Psychosocial Adjustment," *Journal of the American Medical Association,* April 25, 2001: 2094–2100. See also Erica Goode, "School Bullying Is Common, Mostly by Boys, Study Finds," *New York Times,* April 25, 2001: A17.

16. *Talking With Kids About Tough Issues: A National Survey of Parents and Kids,* Kaiser Family Foundation and Nickelodeon, March 8, 2001. Available at <http://www.talkingwithkids.org>.

17. Quoted in Jon Katz, "Voices From the Hellmouth," *Slashdot.org,* April 26, 1999, <http://slashdot.org/articles/99/04/25/1438249.shtml> (August 22, 2000). See also Amy Harmon, "Terror in Littleton: The Outcasts; Theme Song on the Internet: The Pain of Social Ostracism," *New York Times,* April 24, 1999: A14; Jane Dark, "Suffer the (White, Middle-Class) Children," *Village Voice,* May 26–June 1, 1999: 61–62.

18. Aronson, *Nobody Left to Hate,* 133.

19. Aronson, *Nobody Left to Hate,* 20.

20. Aronson, *Nobody Left to Hate,* 155.

21. Aronson, *Nobody Left to Hate,* 160.

22. "President Clinton Talks to Students About Conflict Resolution," T. C. Williams High School, Alexandria, Virginia, April 22, 1999. (The White House, Office of the Press Secretary.)

23. "Remarks by the First Lady to the Columbine High School Community," Dakota Ridge High School, Littleton, Colorado, May 20, 1999.

(The White House, Office of the Press Secretary.) President Clinton spoke at the same event and made much the same argument.

24. Bruce Shapiro, "The Guns of Littleton," *The Nation*, May 17, 1999: 4–5.
25. Aronson, *Nobody Left to Hate*, 9.
26. Aronson, *Nobody Left to Hate*, 177.
27. Aronson, *Nobody Left to Hate*, 159.
28. Quoted in Justin Torres, "Leaders Call for Prayer for Littleton," Conservative News Service, April 21, 1999.
29. Pat Buchanan, interview by Catherine Crier, *The Crier Report*, Fox News Network, April 27, 1999.
30. "No Norms," *Wall Street Journal*, April 22, 1999: A22.
31. Edmund Burke, "A Letter to a Member of the National Assembly," *The Works of Edmund Burke*, vol. 2. (London: George Bell and Sons, 1894), 555.
32. William Kristol, "Good and Evil in Littleton," *Weekly Standard*, May 10, 1999: 7. The statement from Harris is quoted in this article.
33. Charles Colson and Nancy Pearcey, "How Evil Became Cool," *Christianity Today*, August 9, 1999: 80.
34. Pat Robertson, Remarks on *The 700 Club*, Christian Broadcasting Network, April 21, 1999.
35. Versions of this poem appear on hundreds of sites on the web with diverse attributes of authorship. It is often attributed to either a "12-year-old girl in Boston" or "a teen in Bagdad, Arizona." See, for example, "The New School Prayer," The Columbine Angels web site, undated, <http://www.columbine-angels.com/Emails.htm> (October 30, 2001). See also, Anonymous, "The New School Prayer," *Rachel's Journal*, February/March 2000: 29.
36. Ken Ham, "The 'Missing Link' to School Violence," Answers in Genesis web site, April 29, 1999, <http://www.answersingenesis.org/docs/4051.asp> (April 28, 2001).
37. Ham's article does not mention this fact. Eric Harris's "Natural Selection" T-shirt is mentioned in the autopsy report prepared by the Jefferson County Coroner's Office in Golden, Colorado.

    During his public presentations, Darrell Scott plays a videotape that gives an overview of the basic events of the Columbine shooting. The narration on the tape mentions the "Natural Selection" T-shirt, but does not discuss its significance. I have observed this at several of his public presentations.
38. See Dave Cullen, "The Rumor That Won't Go Away," *Salon.com*, April 24, 1999, <http://www.salon.com/news/feature/1999/04/24/rumors> (August 15, 2001); Dave Cullen, "Gay Leaders Fear Littleton Backlash," *Salon.com*, April 27, 1999, <http://www.salon.com/news/feature/1999/04/27/gay> (August 15, 2001); C. Barillas, "Right

Makes Use of Gay Rumors in Colorado Tragedy," *The Data Lounge,* April 28, 1999, <http://www.datalounge.com/datalounge/news/record. html?record=4189> (July 8, 2001). Rumors about the sexual orientation of the Columbine killers have proven remarkably resilient within the gay community itself. See Anthony Chase, "Violent Reaction: What Do Teen Killers Have in Common?" *In These Times,* July 9, 2001: 16.

39. Bob Larson, *Extreme Evil: Kids Killing Kids* (Nashville, TN: Thomas Nelson Publishers, 1999), 8–12.
40. Larson, *Extreme Evil,* 101. Larson has a long record of concern with Satanism. See Bob Larson, *Satanism: The Seduction of America's Youth* (Nashville, TN: Thomas Nelson Publishers, 1989). See also <http://www.boblarson.org>.
41. See, for example, Howard Kurtz and Dan Balz, "Clinton Assails Spread of Hate Through Media," *Washington Post,* April 25, 1995: A1.
42. Newt Gingrich, Remarks on School Violence and Kosovo, Republican Women Leaders Forum, Washington, D.C., May 12, 1999.
43. Quoted by House Majority Whip Tom DeLay (R-TX) during the debate of H.R. 1501, the Consequences for Juvenile Offenders Act of 1999 (House of Representatives—June 16, 1999).
44. Rod Martin, "Littleton," *Vanguardmag.com,* April 24, 1999, <http://www.vanguardmag.com/thevanguard/042699.htm> (July 24, 2001).
45. Peggy Noonan, "The Culture of Death," *Wall Street Journal,* April 22, 1999: A22. See also R. Emmett Tyrrell, Jr., "Islands of Anarchy," *American Spectator,* June 1999: 14–15.
46. "Bauer Announces Candidacy," speech text, Bauer for President 2000 web site, April 21, 1999, <http://bauer2k.com/html/april21.html> (January 17, 2000).
47. Alan Keyes, "When the Righteous Don't Stand," WorldNetDaily Exclusive Commentary, April 23, 1999, <http://www.worldnetdaily.com/news/article.asp?ARTICLE_ID=18663> (July 24, 2001).
48. Quoted in "Christian Coalition: Put God Back in Schools," Associated Press, May 9, 1999.
49. See "Politics, Not Principle, Motives House Votes on Church-State Legislation, Charges Americans United," Americans United news release, June 17, 1999.
50. Hanna Rosin, "Winning by the Book: Columbine Helps Christian Activists Pass Long-Sought Amendments," *Washington Post,* June 21, 1999: A3.
51. Kevin Simpson, "Religion in the Schools: Nation Searches Its Soul on Whether Faith Has a Place in Its Classrooms," *Denver Post,* February 20, 2000: A1; see also Steve Benen, "The Ten Commandments Crusade: Decalogue Disputes Erupt Nationwide," *Church and State,* May

1, 1999: 9–12; Rob Boston, "The Ten Commandments: A Sequel," *Church and State,* July-August 2001: 9.

52. Charles C. Haynes, "Finding Common Ground: Different Faith Debate the Commandments," Gannett News Service, February 22, 2000.

53. The joint letter was published as a full-page ad in *USA Today* on April 7, 1998. The text was also posted on the Focus on the Family web site at <http://www.family.org/docstudy/newsletters/a0001644.html> (July 25, 2001).

54. Pat Robertson, "Press Release: Robertson's Statement Regarding Terrorist Attack on America," *PatRobertson.com,* September 14, 2001, <http://www.PatRobertson.com/partner/Article_Display_Page/0,PTID3826|CHID102165|CIID836236,00.html> (September 15, 2001).

55. William Kristol, *ABC This Week,* American Broadcasting Companies, Inc., April 25, 1999. Kristol's comments came during the "Roundtable" discussion portion of the program.

56. Cover, *Weekly Standard,* May 10, 1999.

57. Andrew Sullivan, "TRB from Washington: Afterlife," *New Republic,* November 22, 1999: 6. See also Beth Loffreda, *Losing Matt Shepard* (New York: Columbia University Press, 2000).

58. Remarks by Rep. Tom Tancredo (R-CO) introducing a concurrent resolution (H.Con.Res. 92), expressing the sense of Congress with respect to the tragic shooting at Columbine High School in Littleton, Colorado (House of Representatives, April 27, 1999).

59. J. Bottum, "Awakening at Littleton," *First Things: A Monthly Journal of Religion and Public Life,* August 1999: 28.

60. Vice President Al Gore, Remarks at the Columbine Memorial Service, April 25, 1999, in Littleton, Colorado.

61. Governor George W. Bush "The True Goal of Education," speech in Gorham, New Hampshire, November 2, 1999, <http://www.georgewbush.com/News/speeches/110299_education.html> (July 24, 2001).

62. Alan Keyes, "When the Righteous Don't Stand," WorldNetDaily Exclusive Commentary, April 23, 1999. <http://www.worldnetdaily.com/news/article.asp?ARTICLE_ID=18663> (July 24, 2001).

63. Bauer had already scheduled the official announcement of his candidacy for April 21, 1999. He did, however, make Columbine the central topic of his announcement speech.

  The disappointing results of Bauer's presidential campaign do not necessarily argue against the political significance of Columbine and Cassie. It is possible that Bauer would have done even *worse* without these appeals. His lack of success can be attributed to a field overcrowded with religious conservatives.

64. Quoted in Fred Barnes, "God, Gary, and the GOP," *The Weekly Standard,* May 24, 1999: 13.

65. "Bauer Says Minnesota Gov. Jesse Ventura is a Bigot," Gary Bauer for President press release, October 1, 1999.

66. Quoted in Eric Gorski, "The Question of Martyrdom," *Arkansas Democrat-Gazette,* August 14, 1999: H6.

67. See Justin Watson, *The Christian Coalition: Dreams of Restoration, Demands for Recognition* (New York: St. Martin's Press, 1999), 124–139. The phrase "the moral clout that comes with victimhood," is from David Gates, "White Male Paranoia: New Victims or Just Bad Sports?" *Newsweek,* March 29, 1993: 3.

68. Quoted in Steve Rabey, "Videos of Hate," *Christianity Today,* February 7, 2000: 21. See also Peggy Lowe, "Suicide Tapes Transcripts," *Denver Post,* December 21, 1999, <http://www.denverpost.com/news/shot1221c.htm> (March 28, 2000); Keith Coffman, "Columbine Dad Plays Killers' Audio," *APBnews.com,* December 21, 1999, <http://www.apbnews.com/newscenter/breakingnews/1999/12/21/columbine-1221_01.html> (July 24, 2001). These statements were taken from an audio tape made by Darrell Scott, father of victim Rachel Scott, when he and other family members of the victims were allowed to view the videotapes made by Harris and Klebold.

69. See Rick Bragg, "Forgiveness, After 3 Die in Shootings in Kentucky," *New York Times,* December 3, 1997: A16. James Malone, "Three Students Killed, 5 Wounded in Shooting," *The Courier-Journal* (Louisville, KY) December 2, 1997: 1A; Dirk Johnson with Gustav Niebuhr, "Deaths in a Church," *New York Times,* September 17, 1999: A18; David Van Biema, "Terror in the Sanctuary," *Time,* September 27, 1999: 43; Dan R. Crawford, Kevin Galey, and Chip Gillette, *Night of Tragedy, Dawning of Light* (Colorado Springs, CO: Waterbrook Press, 2000).

70. See Dennis R. Hoover, "Spiritual Victimology," *Religion in the News* 2 (Fall 1999): 8–9, 23.

71. Quoted in Van Biema, "Terror in the Sanctuary," 43.

72. Quoted in D. F. Olivera, "Christian Faith Suffering in Silence," *Spokesman-Review* (Spokane, WA) September 26, 1999: B8.

73. James B. Jacobs and Kimberly Potter, *Hate Crimes: Criminal Law & Identity Politics* (New York: Oxford University Press, 1998), 5.

74. "Leaders Decry Rising Hostility to Christians," *Los Angeles Times,* September 19, 1999: A8.

75. House Majority Leader Dick Armey, "Religious Bigotry in America," Special Order speech, September 29, 1999. I found the transcript of this speech on the web site of the Traditional Values Coalition (www.traditionalvalues.org). Armey attributed Barry Lynn's remarks to a May 21, 1999, appearance on *Crossfire* (Cable News Network).

76. Janet Chismar, "Christians Bow Before God in Nation's Capitol on National Day of Prayer," *Religion Today,* May 4, 2001; "Bush

Participates in National Day of Prayer," Associated Press, May 4, 2001.

77. Misty Bernall, *She Said Yes: The Unlikely Martyrdom of Cassie Bernall* (Farmington, PA: Plough Publishing, 1999), 139.

78. "Art Linkletter, Columbine's Bernalls, Unite With LifeWayonline To Promote Safe Internet Access," news release (Nashville, TN: LifeWay Christian Resources), May 25, 2000.

79. See the Plough Publishing House web site at <http://www.plough.com>.

80. Catherine Ryan Hyde, *Pay It Forward* (New York: Simon & Schuster, 2000); *Pay It Forward,* prod. Peter Abrams, dir. Mimi Leder, 2 hr. 3 min., Warner Brothers, 2000, videocassette. See also <http://www.pay-itforwardfoundation.org>. See Darrell Scott and Steve Rabey, *Chain Reaction: A Call to Compassionate Revolution* (Nashville, TN: Thomas Nelson Publishers, 2001), 103–115.

81. Quoted in Scott, *Chain Reaction,* 20.

82. Scott, *Chain Reaction,* 21.

83. Samuel Z. Klausner, *Encyclopedia of Religion* (New York: Macmillan, 1986), s.v. "Martyrdom," ed. Mircea Eliade.

84. Quoted in Beth Nimmo, Darrell Scott, and Steve Rabey, *Rachel's Tears: The Spiritual Journey of Columbine Martyr Rachel Scott* (Nashville, TN: Thomas Nelson Publishers, 2000), 163–164. This particular poem, which is quoted in Bruce Porter, *The Martyrs' Torch: The Message of the Columbine Massacre* (Shippensburg, PA: Destiny Image Publishers Inc., 1999), 66, is never shown in her original handwriting as are so many of her writings.

85. Scott, *Chain Reaction,* 32.

86. Reverend Bruce Porter, Remarks at Funeral Service for Rachel Scott, *CNN Live Event,* Cable News Network, April 24, 1999.
   At the conclusion of Torchgrab youth rallies, an elaborate dance-drama depicts a torch being passed from Christ, to the martyrs of the church, to Rachel, and then, when she is cut down by a black-clad "Goth," Christ returns to the stage and hands the torch to members of Rachel's generation. At the conclusion of this dance-drama, a gold-plated torch, engraved with the names of the Columbine victims, with an actual flame is then passed among the members of the audience, who symbolically take up "Rachel's torch."

87. Porter, *Martyrs' Torch,* 60–63, 76.

88. Porter, *Martyrs' Torch,* 80.

89. Bruce Porter, Torchgrab Youth Rally, Myerstown, Pennsylvania, June 23, 2001. I attended this event and heard this remark.

90. Nimmo and Scott, *Rachel's Tears,* 164.

91. Nimmo and Scott, *Rachel's Tears,* 162–164. This is a July 1999 letter sent to Rob Schenck of Ten Commandments, a religious conservative

organization promoting the display of the Ten Commandments in public buildings and schools. It has been reprinted in *Rachel's Tears,* 163–165, and in other publications. See Beth Nimmo, "From A Mother's Heart," *Rachel's Journal,* December 1999: 8–9.

92. Lynn Sweet, "Parents Testify on Gun Curbs, Dems to Seek More Restrictions," *Chicago Sun-Times,* May 28, 1999: 36; Michael Romano, "Columbine Victim's Dad Says NRA A Scapegoat: Slain Girl's Father Says Answer Is Faith In God," *Denver Rocky Mountain News,* May 28, 1999: 4A; Brian Naylor, "House Judiciary Subcommittee on Crime Hears Conflicting Testimony About How To Stop Gun Violence in Schools," *NPR Morning Edition,* National Public Radio, May 28, 1999; Gwen Ifill, "Capitol Hill Hears Both Sides Of Gun Control Debate," *NBC News at Sunrise,* National Broadcasting Co., Inc., May 28, 1999.

The conservative magazine *Insight on the News* published a slightly edited version Darrell Scott's testimony almost a year after it was delivered. See Darrell Scott, "Columbine Tragedy Shows Nation Must Return to a Trust in God," *Insight on the News,* May 1, 2000: 46.

93. "Mission Statement," undated, <http://www.thecolumbineredemption.com/mission.html> (November 12, 2000).

94. This is an allusion to Isaiah 40:3. "A voice cries: 'In the wilderness prepare the way of the LORD, make straight in the desert a highway for our God'" (RSV). This passage is cited by all four Gospels in reference to the coming of Christ. (Mt 3:3, Mk 1:3, Lk 3:4–6, Jn 1:23.)

This message can be found at "Urban Legends Reference Pages," updated February 15, 2001, <http://www.snopes.com/inboxer/outrage/scott.htm> (July 17, 2001).

95. Darrell Scott, "Prepared Testimony of Darrell Scott, Father of Two Victims of Columbine High School Shootings Littleton, CO Before the House Judiciary Subcommittee on Crime," *Federal News Service,* May 27, 1999.

96. Some of Darrell Scott's actions, however, indicate that he is not a typical religious conservative. He met with President Clinton at the White House and invited the president to attend a memorial service in Littleton, Colorado, on the first anniversary of the shooting. Holly Kurtz, "Clinton Invited to Memorial: Columbine Victim's Dad Makes Request," *Denver Rocky Mountain News,* April 10, 2000: 5A. President Clinton did not attend. Kirk Mitchell, "Clinton Won't Visit April 20," *Denver Post,* April 10, 2000: B-04.

Darrell Scott is also interviewed about Columbine in a documentary, "Journey to a Hate Free Millennium," that also examines the role of hate in the murders of gay college student Matthew Shepard and African American James Byrd, Jr. See Coleman Cornelius, "Shepard's Mom Takes on Hatred," *Denver Post,* October 13, 1999:

B-01; "The Film: Journey to a Hate Free Millennium," undated, <http://www.newlightmedia.org/journey/journey.html> (August 16, 2001). The Columbine Redemption web site provides a link to the Daniel Mauser Memorial web site. Tom Mauser, father of Daniel Mauser, who was killed in the Columbine library, is a well-known gun control activist and vocal critic of the National Rifle Association. See <http://www.columbineredemption.com> and <http://www.danielmauser.com>.

97. Darrell Scott, ed., *Important American Documents* (Franklin, TN: Think Big, 2000).

98. Darrell Scott, ed., *America's Christian Roots* (Franklin, TN: Think Big, 2001).

99. Scott, *America's Christian Roots,* 9–10.

100. Scott, *America's Christian Roots,* 5.

101. Scott, *Important American Documents,* v.

102. Darrell Scott seems particularly influenced by the work of David Barton, whom he thanks in *America's Christian Roots,* 2. See David Barton, *The Myth of Separation* (Aledo, TX: Wallbuilders Press, 1992); *Original Intent* (Aledo, TX: Wallbuilders Press, 1996). See also <http://www.wallbuilders.com>.

Scott has also established an additional web site, ChristianAmerica.com. The product page of this site sells Scott's *America's Christian Roots* and *Important American Documents,* as well as Barton's *Original Intent.* "Products: Get a True American History Lesson," undated, <http://www.christianamerica.com/products.htm> (May 19, 2002).

103. See Winfred E. A. Bernhard, *Fisher Ames: Federalist and Statesman 1758–1808* (Chapel Hill, NC: University of North Carolina Press, 1965).

104. Thomas J. Curry, *The First Freedoms: Church and State in America to the Passage of the First Amendment* (New York: Oxford University Press, 1986), 199–207.

105. Curry observed that Ames actually had "a somewhat contemptuous attitude toward the proposed amendments, especially insofar as he perceived them as representing popular rights." Curry, *The First Freedoms,* 214.

106. Scott, *Important American Documents,* ix.

107. Quoted in Scott, *Important American Documents,* ix-x; Scott, *America's Christian Roots,* 50. In the latter work, Scott provides the following citation: (September 20, 1789, Palladium magazine; D. James Kennedy, The Great Deception, Fort Lauderdale, Florida, Coral Ridge Ministries, 1989, p. 3.) But the closest match to this title, Kennedy's *The Great Deception,* published by Coral Ridge Ministries in 1985, contains no quotations by Fisher Ames.

108. In 1801 the name *New England Palladium* was appended to an existing publication, *The Massachusetts Mercury,* which had been established in 1793. Frederic Hudson, *Journalism in the United States, From 1690 to 1872* (New York: Harper & Brothers, Publishers, 1875), 188. The *Palladium* was intended to promote the Federalist party, of which Ames was a prominent member. See Robert Edson Lee, "Timothy Dwight and the Boston 'Palladium,'" *New England Quarterly* 35 no. 2 (1962): 229–239.

The two-volume *Works of Fisher Ames,* with approximately 1,600 pages, does not contain anything from either the *Palladium* or the *Mercury* in September 1789. Seth Ames and W. B. Allen, eds., *Works of Fisher Ames,* 2 vols. (Indianapolis, IN: Liberty Classics, 1983).

Ames did publish an essay in the *Palladium* in January 1801 advocating the continued use of the Bible in children's education, but not containing the statements that Darrell Scott quotes. The essay "School Books" contains no discussion of any legal or constitutional issues and makes no allegations of anything like a "dangerous trend." Ames, *Works of Fisher Ames,* Vol. I, 11–12.

109. The cases in which the "establishment" and "free exercise" clauses were held to apply to the states through the Fourteenth Amendment were, respectively, *Everson v. Board of Education* 330 U.S. 1 (1947) and *Cantwell v. Connecticut* 310 U.S. 296 (1940).

110. Curry, *First Freedoms,* 163–177. Curry concluded, "Church and State in Massachusetts emerged from the revolutionary era much as they had entered it," 177. For an additional discussion of state establishments of religion after the ratification of the First Amendment, see Leonard W. Levy, *The Establishment Clause: Religion and the First Amendment* (New York: Macmillan Publishing Company, 1986), 25–62.

111. For useful discussions of religion and American education, see Warren A. Nord, *Religion and American Education: Rethinking a National Dilemma* (Chapel Hill, NC: University of North Carolina Press, 1995); James W. Fraser, *Between Church and State: Religion and Public Education in a Multicultural America* (New York: St. Martin's Press, 1999).

112. Nimmo and Scott, *Rachel's Tears,* 153.

113. Darrell Scott, "Prepared Testimony of Darrell Scott, Father of Two Victims of Columbine High School Shootings Littleton, CO Before the House Judiciary Subcommittee on Crime," *Federal News Service,* May 27, 1999.

114. Scott, *Important American Documents,* vi.

115. U.S. Department of Education, "Religious Expression in the Public Schools," revised May 1998 <http://www.ed.gov/Speeches/08–1995/religion.html> (July 18, 2001).

This is *not* to say that all specific issues relating to the personal religious activity, or to the thousands of voluntary groups, in the schools have been settled, or that all public school personnel are aware of, or even willing to abide by, these guidelines. The sheer volume of pending free-exercise litigation demonstrates this. But all that litigation also shows that public school students *have* recognized free-exercise rights.

116. Nimmo and Scott, *Rachel's Tears*, 121.
117. Scott, *Important American Documents*, xvi.
118. Scott, *America's Christian Roots*, 10.
119. Grant Wacker, "Uneasy in Zion: Evangelicals in Postmodern Society," in *Evangelicalism and Modern America*, ed. George M. Marsden (Grand Rapids, MI: William B. Eerdmans Publishing Company, 1984), 24.
120. "Christian nation" rhetoric has not only alienated those outside the evangelical community, including potential political allies of religious conservatism, it has failed to motivate many evangelicals. For a useful discussion of the various concepts of "Christian nation" among evangelicals, see Christian Smith, *Christian America?: What Evangelicals Really Want* (Berkeley, CA: University of California Press, 2000), 21–37.
121. Albert Camus, *The Fall*, trans. Justin O'Brien (New York: Knopf, 1960), 76.

CHAPTER 5

1. Virtually every major news organization covered Columbine. The best continuing coverage has been provided by the *Denver Post* and the *Denver Rocky Mountain News.*

    Dave Cullen, a Denver-based writer, produced some of the most useful investigative coverage of Columbine for the online magazine *Salon.com.* Cullen has used this material as the basis for *Cloud Over Columbine: How the Press Got It Wrong and the Police Let It Happen* (New York: Random House, 2002). Cullen broke the story that investigators doubted the Cassie martyr story.

    Wendy Murray Zoba, a senior writer for *Christianity Today,* who covered Columbine for that magazine, has published *Day of Reckoning: Columbine and the Search for America's Soul* (Grand Rapids, MI: Brazos Press, 2000). Zoba defends the Cassie martyr story and does not question the similar stories about Rachel.

2. The most important of these promotional materials are, Misty Bernall, *She Said Yes: The Unlikely Martyrdom of Cassie Bernall* (Farmington, PA: Plough Publishing House, 1999); Beth Nimmo, Darrell Scott, and Steve Rabey, *Rachel's Tears: The Spiritual Journey of*

Columbine Martyr Rachel Scott (Nashville, TN: Thomas Nelson Publishers, 2000); Bruce Porter, *The Martyrs' Torch: The Message of the Columbine Massacre* (Shippensburg, PA: Destiny Image Publishers Inc., 1999).

3. Jefferson County, Colorado, Sheriff's Office, *The Jefferson County Sheriff's Office Report, Columbine High School Shootings, April 20, 1999* (Golden, CO, 2000), CD-ROM. Hereafter cited as *Sheriff's Report.*

For an evaluation of how the Jefferson County Sheriff's Office responded to Columbine, see State of Colorado, *The Report of Governor Bill Owens' Columbine Review Commission* (Denver, CO, 2001).

Many of the families of Columbine victims have filed lawsuits against the Sheriff's Office. Most notably, the family of Columbine victim Daniel Rohrbough alleged that Daniel was shot by a police officer, rather than by Harris or Klebold, and that the Sheriff's Office engaged in "obstruction and falsification" to hide this and other information about its response to and investigation of the Columbine shooting. Kevin Vaughan and Jeff Kass, "Investigating the 'Lies'; Parents, Police Are Miles Apart on What Happened in Columbine Rampage," *Denver Rocky Mountain News,* January 5, 2002: 10A. As of this writing, litigation against and calls for investigations of the Sheriff's Office, by Rohrbough's family, and by other victims' families, continues.

4. Jefferson County, Colorado, Sheriff's Office, *Investigative Materials, Columbine High School Shootings, Released November 21, 2000* (Golden, CO, 2000). Hereafter cited as *Investigative Materials.*

This material provides useful insights into the conclusions presented in the *Sheriff's Report,* which confirms neither of the martyr stories. These statements also provide a useful context for evaluating statements made by the same witnesses to journalists or in materials promoting the martyr stories of Cassie and Rachel. And unlike journalistic or promotional material, investigators collected statements from every possible witness, not just the ones a reporter happened to contact, or those willing to provide testimony in favor of a martyr story.

These witness statements, however, are uneven in quality. Given the circumstances, this should not be surprising. The statements were composed by a collection of investigators with different levels of expertise and experience from an array of local, state, and federal law enforcement agencies. Witnesses were interviewed under a wide variety of conditions and over a range of time, from days to weeks after the shooting. The witnesses themselves, of course, varied in their ability/willingness to recall and describe what they had seen and experienced. And media attention undoubtedly influenced what witnesses recalled. "Students would watch or read coverage of the Columbine shootings," observes the *Sheriff's Report,* "and make conclusions based on some of the impressions presented by the media rather than from their own perceptions." "Findings of the Library Team," *Sheriff's Report.*

5. The courts have ordered a number of items released to the public by the Jefferson County, Colorado, Sheriff's Office. The approximate date of release is in parenthesis. These items are: (1) Littleton Fire Department training video, raw helicopter footage by Channel 4 (April 25, 2000); (2) Two CD-ROM set of the 911 and dispatch audio tapes (radio traffic)(May 11, 2000); (3) Cafeteria surveillance video-tapes (May 26, 2000); (4) Ballistics report (May 31, 2000); (5) Autopsy summaries (February 6, 2001); (6) Klebold autopsy report (February 23, 2001); (7) Miscellaneous Collection (April 10, 2001): draft search affidavit, the CD (audio) of the shoot team interviews, the written transcript of an interview with the Columbine Community Resource Officer, Neil Gardner, and the executive summary of the library investigative team; (8) Two computer-generated evidence logbooks, 973 pages (May 11, 2001); (9) One additional computer-generated evidence logbook. (April 10, 2001); (10) FBI report of interview with Randy, Judy, and Brooks Brown (May 22, 2001); (11) Lab books, 700 pages (June 19, 2001); (12) Seven notebooks of investigative files. Audio cassette of 911 dispatch tape. CD-ROM containing two large crime scene diagrams (August 9, 2001); (13) FBI documents including handwritten sketches, notes, and miscellaneous reports (September 6, 2001). The description of these items and other information is available at the Jefferson County, Colorado, Sheriff's Office web site at <http://206.247.49.21/ext/dpt/officials/sheriff/chsmaterials.htm> updated September 6, 2001 (September 8, 2001).

6. Susan Besze Wallace, "Val Schnurr Knows What She Said on That Horrifying Day," *Denver Post,* September 28, 1999: A2; Hanna Rosin, "Columbine Miracle: A Matter of Belief," *Washington Post,* October 14, 1999: C1. Schnurr's story was told in the early coverage of the massacre. See Rebecca Jones, "Girl Did Not Forsake God," *Denver Rocky Mountain News,* April 27, 1999: 5A.

7. Dave Cullen, "Inside the Columbine High Investigation," *Salon.com,* September 23, 1999, <http://www.salon.com/news/feature/1999/09/23/columbine> (July 7, 2001). For instance, Columbine student Mickie Cain was interviewed by CNN's Larry King on April 21. She told the story of Cassie's heroic death. But, as Cain herself told King, she was *not* in the library during the shooting. Micki Cain, interview by Larry King, *Larry King Live,* Cable News Network, April 21, 1999. Cain told King "she [Cassie] completely, completely stood up for God when the killers asked her if there was anyone who had faith in

Christ. She spoke up and they shot her for it." Cain added, "And that is the most brave thing anyone could ever do, and I—I want that memory to live on and her example for that."

8. Dan Luzadder and Katie Kerwin McCrimmon, "Accounts Differ on Question to Bernall," *Denver Rocky Mountain News,* September 24, 1999: 5A.

9. Some of these include: "Columbine Martyr May Not Have Been," Associated Press Online, September 29, 1999; Sandi Dolbee, "Teenager's Last Words Cause Debate," *San Diego Union Tribune,* October 1, 1999: E1; Andrew Brown, "Faith & Reason: The Martyr Who Died a Rock and Roll Death," *The Independent* (London), October 2, 1999: 7; Jon Carroll, "She Didn't Say Anything," *San Francisco Chronicle,* October 4, 1999: D8; Michael Janofsky, "Far Beyond Columbine, Rancor and Tension," *New York Times,* October 4, 1999: A14; Dick Woodbury, "Columbine: So Who Said Yes?" *Time,* October 11, 1999: 26; Thomas Fields-Meyer and Vickie Bane, "For the Record," *People Weekly,* October 18, 1999: 129.

10. "From the Publisher," in Bernall, *She Said Yes,* x.

11. Quoted in Susan Besze Wallace, "Faith in Cassie's Final Words Wavers as Book Sales Soar," *Denver Post,* September 25, 1999: B2.

12. Zoba, *Day of Reckoning,* 78–79.

13. Zoba, *Day of Reckoning,* 221 note 20. With the permission of Plough, Zoba graciously provided me with a copy of this collection of material entitled, "Excerpts from the Background Material and Selected News Stories Recounting the Dialogue Between Cassie Bernall and her Killer on April 20, 1999," compiled by Plough Publishing House.

14. Zoba's chapter "Tactical Choices" discusses the *Sheriff's Report* and its shortcomings. See Zoba, *Day of Reckoning,* 105–136.

15. "Findings of the Library Team," *Sheriff's Report.* Two of the library witnesses, Brian Anderson and Patricia Nielsen, were injured at the western entrance to the school building prior to entering the library. They are not included in the figure of 12 injured in the library.

16. Some of the investigators' reports use a numbering system that is different from the system used in the *Sheriff's Report.* Tables 16 and 17 are sometimes transposed. I will use the system of numbering and witness locations used in the *Sheriff's Report.*

17. The *Library Team Executive Summary,* released April 10, 2001, lists 48 rather than 46 persons in the library. No witness statements are available from Elisha Encinias, who was in the "Hall Entry," and Makai Hall, who was injured in the western section of the library. It is unknown why their statements, if indeed they were interviewed by investigators, have not been released. Jefferson County, Colorado, Sheriff's Office, *Columbine Task Force Library Team Executive Summary, Released April 10, 2001* (Golden, CO, 1999).

18. Joshua Lapp quoted in Misty Bernall, *She Said Yes*, 12–13. See also Carla Crowder, "Martyr For Her Faith," *Denver Rocky Mountain News*, April 23, 1999: 5A; Eileen McNamara, "A Martyr Amid the Madness," *Boston Globe*, April 24, 1999: A1; Wendy Murray Zoba, "'Do You Believe in God?': How Columbine Changed America," *Christianity Today*, October 4, 1999: 36.
19. Quoted in Luzadder and McCrimmon, "Accounts Differ on Question to Bernall," 5A.
20. Zoba, *Day of Reckoning*, 95.
21. Zoba, *Day of Reckoning*, 95.
22. *Investigative Materials*, JC-001–000480, JC-001–000488.
23. Joshua Lapp and Misty Bernall, interview by Lynn Sherr, "Yes to God," *20/20 Friday*, American Broadcasting Companies, Inc., September 10, 1999.
24. *Investigative Materials*, JC-001–000488.
25. Quoted in Zoba, *Day of Reckoning*, 95.
26. *Investigative Materials*, JC-001–000172.
27. Zoba, *Day of Reckoning*, 89.
28. *Investigative Materials*, JC-001–000–578.
29. Zoba, *Day of Reckoning*, 101.
30. "Findings of the Library Team," *Sheriff's Report*.
31. *Investigative Materials*, JC-001–000146 to JC-001–000147.
32. Zoba, *Day of Reckoning*, 95.
33. *Investigative Materials*, JC-001–000587 to JC-001–000588.
34. Susan Besze Wallace, "Val Schnurr Knows What She Said on That Horrifying Day," *Denver Post*, September 28, 1999: A2; Rosin, "Columbine Miracle: A Matter of Belief," C1.
35. See Zoba, *Day of Reckoning*, 95. The subhead for this discussion is "An Expert Opinion." Zoba, however, does not make it clear why, other than meeting standard education and licensing requirements, McDermott should be regarded as an expert. Zoba does not cite any additional experts who might either agree or disagree with McDermott.
36. Zoba, *Day of Reckoning*, 96, 95. Wendy Murray Zoba, "Cassie Said Yes, They Said No," *Christianity Today*, December 6, 1999: 77–78. In this earlier version of her argument in *Christianity Today* Zoba cites McDermott as providing the specific diagnosis of Post Traumatic Stress Disorder. It is unclear why this concept was not included in *Day of Reckoning*.
37. Zoba, *Day of Reckoning*, 96, 95.
38. Investigators from the Jefferson County Sheriff's Office did explain to the Bernalls why they doubted that the exchange about God between Cassie and her killer even took place. In an interview between Plough editors and the Bernalls, Brad Bernall summarized what the

investigators told them. "They [the investigators] came and said, Cassie was on the left, and these kids that we interviewed they said the exchanges they heard came from the right." From an interview conducted by Joe Keiderling and Chris Zimmerman with Brad and Misty Bernall, June 12, 1999, in, "Excerpts from the Background Material and Selected News Stories Recounting the Dialogue Between Cassie Bernall and her Killer on April 20, 1999," compiled by Plough Publishing House.

39. "Findings of the Library Team," *Sheriff's Report.*
40. *Investigative Materials,* JC-001–000647
41. Luzadder and McCrimmon, "Accounts Differ on Question to Bernall," 5A.
42. Zoba, *Day of Reckoning,* 99. Keep in mind that Zoba argues that Craig Scott's testimony is credible despite locating Cassie's God-conversation on the wrong side of the library. Indeed, the standard Zoba uses to reject Wyant's testimony would also compromise the inconsistent and incompatible versions of events offered by Craig Scott, Todd, and Lapp.
43. *Investigative Materials,* JC-001–000647.
44. Investigators apparently did tell the Bernalls in early June 1999 about the witnesses who supported the "peek-a-boo" version of Cassie's death. In a June 12, 1999, interview with Plough editor Zimmerman, Misty Bernall said that investigators had explained the evidence behind the "peek-a-boo" version of Cassie's death. "The people that sat behind Cassie said that's what happened to Cassie, based upon their interview with them, and they gave a name, and I don't remember what that name was." In the remainder of the interview, neither the Bernalls nor Zimmerman show any interest interviewing "the people who sat behind Cassie," or talking to the person the investigators mentioned by name. "Excerpts from the Background Material and Selected News Stories Recounting the Dialogue Between Cassie Bernall and her Killer on April 20, 1999," compiled by Plough Publishing House.

In all fairness to the Bernalls, we must remember that this took place mere weeks after the profound trauma of their daughter's death. They are not trained journalists, scholars, or criminal investigators. The *Sheriff's Report,* floor plans of the library, detailed chronologies of the order of events, and the witness statements that I have been able to use were not available when Misty Bernall's *She Said Yes* went to press.

45. *Investigative Materials,* JC-001–000459.
46. *Investigative Materials,* JC-001–000319.
47. Quoted in Jason Blevins, "Terror Won't Fade Away: Survivors of Library Killings Paint a Picture of Horror," *Denver Post,* April 29, 1999: A-09.

48. This interview by a local television reporter was replayed on NBC's *Today* show as part of an interview with Pasquale by Katie Couric, "Bree Pasquale Discusses Her Harrowing Experience at Columbine High School," *Today,* National Broadcasting Co., Inc., April 23, 1999.
49. *Investigative Materials,* JC-001–000529. The detail supplied by Bree Pasquale about Cassie's "hands up covering the sides of her face" explains why the tip of a finger on her right hand was blown off by the shotgun blast. Bernall, *She Said Yes,* 14; Summary of Denver Coroner autopsy report on "Bernall, Cassie," April 22, 1999, released to the public February 6, 2001.
50. "Narrative Time Line of Events," *Sheriff's Report.*
51. "Findings of the Outside Team," *Sheriff's Report.*
    The time of Rachel's death at 11:19 A.M. has been called into question. The *Denver Rocky Mountain News* reported on January 5, 2002, "Scott's cafeteria receipt shows that she bought lunch at 11:32 A.M. Another report indicates that the receipt clock was ten minutes fast. That would put the time of her transaction at 11:22 A.M., still up to three minutes after the sheriff says she was shot and killed." Vaughan and Kass, "Investigating the 'Lies,'" 10A.
    It is unclear what significance, if any, this apparent discrepancy may have. So far, no one, least of all her family and other proponents of Rachel's status as a martyr, disputes that she was shot and killed by Harris or Klebold.
52. *Investigative Materials,* JC-001–000229.
53. *Investigative Materials,* JC-001–001118.
54. *Investigative Materials,* JC-001–000757.
55. *Investigative Materials,* JC-001–000196.
56. *Investigative Materials,* JC-001–000197.
57. It is possible, of course, that the investigators simply failed to elicit or to record information that would shed more light on Rachel's final moments. Since we do not have any tape recordings or transcripts of these interviews, it is hard to evaluate this suggestion. (But it is a little hard to believe that any investigator would have ignored information, assuming it was offered, regarding how one of the victims died.)
58. Mark Obmascik, "April 20 Through the Eyes of Survivors," *Denver Post,* June 13, 1999: A-01.
59. Matt Bai, "Anatomy of a Massacre," *Newsweek,* May 3, 1999: 27; John C. Ensslin, "Columbine Victim: Faith Saved My Life," *Denver Rocky Mountain News,* January 27, 2000: 4A.
60. Jefferson County Coroner's Office, summary of Autopsy Report on "Scott, Rachel," dated May 18, 1999, released to the public on February 6, 2001.
61. Bruce Porter, "Update #2," April 22, 1999, distribution list.

A collection of Porter's e-mail messages from April 21 to June 10, 1999, were posted at the Torchgrab Youth Ministries web site at <http://www.torchgrab.org/updates/dispatches.html>. I accessed these on May 13, 2000. These messages are no longer posted on the Torchgrab site. Some of these posted messages contained editorial notations or corrections.

Some of these messages also appear in Porter's book, *The Martyrs' Torch,* but are heavily redacted. Porter advises his readers that he has done this. See Porter, *Martyrs' Torch,* xxiv.

62. Bruce Porter, "Update #5," April 25, 1999, distribution list.
63. Bruce Porter, "Update #8," May 20, 1999, distribution list.
64. Bruce Porter, e-mail to the author, August 16, 2001.
65. Porter, *Martyrs' Torch,* 89.
66. Bruce Porter, e-mail to the author, August 16, 2001.
67. Kevin Simpson, "Who Said 'Yes' Blurs With Time," *Denver Post,* December 16, 1999: A-01.
68. S. C. Gwynne, "An Act of God?" *Time,* December 20, 1999: 58.
69. Simpson, "Who Said 'Yes' Blurs With Time," A-01.
70. Nimmo and Scott, *Rachel's Tears,* 91.
71. Quoted in Sara James, "The Long Journey Back," *Dateline NBC,* National Broadcasting Co., Inc., July 21, 2000.
72. Quoted in Zoba, *Day of Reckoning,* 183.
73. Wendy Murray Zoba, "Re: Day of Reckoning question," June 25, 2001, personal e-mail.
74. Simpson, "Who Said 'Yes' Blurs With Time," A-01.
75. Kevin Simpson, "Apology to Rachel's Kin 'From the Heart,'" *Denver Post,* April 21, 2000: A-08.
76. Simpson, "Apology to Rachel's Kin 'From the Heart,'" A-08.
77. Telephone conversation with Kevin Simpson, June 19, 2001.
78. Simpson, "Apology to Rachel's Kin 'From the Heart,'" A-08.
79. Simpson, "Apology to Rachel's Kin 'From the Heart,'" A-08.
80. *Oxford English Dictionary,* 2nd ed., s.v. "hearsay evidence."
81. Nimmo and Scott, *Rachel's Tears,* 98.
82. According to one story, Rachel had created a mime set to recorded music for a school talent show. During her performance, the audiotape malfunctioned. Klebold was working in the sound booth and got the tape working again. She thanked Klebold for his help, according to Devon Adams, a student who knew both Rachel and Klebold. Zoba, *Day of Reckoning,* 183.
83. Peter Wilkinson and Matt Hendrickson, "Humiliation and Revenge: The Story of Reb and VoDkA," *Rolling Stone,* June 18, 1999: 50. Brown's full statement was "Dylan knew Rachel Scott, and he would not have shot her." Brown quoted on 141.

84. Nimmo and Scott, *Rachel's Tears*, 114; *Untold Stories of Columbine*, Darrell Scott, 80 min., Gateway Films, 2000, videocassette. This confrontation probably did not occur during the Spring 1999 semester. Class rosters released by the Sheriff's department show that Rachel was not enrolled in any of the classes being taken by Harris and Klebold during Spring 1999. See *Investigative Materials*, JC-001–010108 to JC-001–01015 for Eric Harris, and JC-001–010452 to JC-001–010470 for Dylan Klebold.

85. Quoted in Peggy Lowe, "Suicide Tapes Transcripts," *Denver Post*, December 21, 1999, <http://www.denverpost.com/news/shot1221c.htm> (March 28, 2000).

86. Wendy Murray Zoba, "Columbine's Tortuous Road to Healing," *Christianity Today*, April 3, 2000: 81.

87. Porter, *Martyrs' Torch*, 67.

88. *Investigative Materials*, JC-001–010115, JC-001–010470.

89. *Investigative Materials*, JC-001–010378, JC-001–010470.

90. *Investigative Materials*, JC-001–001779, JC-001–001780.

91. Nimmo and Scott, *Rachel's Tears*, 91–92. The same account, with only minor changes, can be found in Darrell Scott and Steve Rabey, *Chain Reaction: A Call to Compassionate Revolution* (Nashville, TN: Thomas Nelson Publishers, 2001), 125–126. Rabey worked on both books. Almost the same account can also be found in Beth Nimmo and Debra K. Klingsporn, *The Journals of Rachel Scott* (Nashville, TN: Thomas Nelson Publishers, 2001), 119.

92. Quoted in Linda Mullen, "Family Forgives Gunmen," *South Bend Tribune*, April 30, 1999: A1.

93. Quoted in Cynthia Bowers, "Rachel," *48 Hours*, Columbia Broadcasting System, June 10, 1999.

94. See, for instance, Brent High, "God Used a Toothache," undated, <http://www.christianstories.com/stories/godusedatoothache.html> (June 25, 2001).

95. Bob Larson, *Extreme Evil: Kids Killing Kids* (Nashville, TN: Thomas Nelson Publishers, 1999), 16.

96. Porter, *The Martyrs' Torch*, 53.

97. One possibility is suggested by December 1999 news stories in *Time* magazine and the *Denver Post*. Both refer to an article in a "local Christian newspaper" or "small Christian newspaper" that cited Castaldo as the source of an account of Rachel's last words. When I contacted the authors of the *Time* and *Denver Post* articles they were unable, more than 18 months later, to provide further information or a copy of the article. See S. C. Gwynne, "An Act of God?" *Time*, December 20, 1999: 58; Simpson, "Who Said 'Yes' Blurs With Time," A-01.

This mysterious article, so far as I am able to determine, is not cited in the written materials produced by ministries that promote Rachel as a modern-day martyr.

98. *The Message of Columbine,* Bruce Porter, 62 min., Torchgrab Youth Ministries, Inc., 2001, videocassette. When I attended a Torchgrab Youth Rally in Myerstown, Pennsylvania, on June 22–23, 2001, Porter told this version of the Rachel martyr story.

99. *Black's Law Dictionary,* 7th ed., s.v. "reasonable doubt," "preponderance of the evidence," and "clear and convincing evidence."

CHAPTER 6

1. *The Man Who Shot Liberty Valance,* prod. Willis Goldbeck, dir. John Ford, 2 hr. 2 min., Paramount, 1962, videocassette.

2. See Scott Eyman, *Print the Legend: The Life and Times of John Ford* (New York: Simon & Schuster, 1999), 487–492; J. A. Place, *The Western Films of John Ford* (Secaucus, NJ: Citadel Press, 1974), 214–227; Tag Gallagher, *John Ford: The Man and His Films* (Berkeley, CA: University of California Press, 1986), 384–413.

3. Hanna Rosin, "Columbine Miracle: A Matter of Belief," *Washington Post,* October 14, 1999: C1.

4. K. Daniel Glover, "The Truth About Cassie Bernall," *IntellectualCapital.com,* October 28, 1999 <http://www.intellectualcapital.com/issues/issue314/item6996.asp> (January 21, 2000).

5. Twila Decker, "Another Girl Likely Said 'Yes' at Columbine High," *St. Petersburg Times,* October 2, 1999: 8.

6. Jon Carroll, "She Didn't Say Anything," *San Francisco Chronicle,* October 4, 1999: D8.

7. Patrick McKinnion, "She didn't say yes . . . ," *Amazon.com* Customer Review of *She Said Yes* by Misty Bernall, October 27, 1999, <http://www.amazon.com/exec/obidos/tg/stores/detail/-/books/0874869870/customer-reviews/3/002–7356050–6548015?show=1> (August 24, 2001).

8. P. Scott Horne, "Cretinously Vile right-wing Christian pabulum," *Amazon.com* Customer Review of *She Said Yes* by Misty Bernall, December 2, 2000, <http://www.amazon.com/exec/obidos/tg/stores/detail/-/books/0874869870/customer-reviews/1/002–7356050–6548015?show=1> (August 24, 2001).

9. Dan Adler, "I Said Yuck," *Amazon.com* Customer Review of *She Said Yes* by Misty Bernall, June 26, 2000, <http://www.amazon.com/exec/obidos/tg/stores/detail/-/books/0874869870/customer-reviews/002–7356050–6548015?show=2&Go.x=12&Go.y=14> (August 24, 2001).

10. T. B., "don't waste your time," *Amazon.com* Customer Review of *She Said Yes* by Misty Bernall, November 6, 1999, <http://www.amazon. com/exec/obidos/tg/stores/detail/-/books/0874869870/customer-reviews/2/002–7356050–6548015?show=1> (August 24, 2001).

11. A reader, "Cynical . . . ," *Amazon.com* Customer Review of *She Said Yes* by Misty Bernall, October 8, 1999, <http://www.amazon. com/exec/obidos/tg/stores/detail/-/books/0874869870/customer-reviews/2/002–7356050–6548015?show=1> (August 24, 2001).

12. Bernard Gundy, "Letters to the Editor," *Salon.com,* October 7, 1999, <http://www.salon.com/letters/1999/10/07/faludi/index.html> (August 25, 2001).

13. Daniel Radosh, "The Martyr of Columbine," *The Nation,* November 8, 1999: 28. See Dinesh D'Souza, "I, Rigoberta Menchu . . . Not!" *Weekly Standard,* December 31, 1998: 27.

14. For an example of *The Nation*'s editorial stance toward Columbine see Bruce Shapiro, "The Guns of Littleton," *The Nation,* May 17, 1999: 4–5.

15. See S. C. Gwynne, "An Act of God?" *Time,* December 20, 1999: 58; Kevin Simpson, "Who Said 'Yes' Blurs With Time," *Denver Post,* December 16, 1999: A-01.

16. See, for instance, "Columbine's Rachel Scott May Have Said Yes," Associated Press, December 16, 1999; P. Solomon Banda, "Who Said Yes to Columbine Gunman?" Associated Press, December 27, 1999.

17. See Kevin Vaughan and Peggy Lowe, "Report Sheds Light on Tragedy," *Denver Rocky Mountain News,* May 16, 2000: 4A; Daryl Lindsay, "A Reader's Guide to the Columbine Report," *Salon.com,* May 17, 2000, <http://www.salon.com/news/feature/2000/05/17/guide/ index.html> (May 20, 2000).
     American Atheists, Inc., also took a keen interest in the findings of the *Sheriff's Report.* See "Final Columbine Report: No Mention of 'Martyrdom' Executions, Christians Being 'Targeted,'" May 23, 2000, <http://www.atheists.org/flash.line/colo12.htm> (May 31, 2001).

18. marissa, "Wow—what imagination," *Amazon.com* Customer Review of *The Martyrs' Torch* by Bruce Porter, June 9, 2000, <http://www. amazon.com/exec/obidos/tg/stores/detail/-/books/0768420466/ customer-reviews/ref=pd_pym_rvi_8/002–7356050–6548015> (August 24, 2001).

19. A reader, "authors/publishers should be ashamed of themselves," *Amazon.com* Customer Review of *Rachel's Tears* by Beth Nimmo and Darrell Scott, June 10, 2000, <http://www.amazon.com/exec/ obidos/tg/stores/detail/-/books/0785268480/customer-reviews/002–7356050–6548015?show=1&Go.x=13&Go.y=14> (August 24, 2001).

20. A reader, "she was not killed for her faith," *Amazon.com* Customer Review of *Rachel's Tears* by Beth Nimmo and Darrell Scott, May 22, 2000, <http://www.amazon.com/exec/obidos/tg/stores/detail/-/books/0785268480/customer-reviews/002–7356050–6548015?show=1&Go.x=13&Go.y=14> (August 24, 2001).

21. Gary Bauer, Remarks at St. Anselm College, Bedford, New Hampshire, November 9, 1999.

22. Governor George W. Bush, "The True Goal of Education," speech in Gorham, New Hampshire, November 2, 1999, <http://www.georgewbush.com/News/speeches/110299_education.html> (July 24, 2001).

23. Timothy Noah, "George W., Folklorist," *Slate,* November 4, 1999, <http://slate.msn.com/code/Chatterbox/Chatterbox.asp?Show=11/4/1999&idMessage=3954> (July 29, 2001).

24. "Bush Remembers Columbine, Emphasizes Character Education," George W. Bush for President news release, April 20, 2000, <http://www.georgewbush.com/news/2000/april/pr042000_ed.asp> (May 30, 2000).

25. Richard John Neuhaus, "The Public Square," *First Things,* February 2000, <http://www.firstthings.com/ftissues/ft0002/public.html> (August 25, 2001).

26. J. Bottum, "Columbine Again," *Weekly Standard,* December 27, 1999: 7.

27. Quoted in Susan Besze Wallace, "Voices of Columbine: The Family of Cassie Bernall," *Denver Post,* April 16, 2000: Sect. I, I-12.

28. Wendy Murray Zoba, "Cassie Said Yes, They Said No," *Christianity Today,* December 6, 1999: 77–78.

    See also Wendy Murray Zoba, "Letters to the Editor," *Washington Post,* October 24, 1999: B6. In this letter, Zoba criticizes Rosin's reading of her *Christianity Today* article. Zoba also stated, "For me, as a journalist, truth is everything." This is an interesting twist on Zoba's "Truth is everything" for evangelicals that she used in her December 6, 1999, *Christianity Today* statement.

29. Wendy Murray Zoba, "Columbine's Tortuous Road to Healing," *Christianity Today,* April 3, 2000: 80.

30. C. M. Zimmerman, "Columbine at Six Months, April 20, 1999–October 20, 1999," undated, <http://www.CassieBernall.org/columbine_6_months.htm> (February 25, 2000).

31. Darrell Scott, interview by Matt Lauer, *Today,* National Broadcasting Companies, Inc., December 21, 1999.

32. Darrell Scott, Remarks at the Youth Alive! held at Marcus Pointe Baptist Church, Pensacola, Florida, June 12, 2000.

33. Beth Nimmo, Darrell Scott, and Steve Rabey, *Rachel's Tears: The Spiritual Journey of Columbine Martyr Rachel Scott* (Nashville, TN: Thomas Nelson Publishers, 2000), 15.

34. Quoted in Zoba, "Columbine's Tortuous Road to Healing," 81.

35. Quoted in P. Solomon Banda, "Who Said 'Yes?' to Columbine Gunmen? Faithful Say It's Immaterial," Associated Press, December 27, 1999.
36. Claire, "The TRUTH for all those concerned about what has been said," *Amazon.com* Customer Review of *She Said Yes* by Misty Bernall, November 26, 1999, <http://www.amazon.com/exec/obidos/tg/stores/detail/-/books/0874869870/customer-reviews/9/002-7356050-6548015?show=%2Bsubmittime> (August 24, 2001).
37. "An Unlikely Martyr?: Littleton Victim's Parents Respond to Criticism of New Book," Plough Publishing House news release, October 6, 1999.
38. Quoted in "Columbine's Rachel Scott May Have said Yes," Associated Press, December 16, 1999.
39. J. Bottum, "Awakening at Littleton," *First Things: A Monthly Journal of Religion and Public Life,* August 1999: 28.
40. Brad Bernall and Misty Bernall, "Tough Love Saved Cassie," interview by Wendy Murray Zoba, *Christianity Today,* October 4, 1999: 43.
41. Darrell Scott and Steve Rabey, *Chain Reaction: A Call to Compassionate Revolution* (Nashville, TN: Thomas Nelson Publishers, 2001), 49–50. A comparison between Rachel's diaries and those of Anne Frank also is made in Beth Nimmo and Debra K. Klingsporn, *The Journals of Rachel Scott: A Journey of Faith at Columbine High* (Nashville, TN: Tommy Nelson, 2001), 31.
42. Chris Zimmerman, e-mail to author, August 18, 2001.
43. Andrea Vinley, "She Lived Yes," *Focus on the Family,* April 2000: 18–19.
44. Quoted in Todd Starnes, "Jars of Clay Dedicates Grammy to Memory of Cassie Bernall," Baptist Press, February 22, 2001.
45. Interview with Senior Pastor Jo Ann Kunz of Hosanna Christian Fellowship in Lititz, Pennsylvania. The event at which the Bernalls spoke was at Lancaster Mennonite High School on October 14, 2000. I spoke with Kunz after the event.
46. Misty Bernall, "Introduction to the Paperback Edition," *She Said Yes: The Unlikely Martyrdom of Cassie Bernall* (New York: Pocket Books, 2000), xvi.
47. Thomas Nelson, the publisher of *Rachel's Tears,* does not release information on the number of copies in print. *Rachel's Tears* did appear twice on the *Publishers Weekly* bestsellers list for paperback religion titles. "Religion Bestsellers," *Publishers Weekly,* August 14, 2000: 212; "Religion Bestsellers," *Publishers Weekly,* September 11, 2000: 44.
48. Quoted in Hanna Rosin, "Columbine Miracle: A Matter of Belief," *Washington Post,* October 14, 1999: C1.
49. Quoted in Todd Starnes, "In Community Shocked By Violence, Southern Baptists Ties Prove Strong," Baptist Press, March 9, 2001.

INDEX

secularism, 5, 27, 110
secularization, 26, 78, 102–3, 155, 159
"separation of church and state," see church-
    state issues
September 11, 2001, ix, 1, 3, 51, 94
Shepard, Matthew, 95, 192–93n.96
Sheriff's Office, Jefferson County, Colo.
    criticisms of, xi, 115–116, 154, 196n.3,
        201n.51
    investigative materials, 116, 119–30,
        139–40, 196n.3, 196–97n.4, 197n.5,
        198n.16, 17, 201n.49
    Sheriff's Report, 6, 21, 116, 118–19, 123,
        125–30, 144, 150–51, 154, 157
She Said Yes (Bernall), 10–11, 29, 35–39, 71,
    100, 117–20, 145, 151–53, 155,
    158–59
"She Said Yes," derivatives, 36–37, 40, 44–45,
    173n.51, 176n.99, see also Smith,
    Michael W.
Shoels, Isaiah, 123
Simpson, Kevin, 133–34
Slashdot.com: News For Nerds, 82–83
Smith, Christian, 26
Smith, Lacey Baldwin, 15
Smith, Michael W., 37–38, 46, 99, 158, 172n.39
Southern Baptist, 38, 100, 136, 160
standards of proof, 143–44
Stark, Rodney, 17
Stephen, 18
Sullivan, Andrew, 95
Supreme Court, see church-state issues

Tabor, James D., 18
Tancredo, Tom, 95
Taylor, Mark, 131, 137
Teen Mania, 32–33, 55, 65, 178n.16
Ten Commandments, see church-state issues
Tertullian, 17, 20
"This Is Your Time," see Smith, Michael W.
Thomas Nelson Publishers, 59, 207n.47

Time, 2–3, 33–34, 40, 42, 53, 81, 98, 132, 150
Todd, Evan, 81, 121–22, 125, 127
Tomlin, John, 51, 123, 137
Torchgrab Youth Ministries, Inc., see Porter,
    Bruce
"Trench Coat Mafia," 25, 89
Turse, Nicholas, 25
Tyler, Ty, 170n.23

Untold Stories of Columbine (Scott), 62, 78

victimization politics, 98–99
violence in entertainment, 3, 80, 85–86, 90, 92
Voice of the Martyrs, 42, 55, 178n.17

Wacker, Grant, 111–12
Wallace, William, 18–20
Wall Street Journal, 87–88
Washington Post, 33, 41, 93, 149, 159
"Watch the Lamb," 61
web site tributes, 2, 10, 30–32, 56–57, 168n.6
Wedgewood Baptist Church shooting, 55, 98
Weekly Standard, 88, 94, 152–53
Weiner, Eugene and Anita, 14, 16–17, 23
West Bowles Community Church, 36
Whatever It Takes—The "She Said Yes" Music
    Project, 37
Word Publishing, 35–36, 38
WWJD, 37, 43, 97, 139–40
Wyant, Emily, 117–118, 126–27, 200n.42

"Yes, I Believe," products and web site, 37,
    45, 47–48
youth ministry, see evangelicalism, youth
    ministry

Zanis, Greg, 63, 182n.54, 55
Zimmerman, Chris, 118, 153–55
Zoba, Wendy Murray, 118–20, 122–26,
    133–34, 139, 153, 155, 158, 195n.1,
    198n.13, 200n.42, 206n.28